Every Room a Garden

Other books by Alice Skelsey

Farming in a Flowerpot
Growing Up Green *with Gloria Huckaby*
A Working Mother's Guide to Her Home, Her Family and Herself

Every Room a Garden

by Alice Skelsey and Cecile Mooney

Illustrations by Tom Stoerrle

Workman Publishing Company
New York City

Copyright © 1976 by Alice Skelsey and
Cecile Mooney.

All rights reserved. No portion of this book may
be reproduced—mechanically, electronically or
by any other means, including photocopying—
without written permission from
the publisher. Published simultaneously in
Canada by Saunders of Toronto, Inc.

*Library of Congress Cataloging in Publication
Data*
Skelsey, Alice Fulton
    Every room a garden.

    1. House plants in interior decoration. I.
Mooney, Cecile, joint author. II. Title.
SB419.S52   747'.9   75-20176
ISBN 0-911104-64-X
ISBN 0-911104-91-7 pbk.

Cover illustration: Tom Stoerrle

Workman Publishing Company, Inc.
231 East 51 Street
New York, New York 10022

Manufactured in the United States of America

First printing September 1976

    3   5   7   9   8   6   4   2

With special acknowledgment to Anne Skelsey Helvey, whose apartment served as an extra living laboratory for many of the plants and lights used in this book, and who helped document and describe their use, care, and performance.

Contents

Plants and you

This book has taken a long time to write. It will probably take a long time to read. We hope so. Because you will then be doing what we have done—learning about, living with, and loving dozens of plants in all kinds of settings all around the house. You will no longer be content with simply buying a few plants to place here and there. Now you will want to think about and savor these beautiful companions. You will be looking at plants with new eyes. The shape of the leaves, their texture, their subtle shadings, their shyness or their drama—all will seem quite remarkable to your design eye.

You will discover a whole new world of plant possibilities: Plants you thought you never could grow because you didn't have enough light for them will flourish under the lighting you can now arrange for them; vegetables and herbs that you might ordinarily consign to the kitchen will delight in bedroom or bath.

Every room will become a backdrop for greenery, tempting you to consider pedestals and platforms, trellises and trays, all manner of garden show-offs that you can make yourself.

You will check and recheck the specific needs for each kind of plant and in the process will come to feel at home with botanic names as well as common ones.

You will find that the plants you choose can be as much a reflection of your own personality as any of your most treasured objects are. The way you display your plants—what you put them in, where you place them, how you care for them—will become an enormously satisfying occupation.

Some of your plants will die. Living things do that. Those that meet a premature demise will challenge you to restudy the basics of plant care rather than shrug off the end of the relationship as a case of no green thumb.

We have worked with and cared for and loved each of the many plants described in this book. We have created hundreds of settings for them, from large focal points in a room to small cameos on a table. And we have learned all over again that the true plant expert is the person who really *sees* each plant. That simple involvement will lead you to care for your plants properly and give them the important place they deserve in your home and your life.

You will love living with every room a garden.

Some Basics

Making the most of light

Some plants require less light than others, and some can hang on to life for a surprising length of time with inadequate light; but if you want to grow a number of plants all around the house, it's important to capture every ray of light that you can.

So what do you do if you don't get enough sun? Or your windows are shaded by the building next door? Or you live in the northern part of the country, and daylight hours are just too short through much of the year?

Knowing which plants require less light than others can obviously be a big help, but you don't have to limit yourself to low-light plants. Look over some of the following suggestions for making the most of the natural light you have and for making good use of artificial light. By giving an added boost to the light you already have, you may be able to energize plants that have been merely marking time and provide yourself with the opportunity to grow many different kinds of plants.

NATURAL LIGHT

To make use of every bit of light available, size up the natural light potential in each room—from sunlight coming through a south window to bright but indirect light through a north window.

Which windows get direct sunlight? For how long each day? (Remember that the amount and intensity of sunlight will vary from summer to winter as the sun shifts position in the sky. A south window with a wide overhang may not get as much direct sunlight in summer when the sun is high in the sky as it does in the winter when the sun is lower and the rays, though weaker, can slant in under the overhang.)

You should also consider the amount of reflectivity from outside that may be increasing the amount of light inside: the white brick wall of a building across the street, for example, or a cement courtyard down below, or light-colored asphalt rooftops on the lower building next to yours.

Next, consider what you can do to help increase and capitalize on the natural light available to you. Here are some suggestions:

🌿 Make it possible for every available ray of natural light to find its way inside by giving special thought to window treatments. Heavy curtains and draperies that block out light or screen off large hunks of the windows will not be a part of the plant lover's thoughts on interior design. (See pages 240–254 for window treatments that do justice to a room without blocking out light.)

🌿 Once the maximum amount of light is allowed to enter, consider ways to make the most of it. When you choose paint for your walls, keep your plants in mind. Whereas dark walls will absorb most of the light that falls on them, white walls will bounce most of the light right back into the room. Plants that would not thrive in a room where walls are brown can perk up when walls turn white. What's more, clean, pure-white walls will reflect more light than off-white or dingy white. To give you an idea of the approximate difference in reflectance values of colors: white reflects 90 percent; lemon yellow, 65 percent; light blue, 42 percent; brown, 24 percent.

Color in Our Daily Lives is a good basic book that includes a section on illumination. It was prepared by the National Bureau of Standards and is available from the U.S. Government Printing Office, Washington, D.C., for $1.70.

� Mirrors obviously offer great reflectivity, and a wall opposite a window is the best one to mirror. Two adjacent walls of mirror will also bounce light back and forth, and a mirrored corner of a room can allow a plant there to thrive rather than merely exist.

� Shiny foil, vinyl, and Mylar wall coverings are also highly reflective. Metals can also be bright and beautiful, from stainless-steel tiles to galvanized tin siding. Used bravely but judiciously, metals can be good plant-endearing choices not only for baths and kitchens but for a wall or ceiling in other rooms, such as a study, office, or den.

� Ceilings offer large expanses for light reflection, too, and the plant lover will consider painting with nothing but white if low light is a problem.

� Floors can also deliver large reflectance benefits. Shiny white, painted floors with a protective polyurethane coating are not only beautiful but generous with the light dividends they pay in dark places.

� When using sheer curtains to screen plants from direct hot summer sun, the choice of white for the curtains can increase the light farther away from the window.

� Furniture arrangements can free window space for occupation by plants. A sofa under the window might be repositioned at right angles to the window so that floor or shelf space is freed for plants to catch the rays. Plants also offer the perfect opportunity for doing away with the table-lamp combination that somehow became linked with the picture window when it first appeared and has never gone away even though it was never a good idea. Picture windows can make ideal gathering spots for plants, and if the sill is nil, shelves and steps and other techniques can be used to provide space. (See Window Stretchers, page 93.)

� Good housekeeping helps. A thin film of dirt or grime on windows can prevent a great deal of light from coming through. Taking screens down in winter lets more light through when you need it most. Keep plants clean. Dusting and washing their leaves can help them make more use of the light they receive.

🌆 Check outside to see if a pruning job on foundation plants or nearby trees can let more light in. If they are your shrubs or trees, no problem. If they are the building owner's trees, negotiations for judicious pruning might pay off. Before whacking on a tree, however, consider the type and its location. On the south side, for example, a deciduous tree—one that loses its leaves in winter—might filter the direct hot sun during the summer months and actually protect windowsill plants as well as help keep the house cooler. In winter, when the branches are bare, the sun's welcome rays benefit the plants and help warm the house.

With all of the above in mind, you may now be looking at the rooms in your house from a different point of view. You will see the sunny spots as places to expand upon; the areas where added reflectivity will pay off; the room where draperies are now ruled out and shades are in; and the places where you will need supplemental artificial light if you want plants to flourish there.

ARTIFICIAL LIGHT

Does it really help? Yes, it most certainly does. And here, as with natural light, it helps if you size up the artificial lighting you already have, from table lamps with incandescent bulbs to strip-lighting with fluorescent tubes. Where do you have it, and what purpose does it serve? The inventory helps because you want this light to work double: to serve what illumina-

tion needs you have while providing light for your plants, too.

If you are adding to or changing the lighting in your home, or thinking of building or remodeling, then be sure to take the time to shop around. Find out what kinds of lights and fixtures are available, what will make a good light environment for each of your rooms, what purposes light can serve, what you want it to do in your home, and of course, how it might be teamed up to help your houseplants prosper.

You may, for example, decide to eliminate the incandescent lights in the center of the kitchen ceiling. They are inefficiently placed there because no matter where you work around the edges of your kitchen—counter, stove, sink—you are always working in your own shadow. So you install fluorescent fixtures under the kitchen cabinets, not only giving you better light for working but also providing a beautiful, inviting place for plants.

And what about something so simple as the reading lamp next to the living room chair? For a plant on the table next to the lamp, that extra light can help. Use shades with a white or metal interior for all lamps that are used with plants. And keep all lamps and fixtures clean to get the most out of the light you are paying for. When bulbs and tubes grow old, turn dark, and become less efficient, rotate them off to another fixture where light delivery is not critical, and give the plants a boost with a new bulb or tube.

While artificial lighting cannot begin to compare with the intensity of sunlight, the longer exposure to artificial light (fourteen to sixteen hours daily) and the dependability (no cloudy or rainy days) help compensate to provide plants with a good growth environment.

Fluorescent lights have turned out to be the greatest thing that has happened to indoor gardening since the African violet. In fact, when fluorescent light teamed up with the violet, the combination proved to be one of the most productive encounters in the whole saga of indoor gardening. Neither would likely have achieved its place in the hearts of millions of houseplant lovers without the other.

Violet growers pioneered in the use of fluorescent lights for indoor gardening and were rewarded with plants that have reached dizzying heights of beauty, form, and variety. At the same time, improvements have been made in fluorescent lights to extend their usefulness over a wide range of growing conditions.

However, fluorescent plant lights have not been greeted with much enthusiasm by interior designers. The light is generally considered cold and unflattering and the fixtures something less than handsome. Fortunately, new tubes coming on the market promise a better light for people as well as plants. They produce a more comfortable light to live with, one that is closer to daylight than previous fluorescent plant lights. Of the commercial tubes (as opposed to those sold specifically for plants), Deluxe Warm White produces a more flattering light than any of the several other "whites." It harmonizes well with incandescent light and is kinder to furnishings and face. Deluxe Cool White is not quite so kind, but many people like its crisp light for kitchen use.

The specially designed fluorescent plant light stands and carts are generally rigid-looking, ungainly, unattractive display places for plants. Much better—and far more attractive—are those fluorescent fixtures that are especially designed for a slim, narrow fit under shelves and cabinets. Some things to know about fluorescent lights and plants:

🌿 Fluorescent light is far more efficient, and uses far less energy for the light delivered, than incandescent light. Fluorescent tubes also last much longer than incandescent bulbs.

🌿 Wattage is measured by the foot; 10 watts to 1 foot. For example, a 24-inch tube is 20 watts; a 48-inch tube is 40 watts.

🌿 Fluorescent tubes give off very little heat. Plants can be as close as a few inches to the tube without harm.

🌿 You can concentrate more light on your plants by teaming up two tubes side by side. Space the tandem tubes 6 to 8 inches apart for more growing space under the lights and better use of the light.

🌿 Use the longest length of tube possible because the light loses intensity at both ends of the tube. Also, rotate plants from the ends to the middle every so often to give each one its fair share of the light.

🌿 Fluorescent lights are easy to install. Fixtures and tubes of varying lengths are widely available, and most can be plugged into a regular outlet. Ready-made fixtures can be bought that can accommodate any number of tubes from one to four.

🌿 Fluorescent tubes gradually lose their strength and should be replaced before they burn out. Count on about a year if the tubes are used on a sixteen-hour daily basis.

🌿 Commercial tubes and plant tubes are interchangeable in fixtures.

🌿 If using commercial tubes, a combination of warm white and cool white tubes is a superior energy source for plants than either one alone.

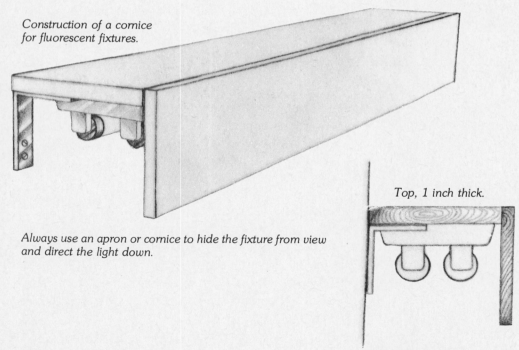

Construction of a cornice for fluorescent fixtures.

Always use an apron or cornice to hide the fixture from view and direct the light down.

Top, 1 inch thick.

Face board, ½ to 1 inch thick.

Paint interior white.
Place one bracket at each end, and use one for every 4 feet of cornice.

PLANT-GROWTH LAMPS

Light is made up of the different wavelengths that make up the color spectrum. Among the colors in the spectrum, blue, red, and far-red light provide the type of energy most useful to plant growth. Plants don't make much use of the yellow-green part of the spectrum; they reflect it rather than absorb it. On that account, special plant-growth lights, which are designed to provide the energy that plants can use, sacrifice the yellow-green part of the light spectrum for the blue and reds. It is the preponderance of blues and reds that make the light cast by these lamps visually unpleasing. Attempts have been made to make these lamps emit a more natural light, but unfortunately, the more natural the light, the less special it becomes as a plant-growth light. You get less efficient plant performance in exchange for a more pleasing illumination effect.

Incandescent light uses more energy and costs more for the amount of light delivered than fluorescent. So if energy efficiency is the only consideration, fluorescent tubes will win.

On this basis, some concerned citizens might well rule out incandescent light as wasteful, but don't sell its advantages short before you look into it rather carefully. For example, a whole new world of lighting possibilities for plants exists today with new track systems and cool-type incandescent bulbs.

With its classic design, track lighting can ingratiate itself in any room in the house. It can add something to the appearance of a room, which fluorescent lighting rarely does. And esthetics should not be lightly dismissed; there's no doubt that well-lighted rooms have an enormous impact on our indoor environment.

Don't overlook the fact that you can offset the difference in energy use between incandescent and fluorescent by cutting down in other ways, ways that will also benefit your plants. For example, your thermostat can be turned down to 68 degrees in the winter; many plants would love it even more at 62! You can caulk and weather-strip your windows to keep cold out and warmth in and at the same time provide a more draft-free place for your plants on the sill. Then you can balance off some of the energy saved with a beautiful lighting system that would be more than a bargain for the trade. Consider what track lighting with its great flexibility can do:

🌿 It can eliminate the cluttered look of a lamp here and a lamp there.

🌿 It can act as general lighting as well as accent, washing a whole room in light or highlighting a single object or part of a room.

🌿 It takes up no floor space while meeting many lighting needs.

🌿 It can be installed almost anywhere on walls (both vertically and horizontally), as

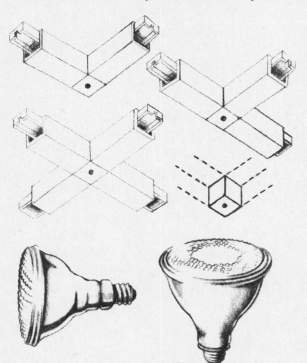

Various track lighting connections can combine with cool-type bulbs to increase the light for any part of the house.

well as on ceilings, and by almost any do-it-yourselfer.

🌿 It can use different kinds of lamps on the same track—drop or pendant types, chandeliers, or the familiar flood, canister, and spotlight shapes clipped on anywhere along the track.

🌿 It can form almost any pattern, with single tracks from 2 to 8 feet in length, and with "L," "T," "X," or "Corner" connectors.

🌿 It can be built into the ceiling or wall or simply plugged into an outlet (with a bit of planning, the cord can be concealed along the edge of a doorframe or bookshelf or such).

As for the incandescent bulbs, the new cool types do not give off as much heat as do regular floodlights, a major advantage for plant growers, since heat has always been a major limitation in using incandescent light close to plants. Cool-type bulbs can be used within 1 foot or so of the plants without burning their foliage.

Cool-type bulbs must be used in ceramic or porcelain sockets, so it will be important for you to check fixtures before you buy. Most of the heat from these bulbs is discharged from the back instead of the front, and that is why, for safety reasons, a ceramic or porcelain socket is indicated. These sockets also help ensure maximum operating life of both lamp and socket.

Lightolier, a leading manufacturer of track lighting, offers a wide selection of track fixtures

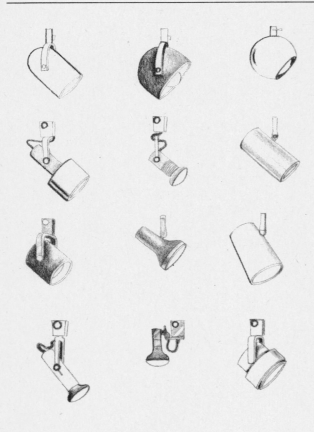

with sockets that will take cool-type bulbs. Other manufacturers of track lighting include Gotham, Halo, Prescolite, Progress, Swivolier, and Thomas Industries.

When considering a track-light installation, check the manufacturers' catalogs for performance data on various lighting arrangements.

For example, lighting levels can vary a great deal depending upon the angle of the lights and the spacing between lights. (The world of track lighting is a fascinating one, and this fact-finding mission won't be a chore.)

PLANTS' RESPONSE TO LIGHT

Plants react to any abrupt change in their routine, including the amount of light they receive. For example, when you bring a plant indoors after a summer outside or home from a greenhouse, there is usually an abrupt and sharp drop in the amount of light it receives. The plant may not curl up its leaves and die on the spot, but in the following days and weeks, older leaves on the plant may begin to yellow and drop.

Assuming it receives the minimum amount of light required to live at all and is given proper care, *which means less water and less fertilizer because it is in a reduced-light situation,* the plant will gradually adjust. The new leaves that develop will be better adapted to the lower light.

To avoid as much leaf drop as possible, as well as other adverse reactions from the plant, a good rule to remember is this: Accustom plants gradually to changes in their environment, including light. Plants can, for example, adjust quite successfully to a shuttle system within the house—being moved back and forth, out of darker spots and into brighter ones. But they need time to make this sort of adjustment to become accustomed to the routine. They cannot simply be taken from a dark spot and put into full sunlight without suffering. Accustom them to moving back and forth from low to bright light gradually, and they will set their systems accordingly and adjust to the routine.

While a number of plants, especially foliage types, do not like direct summer sun, almost all plants like as much light as you can give them indoors. Even low-light plants respond to more indoor light with more vigorous growth. As a general guide, thick-, spiny-, or hard-leaved plants are more likely to enjoy direct sun. Soft- or thin-leaved plants are more likely to be damaged by the sun's rays. Plants that flower usually require more light than foliage plants.

When plants become tall and spindly, they are signaling you for more light. Plants will bend toward the light, so plan to turn them regularly if you want them to develop symmetrically.

While plants can benefit from artificial light for periods up to sixteen hours a day, they also need a rest period. Automatic timers can be helpful in managing day and night for your plants. The timers are not too expensive and worth it if you have a number of plants growing under lights in various places about the house.

Regular cornice lighting, kitchen cabinet lighting, and such are easy enough to keep up with if you simply time them to your own routine of rising and retiring. Turn them on in the morning (after you bring in the paper), and turn them off at bedtime (after you put out the cat).

Plants can profit from the light cast by an ordinary reading lamp, and as you consider plants for the home, consider ones that can snuggle under these lamps. The area will be warm but not too hot for many plants, but do avoid those that definitely dislike warmth. It takes at least a 75-watt bulb to produce enough supplemental light to be of any benefit to the plant.

If you have a place in your house—a basement or garage, for example—where you can concentrate on gardening and not care much, if at all, about the looks of things, an efficient and very inexpensive route to go is plain ceiling-hung fluorescent fixtures. Commercially assembled tiers of lighted trays or carts with lighting fixtures can be the answer for spare rooms that can be devoted partly to hobby gardening—rooms where you can forget about esthetics and use lighting for its functional value alone. (See page 205 for a tier treatment with high design interest.)

Potting and repotting

For first potting, start with the smallest container the plant will comfortably fit (some ferns are occasional exceptions), and move the plant into progressively larger pots as it grows. Remember that a small pot to begin with is just as important to the plant as repotting is later on. If the first pot is too large, the plant will suffer from all the moisture in the excess soil, and more of its efforts will be forced into root growth instead of top growth.

In choosing a container, make it a hard-and-fast rule never to pot a plant directly into a container that does not have a drainage hole. It takes finely tuned watering to keep a plant happy without adequate drainage. If you have a number of plants, this is pretty difficult to do.

Drainage holes can be made in plastic containers quickly and easily with a small soldering iron. If drainage holes cannot be made in a particular container, use it as a cachepot rather than planting directly in it. Find a smaller plastic pot, can, anything that has a hole in it or can have holes punched in it, pot the plant in that, and then put it in the show-off container. Prop the plant up off the bottom of the cachepot so that it won't stand in the water that drains off and collects in the bottom. You don't want the plant pot left standing in drainage water, so pour the excess water out before it goes sour and dank or rises too high. If you are using a pot that's going to be too heavy to lift, choose a cachepot or container large enough so that there's some space between the sides of the cachepot and the pot through which water can be siphoned off (you can use a gasoline siphon or a long, slim kitchen baster). Another way to remove water is to slide the end of a terry towel down the side of the pot to the bottom of the cachepot and let the water soak into it via capillary action. (See page 33–34.)

For smaller pots, a piece of sponge cut to fit the bottom of the cachepot helps soak up excess water. The sponge should be replaced or washed and dried every so often to keep it from souring.

If you have a large plant—a house tree, for example—where the size of the pot and the weight of the plant make lifting impossible and you (ill-advised but stubborn) want to use a cachepot and don't want it to look double-potted, you can follow this method: Choose a clay pot with a drainage hole—one that will fit within your decorative container. It is important that the pot be clay because it is porous and moisture can soak through the sides. Make a bed of dampened unmilled sphagnum moss inside the cachepot on top of a thin layer of gravel. Put the planted clay pot in the cachepot, and then surround the sides of the clay pot and cover the top of the soil with more dampened moss. Water the moss as it dries, and the plant will take its moisture from the dampened moss atop the plant and from moisture that seeps through the sides and bottom of the pot. You will also have a much-better-looking planting than those that are double-potted with perlite, which holds moisture but whose white, plastic-like granules do violence to the looks of a planting.

BASIC STEPS IN POTTING PLANTS

Screen the drainage hole so that soil will stay in but water can drain out. Broken pieces of clay pot—"shards"—are the tool of the classic gardener. If you don't have broken clay pots lying about, pick up a yard of plastic screening from the hardware store. Cut into small squares, it will make enough drain covering for dozens of pots.

Add a thin layer of pebbles to keep the screen in place and provide drainage room. (If your pot has three or four drainage holes, the pebble layer is not really necessary.)

Add moistened soil mix. Always use moistened soil mix when potting or repotting. A dry mix can actually dehydrate a plant by robbing moisture from the roots.

Put the plant in the pot—no deeper than it has been accustomed to (tomatoes are an exception). Hold the plant with one hand, and fill in around it with more soil. Firm up the soil around the stem with your hands, and then give the pot a couple of good clunks on the table to settle the soil. Add more soil if needed, up to about 1 inch from the top of the pot. If you make sure not to have soil too near the top rim, you'll save yourself much teeth-gnashing over water overflowing the top, especially if you have hanging pots.

Water the plant, and put it in a low-light place for a few days; then gradually accustom it to more light. Go easy on water and food while the plant begins to put out new roots.

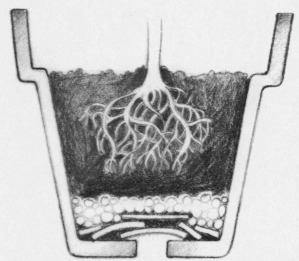

Start by screening drain hole. Add thin layer of pebbles.

REPOTTING

Repotting plants can be a drag. Even the most devoted gardeners will confess to putting off longer than they should the transfer of a plant that has outgrown its container to one more fitting to its size. Unfortunately, if a plant stays in a too-small pot too long, it can strangle

Repot to the next largest size as the plant outgrows its quarters.

on its own roots. If roots are pushing through the drainage hole (another good reason for having drainage holes to begin with), then you and the plant have no time to waste. (There are always exceptions: the Kafir lily, for example, is one plant that likes being potbound.)

To repot, water the plant several hours in advance. Then rap the pot sharply with the palm of your hand or against the edge of a bench or counter. Turn the pot on its side, and tilt it over so that the plant slides out of the pot and into your hand with the stems winding up between your outspread fingers.

Gently remove as much of the old soil as you can, being careful not to damage the roots of the plant. Have a new container of the next-larger size ready with new moistened soil mix in

the bottom. Position the plant in the pot, and add additional moistened mix around the sides. If the plant settles too low in the pot, lift it carefully and add more soil beneath. Firm the new soil around the root ball; water the plant thoroughly; let drain thoroughly. Keep the plant out of direct sun, and be conservative with water while the plant adjusts and begins to put out new roots.

ALL ABOUT DIRT

Most houseplants will do fine in any potting medium that drains well but still holds water long enough to allow plant roots to absorb moisture.

Your choices for a potting medium can include dirt from your own backyard, so long as it is not impenetrable hard clay. Dig the dirt when the ground is *not* wet, and if it doesn't *seem* crumbly enough (which will likely be the case), add some peat moss or other soil conditioner to lighten it up. Never start seeds in dirt that hasn't been sterilized; if you do, a nasty affliction called "damping off" will kill your seedlings almost as soon as they have sprouted.

You can also buy dirt. It is sold by the bag, and once packaged, it acquires the name of soil or loam or topsoil. It is usually soft and loosely textured.

Or you can do what more and more gardeners are doing—use soilless mixes. Their popularity has grown enormously in the last few years since the development of some of the basic mixes at Cornell University. The disadvantages of soilless mixes are that they dry out fast; they tend to pack; they are so light the particles float around in the pot when the plant is watered, thus disturbing the roots; they cost money when soil in your own backyard is free; they require the regular addition of fertilizer because most of them have no nutrients for the plants.

While all of the above may be true for one type of mix or another, the indoor gardener will still find advantages in the soilless mixes, not the least being that many of us don't have backyards with free soil available. Other advantages are that mixes can be specially prepared for differing plant needs and that they provide a basically sterile potting medium, a must when starting seeds. Mixes are also lightweight, an important factor when hanging plants and for use in large containers that may need to be moved about. Specially prepared potting mixes are sold for planting cacti, African violets, and orchids and for general houseplant use; but surprisingly, most of these prepackaged mixes reveal not the slightest hint of their ingredients, much less proportions. Consequently, you really have little idea of what it is you are buying.

Most indoor gardeners who have gone beyond a few plants eventually begin to create their own mix recipes, trying various proportions and combinations of peat, perlite, vermiculite, humus, limestone, charcoal, shredded fir bark, builder's sand, plant food, not to mention other diverse items such as tea leaves, egg shells, leftover table scraps whirled to a soup in a blender, and other organic goodies. The various ingredients can be purchased separately; they're fun to fool with; and they sharpen and enhance your involvement with your plants.

Here are a couple of beginning mixtures that are simple to make. The measurements are by volume, not weight; by quarts, for example, not pounds. Remember, too, that the proper texture in a mix is more important than the richness. It should be loose and well drained.

Good basic mixture for most houseplants, made from ingredients readily available in hardware and gardening stores:

    2 parts milled sphagnum peat moss
    1 part vermiculite
    1 part perlite

Mix all of these ingredients thoroughly, and keep in a covered container; a plastic trash container with a lid is ideal.

For plants, such as cacti and succulents, that require a faster-draining mixture and like to dry out between waterings, try:

    1 part milled sphagnum peat moss
    1 part ground fir bark
    1 part coarse builder's sand

Remember that fertilizer must be added according to the plants' needs because these mixes basically contain no nutrients.

A word about reuse of your potting mix:

After some time, peat moss breaks down into finer and finer particles and tends to pack down; it will eventually interfere with good drainage. (It also tends to form a crust on the surface of the soil, which is why it is a good idea every so often to cultivate—break up—the surface of the soil gently to loosen it so that water can penetrate more easily.)

A plant that is being repotted deserves a new pot of mix. However, if you have a large batch of fresh mix, you can pour some of the old mix into it and stir it well to recycle it and get a little more mileage out of it without sacrificing quality or hurting the plants.

GLOSSARY

Fir bark is just what it says it is: fir bark, ground up in various sizes. Larger, chunky sizes are preferred for potting up various kinds of orchids. Fir bark in soil mixes ensures good drainage. Plants that like to go dry between waterings do well with fir bark in the mix.

Perlite, or sponge rock, as it is also called, is an inert ingredient, a naturally occurring mineral. It soaks up and holds moisture and is useful in keeping soil mix light and loose so that both water and air can penetrate.

Vermiculite is also a mineral, also absorbent, also excellent for adding texture to soil mix.

Peat moss is called a lot of different things: sphagnum peat moss, milled peat moss, and so on. There is a big difference between the milled and unmilled sphagnum peat moss. Unmilled sphagnum peat moss is the long, coarse branches of the moss. It is superabsorbent and soaks up water like a sponge. It is especially useful in double-potting and in lining hanging baskets. Milled sphagnum peat moss has been ground up fine and is used as a basis for most potting mixes.

Builder's sand is also just what it says it is: the sort of sand used by builders in mixing cement. Don't use beach sand or aquarium sand in its place; they are much too fine to provide good drainage.

Humus is made up of decayed vegetable and animal matter. Its rich brown color and soft texture are irresistible to the indoor gardener who has little chance to dig in the good earth. Packaged humus contains enough plant nutrients to start plants off without additional plant food for the first few weeks. Try substituting for peat moss in soil mix.

Watering and feeding

Knowing when to water and feed, and how much, requires a one-to-one relationship with each plant you own. Consider all of the variables: type of plant, type of container, amount and kind of light, different kinds of potting mixes and plant foods, the seasons, the temperature, and the humidity. For all of the general advice that you may read, down at the bottom line the "how much" and "when" will be between you and your plants. Your success will depend on how much you observe each plant's needs in the environment you have created for it.

WATERING

The following basics, which you will eventually learn on your own anyway, can help avoid any plant declines or deaths while you are getting acquainted with their individual needs:

Don't set up a regular schedule for watering your plants, but do set up a regular schedule for checking on them.

Plants generally need watering more often when:

    making active growth
    in clay pots and other porous containers
    on bright days
    in small pots
    when roots fill pot

Plants generally need watering less often when:

    resting or dormant
    newly potted or repotted
    in nonporous pots, such as plastic
    on cloudy days
    in large pots

Learn the general water requirements for each of the plants you own. These requirements fall into three broad categories:

Plants that like to be on the moist side. Never allow these to dry out completely. Keep evenly moist—*not* soggy, but never dry. Some ferns, for example, like an evenly moist soil.

Plants that like to dry out between waterings. Most houseplants will fall into this category. Water these plants thoroughly; then do not water again until the soil feels dry to the touch.

Plants that like to go bone-dry between waterings. Many cacti and succulents fall into this group. Water thoroughly; then let soil go dusty dry to the touch. Dig your finger in beneath the soil surface to feel for traces of moisture before watering again.

Provide for humidity, especially in the winter, and especially if you have a forced hot-air heating system, which draws moisture out of the air like a blotter. Enough humidity can make the difference between thriving and struggling plants. You can also do your health and complexion a favor by putting moisture back into the air. Ways to do so:

Install a humidifier. There are types

that can be either attached to the heating unit itself or installed as a separate unit. They are not extravagantly expensive and can bring the humidity level up to where both you and your plants will be far more comfortable.

🌿 Lower your thermostat in winter. A 68-degree setting may put you in a sweater, but you, your fuel bills, and your plants will be better off with lower temperatures that mean higher humidity. If not 68, no more at most than 70 degrees.

🌿 Mist your plants regularly and often. If you have a number of plants, keep a mister handy in each room. Plastic spray bottles of the type used for household detergents will provide for a lot of mistings before needing a refill. Small brass misters are good-looking enough to be a permanent part of any room's accessories.

🌿 Place plants on trays or saucers that are filled with pebbles so that water can drain off but remain to add moisture to the air. (The plant containers are up on the pebbles out of the water, so the roots won't be soaked.) Open containers of water tucked among a grouping of plants can also boost humidity around the plants. If you have open radiators, look for shallow metal trays to fit the top, and keep them filled with water.

HOW TO WATER

Always saturate the soil when you water, even for plants that like things on the dry side.

All plants, if properly potted in soil that drains well, will be better off with a good soaking when they need water than if they get only enough water to tease the roots.

Try not to let your plants reach the wilting stage before watering them. When plants are allowed to go too dry, the newest growth is usually damaged first. Young foliage wilts, browns, and dies. Some plants suffer if they go dry for only a day too long.

Your sense of touch is important in knowing when potted plants need water. Touch the leaves as well as the soil. Learn the feel of leaves that are either papery dry or limp from lack of water. Leaves of a healthy, properly watered plant have a certain springiness to them, and you will recognize this feeling only by experience. Touch the leaves of your plants as you care for them; it's a bit like taking their pulse.

Do not apply water too rapidly to plants, especially those that like to dry out between waterings. If you dump water on all at once, it will run straight through the pot, too fast for the soil to soak it up. You, in turn, seeing the water exiting from the drainage hole, will not only stop watering but perhaps empty the saucer as well because you know that plants shouldn't stand in water. Result: The plant winds up with too little water, even though you may have applied a lot. Water slowly. Apply a little water, wait for it to soak in, and then apply more, letting it slowly make its way through the pot. If you are watering from the bottom of the pot, pour the water into the saucer or tray in which the plant stands; then let the water remain for at least a half hour so that the plant can soak up what it needs. Then pour off the excess.

WHEN YOU ARE AWAY

For short periods of time, a few days to a week: Fill the bathtub with ½ inch or so of water. Line the bottom with a thick layer of folded newspapers (the papers will soak up a good bit of the water). Place plants in the tub (removed from their cachepots, if any). Drain the tub of any excess water. Close the shower curtain to cut down on light and maintain humidity. When you return, remember to allow your plants time to readjust when you move them back out from the dim light. Don't plop them down in the bright sun until they've had a chance to become accustomed to gradually increasing light.

Wicking can be a successful technique for watering your plants when you must be away for a longer period of time and your plants must be left on their own. It is most useful for those plants that like to be evenly moist, such as some of the ferns and African violets and their relatives. (Many gardeners use wicking for these plants as part of a standard watering method to cut down on the amount of time involved in the daily routine of watering.) Wicking, however, is not for plants that like to go dry between waterings.

To make the wicks: Cut old nylon stockings crosswise in ½-inch-wide pieces. Stretch these circles of nylon as much as possible, and then cut them open to make strips. If your plant is already potted, push 3 or 4 inches of the strip up through the drainage hole with a slim stick or knitting needle. Put the other end through a hole punched in the cover of a container of water (plastic food cartons such as margarine tubs and frozen dessert bowls work well). Place the pot on top of the container. Water the plants thoroughly from the top to start the capillary action. The container should be filled with water to which a small amount of plant food has been added; the extent of the dilution—whether one-quarter strength or one-tenth strength or whatever amount—will depend upon how large the container is and how long the water supply will last for the plants. Look at the amounts recommended for the fertilizer, and calculate from there. (To see capillary action at work, let the tip end of a dry towel ex-

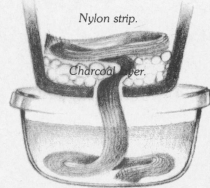

Nylon strip.

Charcoal layer.

tend over the side of the bathtub into the water. Check back later, and you will find the whole towel wet. That is capillarity at work, and that is how wicking works to make moisture available to a plant's roots.)

If you are potting or repotting a plant, you can wick the pot at that time. Pull the wick up through the drainage hole, put a thin layer of gravel or charcoal in the pot, spread the wick out in a circle on the gravel and then fill with soil.

A whole tray of plants can be wick-watered by placing a piece of hardware cloth (½-inch mesh) over the top of a tray that is 2 or 3 inches deep. Bend the hardware cloth over the edges. The wick from each pot can be placed through the mesh of the hardware cloth into the water below.

Nylon seine twine (available where fishing supplies are sold) can be used in place of strips of nylon hose. The size of twine can vary from No. 18 for small pots under 2 inches in size up to No. 48 for larger pots over 4 inches.

TREAT YOURSELF TO PROPER WATERING EQUIPMENT

You will not regret investing in a good, well-designed, solidly built watering can—one with a long-reaching spout and a large, easy-to-hold handle and designed in such a way that there is no dripping from seams when various nozzles are used on the spout. Such a watering can will put water where you want it without undue stretching on your part and without splattering soil and water every which way.

A flexible hose with a gentle-spray attachment to affix to a sink, shower, or tub can help you with watering plants as well as with giving the foliage a bath when needed. The latter is a highly recommended method for controlling insect infestations.

If you can reach your plants, in place, with a hose and wand attachment affixed to a faucet, you have an ideal setup for watering with a minimum of work. Available at hardware stores are coupling attachments that can be placed on a faucet so that a screw-on hose can be used. Check these out, as well as the flat-type hoses that take up little space when not in use.

For watering hanging baskets, consider the pulley as a device for lowering the baskets within easy reach (see page 271). Otherwise, plan to have a sturdy stool on hand, and use a lighter-weight watering can with a shorter spout that can be managed easily in a small space.

FEEDING

Plants need a balanced diet, just as people do. The basic four as far as plants are concerned are nitrogen, phosphorus, potassium, and trace elements. Whatever plant food you buy, you will find that the first three of these ingredients are identified through numbers, whether a 15-30-15 formula, or a 12-36-14, or any of many other combinations. The numbers refer to the percentage of nitrogen, phosphorus, and potassium in the fertilizer formula. The numbers are always given in this order: the percentage of nitrogen first, phosphorus second, and potassium third.

You will also find a wide variety of plant fertilizers on the market, some intended for use with particular kinds of plants, such as African violets, orchids, and cacti, and others for general houseplant use. Follow directions on these fertilizers carefully, being certain that you never exceed the recommendations for amount or frequency of application. As a matter of fact, you will be on much safer ground if you plan to skimp on the amounts recommended.

Almost all gardeners have their own fertilizer favorites, and some gardeners believe that alternating different plant foods benefits the plants by supplying them with a more varied diet. All good gardeners experiment with fertiliz-

OTHER DIETARY TIPS

🌿 Never feed a plant that suddenly turns sickly; you simply add more stress to the roots.

🌿 For plants that have reached as large a size as you wish or can accommodate, feed sparingly and infrequently so that you do not encourage growth. A maintenance diet is what you are after here.

🌿 For plants overdue on watering, use plain water first, and then follow with fertilizer to avoid burning the plants' roots. A straight dose of fertilizer to dry roots can kill a plant dead away.

🌿 Flush plants with plain clear water to rid the soil of fertilizer salts that build up over a period of time. You can see these salts as the white substance that forms on the sides of clay pots or as a salty-looking layer on top of the soil surface. In either case, the plants are already overdue for flushing or repotting in new soil and clean pots. Best way to flush: Take the plant to a sink or tub, and let water run slowly and gently through the soil for a couple of minutes. If the plant is too large to carry to the sink or tub, then water it in place four or five times in succession with tepid plain water.

ers carefully, however, knowing that plants can suffer severely from overfeeding, just as they can from overwatering.

If you have a number of plants to tend and are reasonably busy with other pursuits (school, family, job), you will find it easy to forget what plant was fertilized when. The best solution to feeding a lot of different kinds of plants is to create a system and keep it as simple as possible.

First, identify the cacti and succulents in your collection of plants. These are to get less fertilizer than other plants, just as they also get less water. Next identify any other plant whose specific diet you wish to tend to on an individual basis: a house tree, for example, an expensive orchid, or any other specimen or favorite plant.

For all the rest, you can try one of two feeding methods:

Use a very weak solution of houseplant food each time the plants are watered during their growing season. About mid-October, the end of the active growing season for most of your plants, give each a fish emulsion tablet, water well with plain water, and then feed no more until early spring, when you begin the weak fertilizer regimen again.

Many gardeners find this sort of constant feeding through the growing cycle good for the plants and easy to accomplish. Once a month the plants are watered thoroughly with plain water to eliminate any buildup of fertilizer salts.

The gardener who wants to simplify further can consider the use of fertilizer pellets. These are applied to the surface of the soil, and the nutrients are released slowly over a period of three to four months as the plant is watered. Thus, two or three feedings a year are all you need concern yourself with. Once the fertilizer is applied, you obviously have little opportunity to experiment with other plant foods in varying amounts to see if your plant prefers one diet to another. But if you are busy and wish not to worry that your plants may be going hungry, slow-release fertilizers can be the answer. The risk is in forgetting when you applied a dose and following up with another dose too soon. For most plants, think March 1, June 1, September 1; use less than the recommended amount; and you and your plants will be okay.

Taking care of them all

When you have plants in every room, their care becomes an important commitment of both time and knowledge. Whatever you can do to make it easier and more convenient to care for them will add to your enjoyment of them. Here are some ways to help you provide dependable care for all your plants:

Label all your plants with both their common and their botanical names when you first get them home. If you have more than a few plants, it's not easy to remember all of the names, particularly the botanical ones. The latter are important to know. Common names vary too widely to be dependable, and if you wish to learn more about your plants, such as their native habitats and their culture under various conditions, from reference works, you will need the botanical name to conduct your search.

Include some kind of marking code for each pot to indicate watering needs (evenly moist; dry between waterings; bone-dry between waterings) as an aid to you and others who may be helping out with plant care. Whether just an initial marked on a pot rim with an indelible pen or a small piece of colored tape, a water code can keep you from overwatering or underwatering. Plants have varying needs.

Create a special place to keep a small nursery of cuttings. A beautiful bottle or collection of bottles all in one place can do a lot for a room, whereas plant cuttings in cheese and jelly jars plopped here and there on windowsills and counters are a depressing way to handle the new life they represent. The same applies for cuttings rooting in soil; give all your plants-to-be special attention so that the appeal of these fledglings is not wasted.

Have an intensive care unit where an ailing plant can be kept isolated from the others and where it has the best chance for recovery. Smaller potted plants could take a rest cure in an aquarium. Put a layer of sand or vermiculite on the bottom of the aquarium. Place it where it can get good light but not sun. Put any plant in need of special care in the aquarium; mist to keep humidity high; don't water or feed; and give the plant a chance to recover. Avoid the chicken-soup syndrome—sickly plants do not need more food and water. It is best to go the other way: Isolate the plant; cut down on water and food; you can even prune part of the plant back to ease the burden the roots carry; and then wait and see how the plant does.

When acquiring plants, keep in mind your own limitations, not only of space and light, but of time. Don't have so many that you are simply not able to give them the care they need. Plant euphoria is latent in all gardeners, and plant shops and plant catalogs can bring on a severe case. If your will weakens, think of the number of containers involved, the potting mix and other essentials to be acquired, and the hours of care your plants will require. Any room can become a garden when the plants are in top condition; even a single plant can sing out its green presence so long as it is healthy and well-groomed. Avoid a clutter of many pots of this and that in various stages of anemia.

Be especially careful not to overdo the care of new plants. It is quite possible for a plant to drop most of its leaves while it is adjusting to a move from a high-light environment (greenhouse) to a lower-light environment (your house). A plant's need for food drops sharply when it is placed in a lower-light situation, and to help plants make the transition you should cut down on food and water. Pick off any yellow or dead leaves to keep the plant looking its best and so you'll be able to spot new growth as it appears.

Put together a care kit for each room. If you have all of the things close by that you need to care for your plants, it is much more likely that they'll get that care when they need it. If you have alcohol and cotton swabs on hand, a mealy bug you spot can be banished then and there. If you must make a special trip upstairs, downstairs, to another room for the items you need, then the mealy bug and additional offspring may live to fight another day because of the inevitable interruption that prevents your return.

The following items should be in a care kit in each room. None is so expensive that you cannot have duplicates.

A watering can and a reserve back up container—a gallon-sized plastic milk container, a pitcher, a jug. The idea here is to have water close at hand at all times so a plant can be watered when in need without the bother of locating a watering can, going to the kitchen or bathroom, filling it, and returning. If you fill all the jugs at one time, you'll have enough water for a number of rounds of watering and you will minimize retracing steps. The water in the back-up container is used to replenish the watering can.

A mister—whether the professional pump type, the garden-supply spray containers, the classical brass, or an empty spray bottle formerly filled with a household cleaner.

Bottle of alcohol for treating insect pests, and cotton swabs for applying the alcohol to joints between leaf and stem and other hard-to-reach parts of plants.

Soft cloth for dusting and cleaning smooth leaf surfaces.

Soft brush (such as pastry brush) for cleaning fuzzy leaf surfaces (such as those of African violets).

Scissors or shears for trimming and pruning. Use these often to spruce up plants, removing leaves that are fading, and shaping plants to encourage branching.

Plant food and measuring spoons. It is essential that you be precise in the use of plant food and also consistent. Having both the plant food and the measuring utensils on hand can ensure that plants are fed when they need to be and that they are not overfed.

Kitchen fork. Use this for carefully loosening the surface of the soil once in a while so that water can penetrate more easily.

Soft terry towel for mopping up the inevitable drip.

GUARDING AGAINST INSECT ATTACK

When you have lots of plants about the house, you should be especially watchful against insect attack. You stand a real chance of a wipe-out if an insect invasion goes un-checked. While good preventive measures (in-specting plants before they are brought in; using sterilized soil) will minimize the chance of an insect attack, bugs can still surface occasionally and raise havoc with your plants. The best ways to keep insects under control are to move against them the minute you spot evidence of their presence and to observe the following preventive measures:

Every time you water your plants or visit with them, inspect for evidence of insects. Turn leaves over, and look at the undersides—not every leaf every time, obviously, but here and there.

Inspect carefully any newly acquired plants, whether received from a friend or purchased at the store or by mail order.

Inspect any plants that you have put out-doors for the summer before you bring them back in. Rinse the plants and pots off well, using a sprinkling can or a hose turned to soft shower.

Rinse or wash carefully any plant where an insect has been spotted.

If the insect threat is more extensive and further treatment is necessary, you can rely on the following two techniques for taking care of most of the insects you are likely to encounter: rubbing alcohol, administered by cotton swab or from a small fine-mist atomizer; or a pest strip either hung near your plant collection or cut into several small pieces and tucked into a plastic bag along with any clearly infested plant. Keep out of sun.

There are four insect enemies that you are likely to encounter at some point in your plant career—aphids, mealybugs, mites, and scales.

Aphids. One sign that these tiny insects are at work is a sticky, glossy substance on the leaves of a plant. This is the honeydew excreted by the aphids. Usually you can find the aphids (you'll have to look closely; they are less than ⅛ inch long) clustered on the undersides of the leaves or on new and tender stems, leaves, and flower buds. There are several species; they

Aphids.   *Mealybugs.*

come in green, pink, red, or black, and they feed by sucking out the plant juices.

If caught early, they can be washed off with plain water or dab them with alcohol. If they have gotten away from you, put the plants in bags with pest strip pieces. Put out of direct light for several days. Repeat treatment in a week if necessary.

Mealy bugs. You'll recognize these pests by their white, mealy appearance, looking like tiny blobs of dry soap powder. In another stage they appear as small oval specks. They can literally take over a plant. Watch for them at the joints between stem and leaf and along the veins on the undersides of leaves. These nasties also suck plant juices, stunting, weakening, and sometimes killing the plants.

Wash the plant or dab or spray with alcohol. Repeat whenever you spot the merest white speck that suggests the return of the mealy bug. Constant vigilance is the best deterrent when dealing with this plant pest.

Mites. These insects are so small you're not likely to spot them until they have formed a fine web underneath the leaves where they gather. The damage they do shows up in a whitish or yellowish speckling on the top of the leaf. They are more difficult to be rid of than aphids or mealy bugs. Cut off the infected leaves, and dispose of them; isolate the plant from others; and bag it with a piece of pest strip.

A real mite infestation is bad news indeed,

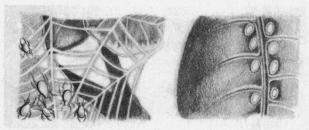

Mites.   Scale.

and rather than play host to an infested plant that can't be cured, bid farewell to it for the good of the flock.

Scale. This is another pest you can spot by the sticky, glossy substance it produces on the leaves of plants. Scale is more time-consuming to remove by washing than are the other insects listed. A spray soft enough to keep from injuring the plant is usually not strong enough to dislodge the scale. On some plants—citrus, for example, of which scale is especially fond—the leaves are big and sturdy enough so that you can take them one at a time, and wash each one with a soft cloth wrung out in warm, soapy water. Be especially careful to wash the undersides of the leaves. Also inspect the branches and trunk carefully. Some scale will nearly match the color of the branches and can be easily overlooked. Be warned that this is a time-consuming task. Repeat the washing as often as you spot a single scale—and you are likely to spot a few of them over a period of weeks. Such a wash treatment is a highly effective control if you stick with it.

As You Enter

In Step with Plants

Weekend cottage dwellers saddened by the sight of plants parched from a week's neglect would find this stairway entwined with green a delightful surprise. And just as surprising as this lush display is its simplicity—plain, ordinary sweet potatoes thriving happily in water, presenting no worries about care while you're away during the week. (If your stairway doesn't have balusters, you can stretch cord and have the sweet potatoes train to that.)

A collection of brown-glass baked-bean jars are the containers here. Heavy-duty, double-faced adhesive tape (the kind often used to install mirror tiles) fastens the jars to the steps. It provides a good tight bond to keep jars and pots safe from accidental bumps.

Obviously, sweet potatoes can be used anywhere, not just to green a stairway in a summer cottage. To start them at any time of year, simply put them in water: about two-thirds of the potato in the water, one-third out. Keep the size of your containers in mind when you buy the potatoes so you don't buy ones that are too fat to fit. Long, skinny potatoes are the best buys, since you can cut them in half and get two plants out of one. Put the cut end down in the water, and prop up with toothpicks if necessary, so that about a third of the potato is out of the water.

If you do want them for a summer house, start them at home in April so they will be vining and ready to move into place by the first summer weekend. Simply replenish the water level as needed, add a dose of fertilizer every three or four

Sweet potatoes: a low-maintenance vine, perfect for a weekend home.

weeks, and the vines will stay bright and lively all summer.

Plants that climb, plants that trail, plants with symmetry—all look great with stairs. The trailers in the wide windowsill of the 1914-vintage stairway, shown on the next page, are big-leaved, hearty members of the cissus genus, which also includes the kangaroo vine and grape ivy.

Small-leaved ivies or other tiny trailers would be overwhelmed by the mass of the stairs.

The spider plant on the newel post will eventually grow too big for its place, but not before it sends out more plantlets to drape around its ready-made pedestal. In the meantime one of the plantlets is being groomed in another part of the

Tiles laid on the diagonal create an illusion of depth.

house to replace its mother when the time comes. (For more about rooting, see page 287.) The spider plant's container is secured in place by double-faced tape.

The entryway here—the kind often found in brownstones, row houses, and semidetached homes built in the teens and twenties—has lovely intricate molding which has been highlighted with a light finish to bring out the detail that the original dark finish obscured. The stairwell wall boasts a collection of mirrors that were cut to fit an assortment of frames gathered from here and there. Mirrors and plants have an affinity for one another.

The stairs were painted a glossy white for a crisp touch and to camouflage several badly mismatched steps from a previous repair job. Traditional at heart, the owners chose to have a carpet runner on the stairs. (You could upholster your stairs if you're after a more contemporary look.)

Many a houseplant fan becomes an instant convert to the training of indoor climbers after seeing the wax plant perform. The thick, sturdy leaves of the wax plant are every bit a match for the circular stairway pictured opposite. As it twines, the woody vine can be held in place by small pieces of transparent tape fastened around the stair pole. (Before attaching the tape to the pole, face a short center section of it with another piece of tape, smooth side out, so a nonsticky surface rests against the vine.)

Wax plant: for more about this flowering beauty, see page 199.

Stairways often mean second-story railings and balconies and other lofty places where plants can trail off into space. Pick plants that are thick and luxuriant so they foam up out of the pot and cascade over it. To obtain a full effect, use several plants to a pot, and pinch back regularly during growth periods to encourage branching.

The loftier the spot, the greater and sturdier the mass of green should be. Swedish ivy will produce a full, billowing mass of green. Other good choices: heartleaf philodendron, some of the large-leaved inch plants and wandering Jews, kangaroo vine, grape ivy, arrowhead, and pothos.

Stairways also have landings, many of them simply halfway places with nothing much to recommend them either architecturally or esthetically. Both can change dramatically when a garden area is installed, complete with a wall-to-wall flower bed.

One newcomer to indoor gardening, in search of more space for more lights for more growing room for more bloomers, put together a hobby spot (pictured on the following page) by claiming less than 12 inches of a split-level landing and using two 4-foot fluorescent tubes, track lighting, and shelving.

A chance encounter with an African violet that bloomed nonstop for months under the fluorescent light of a kitchen cabinet led from one violet to another and inspired this whole new world of flowering plants that belong to the same

A stairway landing cum gardening center. Fluorescent tubes are faced with apron so that they will not be seen by passersby.

first violet, a little patience, study, and trial and error paid off. One or another of the plants can be counted on to keep the flower bed in bloom throughout the year. To help keep humidity up to the gesneriad family's tastes, the containers rest on pebble-filled trays where water can drain, and the plants are obliged often with a misting from householders who pause to admire the flowers while going up and coming down.

Biggest help for this gardener: *The Gloxinian,* the bimonthly publication of The American Gloxinia and Gesneriad Society (Box 174, New Milford, Connecticut 06776). "I love it. Gardeners write in to share their failures and tell what went wrong, as well as how they succeeded, and it encourages you to keep trying and experimenting with your own plants till you get to know them."

family as the African violet. The indoor flower bed now includes temple bells, Cape primroses, flame violets, and gloxinias. While none of these flourished for their owner as effortlessly as did the

Plant groupings

What was once a dark and gloomy entrance hall now boasts a ceiling-to-floor wall of art directly opposite the front door. A long tray for the plants rests on a platform raised slightly above the floor. The repetition of the strong horizontal line of the platform, tray, painting, and ceiling spells modern. (Avid fans of architect Frank Lloyd Wright are convinced that he invented the horizontal line.)

For visual balance you'll need a tall plant here, but one with a reasonably narrow growth habit so that it won't take up much room space. A fiddleleaf fig is a good choice (for other narrow plants, see page 227). This fig has great, lovely lyre-shaped leaves, each attached directly to the main stem. Architecturally it has the feel of a column. Smaller companion plants in this group include mock orange (narrow leaves, thick and bushy in contrast with the tall fig) and the rooting fig for a low, branching look that ties the floor, platform, and wall together.

In the small foyer shown on the next page, the plant grouping is teamed with a large framed pastoral scene and fenced in with an antique fireplace fender. The striped dracaenas paired at one end are tall enough to blend into the wall picture; a single dumb cane does the same thing for the other side. Other greenery fills in the back middle, and ivy leaves weave their way through and over the fender.

To translate this idea into a more informal, airy, garden-room look, use a wall covering of an arbor mural or in a treillage or cane pattern. For the fender, substitute miniature white picket fencing or wire flower-bed fencing (available at

The platform (¾-inch plywood) is propped up on 2-by-4s laid flat and hidden out of sight. Ceiling-mounted fixtures provide light for the plants.

Dracaena, dumb cane, and other greenery grouped together on a waterproof tray.

garden and hardware stores). Try peace lilies for the background; their white spathes add bloom to the garden. Come spring, for a few dollars you can fill in with flowering bedding plants (see page 104). Or try begonias.

Don't be afraid of using a big picture on a small wall. And don't be frightened at the cost of an outsize picture. Really large ones are usually good buys at flea markets and junk shops because few people feel they have the space for one. Also take a look at wallpaper murals; they can be beautiful and surprisingly low in cost.

HINTS FOR GOOD GROUPINGS

A successful plant grouping should combine plants of varying heights and a trailer or two to anchor the arrangement to the tray. Choose plants with similar light and moisture requirements. Place the taller plants in the background, to one side or the other, or on both. Raise any that need to be higher by putting the pot atop an upside-down pot or some other propper-upper.

Don't have too many different kinds of plants; at most, four or five. And don't crowd in too many plants; leave enough room so that each one's foliage has a chance to shine. In a large grouping, choose at least two kinds of plants to be represented more than once.

PLANT TRAYS

The two essential requirements of a tray are that it be waterproof and that it be deep enough to hold a good layer of gravel or marble chips or perlite or pine-bark mulch or some such bed for the pots to sit upon. Ideal plant trays can be found in houseware departments: roasting pans, sheet-cake pans, and large, heavy-duty vinyl or rubberware containers of various types. Hardware stores and auto supply places carry large oil-drip catchers and oil-changing pans that are both suitable. Darkroom trays from photographic supply stores make handsome, durable plant trays in their own right. In junk shops, old refrigerator drip pans and old electric frypans (handles removed) can be had for next to nothing. Kitty-litter trays are another possibility. Plant shops and catalogs also offer a wide range of plastic and metal trays. With all the alternatives, you'll have no trouble finding trays varied enough in shape and size to combine to fit almost any dimension. Eventually, your trays will have to be refurbished or replaced due to rust or cracking, but you can expect years of service out of most of them.

If you don't have, or can't spare, a fireplace fender to define your plant grouping, and if the picket-fence, lighthearted approach is not your style, then make your own frame to corral trays of plants into a unified grouping. Cut 1-by-4s to the desired finished size, miter corners, and glue and nail together. For a finishing touch, add a top trim of 1-by-2s laid flat on the top edges. Miter corners, glue, and nail in place.

Plan to put a double thickness of moisture-barrier paper (sold in building supply places) or other thick vinyl sheeting under the trays. Allow enough plastic to fit under the trays and an additional 4 inches or so all around so that it can be stapled right to the inside of the frame. This extra liner provides insurance against water damage to floor or carpet from any overflows or spills and eliminates the mess and time of mop-up duty.

The arrangement here would be more effective with fewer kinds of plants. See opposite page for hints for good groupings.

Green screens

Plants perched on clear cubes.

To add privacy to a living room when the front door opens directly into it, to make an entrance hall when there isn't one, consider the clear cube. Bracket several cubes together, stack them in a pleasing configuration at right angles to the wall, cover with plants, and *voilà*—an appealing room divider and a cozier room.

If the light level is low in your pretend-foyer, you can install track lighting on the ceiling or on the opposite wall. In the cube treatment pictured here, small lamps with incandescent cool-type lights are keeping the plants alive. The special cool-type bulbs were chosen because they don't produce much heat (see page 23).

OTHER SCREENS

Green screens can divide rooms throughout the house. A traditional folding screen (like the one shown on the opposite page) is a fine room divider—you can hang plants on one side and pictures on the other. An étagère is a solution for those who prefer a see-through divider, and ceiling-hung Lucite or Plexiglas shelves serve the same purpose. The shelves can be cut to whatever length and width you want. Drill holes in the four corners, string the shelves together with chain link, and anchor the whole into a stud in the ceiling. The top shelf shouldn't be positioned too close to the ceiling, or you'll cramp the top plants. If the screen is going to be

ON CARING FOR PLASTIC

Protect plastic cubes and shelves from scratches by covering the bottom of cachepots or saucers with felt, cut to fit, and secured with moistureproof white household glue. Be careful when cleaning: no abrasive cleaners, no substances with solvents in them. Keep a separate sponge for dampening and removing dust; keep it free of grit—even this can scratch.

Anchor pots in place with double-face adhesive tape.

The other side of a green screen offers an opportunity to create a small, quiet place.

in the way of a lot of action—meaning kids—anchor it to the floor with large eye hooks.

For a look that's straight out of the garden, construct a lattice screen. Paint and attach lengths of 2-by-4 to both the floor and the ceiling. Spray-paint lathing the same color as the 2-by-4 supports. When dry, attach to the 2-by-4s in a lattice pattern with small nails or a staple gun. Bank or hang the lattice with small- to medium-leaved plants like the trailing columneas, some of the inch plants, and wandering Jews.

If you want to go all the way with an outdoors look, the screen pictured here —made of cedar stained dark brown—should appeal. The end uprights are 2-by-4s, and the other vertical strips, on which the vines are trained, are 1-by-2s. The screen, which is heavy, is anchored to 2-by-4s at both the floor and the ceiling. You could add a plant tray in front of the screen (see page 49 for the how-to).

When it comes time to pick out a vine, choose just one kind. Here are a few large-scale sturdy types you might make your choice.

*The heartleaf
philodendron is vigorous,
and its rapid growth can
make a green screen a quick reality.*

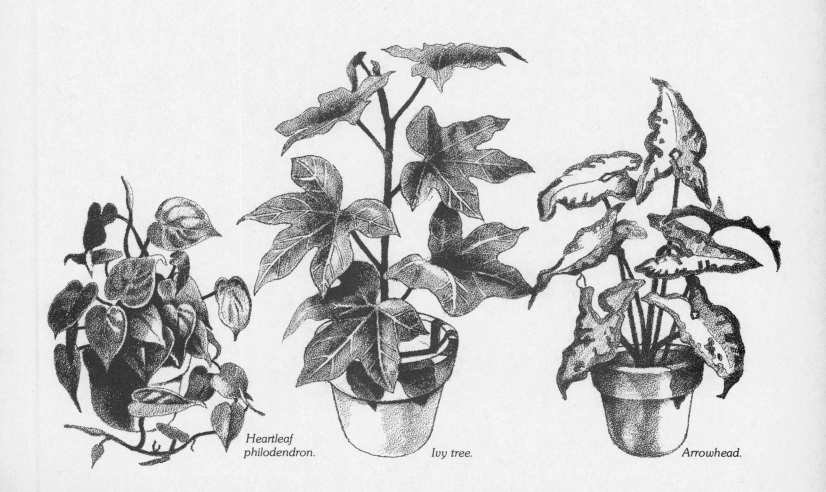

Heartleaf
philodendron.

Ivy tree.

Arrowhead.

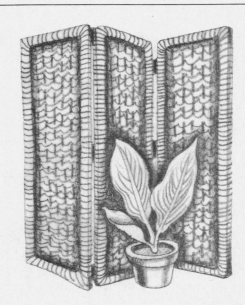

House trees

The owner of this split-level contemporary wanted just one plant for the foyer—a tree, and a large, dramatic one. A stroll through a botanic garden inspired the choice of a banana plant, but a search through catalogs and plant shops turned up only dwarf varieties. Though the

dwarfs make beautiful house trees, they grow only about 5 feet; whereas full-size banana plants can reach a height of 15 to 18 feet in a single summer. Growth will be less indoors than outdoors but will still be big-scale.

Unfortunately, about the only way to get hold of one of the big ones is through a friend who owns a plant and will part with an offshoot. Not having a banana-plant enthusiast among her friends, the owner of this home grew the banana plant from seed. (Source: George W. Park Seed Co., Inc., Greenwood, South Carolina 29647. *Musa arnoldiana,* 3 seeds $.65; *Musa ensete,* 5 seeds $1.00.)

ON BUYING A HOUSE TREE

Buying a house tree calls for a certain amount of courage. The size of the plant itself—and its cost—can produce misgivings and uncertainties. If you are buying a reasonably large tree, keep the following guidelines in mind:

Measure the height and width of the space your tree is to occupy, and measure the tree before you take it home to be sure there is enough room for it. Trees need freedom of space to grow up and grow out. They shouldn't be crowded by other plants or furniture or walls.

Select a container that has, or can be provided with, adequate drainage holes.

If you have selected your tree and are not happy with the container it is already in, buy one you like and have the tree repotted before you take it home. Some plant shops charge;

HOW TO GROW A BANANA PLANT FROM SEED

Soak milled sphagnum peat moss in a pail of water for an hour or so; then squeeze out the excess water, and fill small peat pots with the dampened moss. Place each seed 1 to 1½ inches down in the moss, and cover with more moss. Most important: keep the moss moist at all times; do not let it dry out, or the seeds will not germinate.

Keep the pots in a warm place but not in direct sun. Soon—in three or four weeks, maybe less—a green spearlike sprout will break through the soil. Within a few days it will be 3 or 4 inches tall and ready to be planted, peat pot and all, into a larger pot.

Use as large a container as you can manage. A good choice is a 14-inch clay pot (6-gallon size) on a shallow tray which can be kept almost continuously filled with water. If available, ordinary garden soil, not too clayey and not too sandy, can be used for potting. Add a thick layer of gravel to the pot first and then the dirt or potting soil mix if you have no access to the real thing. Place the container where it is to remain before you fill it for planting; it will be too heavy to rassle around after it is filled.

The banana's growth is dramatic.

Within less than a month, the plant will be over 1 foot high, with four or five long leaves unfurling one after another from a central stalk. From then on, growth will be slower but steady, and in a matter of months, your banana plant will have taken on stately proportions. The leaves stretch out in a large rosette, so the plant needs room both high and wide.

Three main things to know about raising a banana plant (which is actually an herb, not a tree):

Bananas are heavy feeders. Apply a general houseplant fertilizer at half strength once a week. Add a treat of manure tea (packaged dried manure, available from garden shops and catalogs, dissolved in water to make a weak solution) once a month.

Bananas like lots of water; they drink so much that water beads up in large drops on the topside of the leaves. Keep the plants evenly moist, and never let the soil dry out completely.

Bananas do best in an outdoor, sunny spot in the summer, but they will also thrive in bright indoor light. The foyer illustrated on the preceding page, with its clerestory window and large glass sidelight, has proven a happy spot for this banana grown from seed.

others do not. In any event, the charge is usually nominal and worth it to avoid the encounter at home.

🌿 Avoid double potting for a house tree. Because the tree is heavy, you will not be able to lift it out of its container to check whether it's standing in water or not getting enough water. Save yourself much worry and indecision (especially if your tree shows signs of ailing and you need a diagnosis on the water situation) by having a single container that can sit in a shallow-lipped saucer or atop a drain pan or tray filled with pebbles or marble chips.

THE FIG FAMILY

Probably the most successful of all house trees are the members of the fig family. They adapt well to being indoors and make vigorous, healthy plants. The rubber tree is the best known and one of the family's fastest growers—probably the main reason for its popularity. It can put on 3 to 4 feet of growth in a year's time. Such speedy performance puts it high on the list of any budget-minded person who can't afford to pay for 5 feet of green at a whack but can manage a 2-foot plant and a year's wait. Upon approaching a desirable height, the rubber tree can be kept within bounds by pruning it from the top, which, in turn, will produce branching.

Another fig family member is the fiddleleaf fig. It has large, leathery leaves indented on the sides.

Actually, the leaves look more like lyres or huge oak leaves than they do fiddles. It makes a splendid choice for a tree when large-scale-in-a-small-space is what you want.

Then there's the Indian laurel, with its small, smooth, shiny dark-green leaves. It looks like a real outdoor tree and makes a good subject for topiary. Its cousin, the weeping fig, looks a lot like it. The leaves are a bit larger, and the plant assumes a beautiful free-flowing form if given the space; whereas the Indian laurel remains more erect.

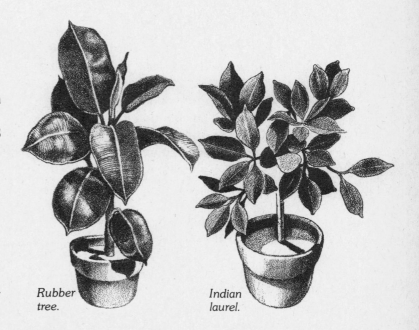

Rubber tree.

Indian laurel.

GROUND BEDS

Given a sizable amount of space—a large living room, for example—you might want to step up from a single potted tree to a ground bed where a tree can keep company with other plantings. Here, a redwood bed houses an heirloom cactus and a satellite collection of smaller cacti and succulents. A base of ¾-inch exterior plywood was cut first to fit under all. Then the higher bed was built from four 2-by-8s, and the wrap-around L-shaped bed from four 2-by-6s. Both beds were lined with moisture-barrier paper—both bottom and sides—and the floor beneath the bed was covered with a protective liner, too. A sandy soil was added, the plantings were made and topped with washed river stones.

As most other plants need more soil depth than do cacti, if you were planting, say, a weeping fig, you'd want to make the higher beds out of 2-by-12s. The weeping fig could be topped with pine-bark mulch and surrounded with a green carpet of creeping fig in the lower bed. A grapefruit tree would also love being housed here; surround its glossy green shrub shape with ivy on the lower level.

PALMS ARE POSH

Despite their upper-crust looks, palms are among the least demanding of houseplants. A modicum of care will keep them happy. There are

Cactus and succulent ground bed.

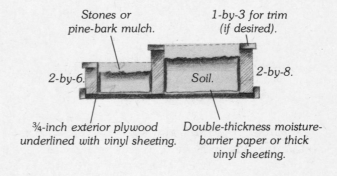

Stones or pine-bark mulch.

1-by-3 for trim (if desired).

2-by-6.

Soil.

2-by-8.

¾-inch exterior plywood underlined with vinyl sheeting.

Double-thickness moisture-barrier paper or thick vinyl sheeting.

dozens of palms to choose from; here are three that make great house trees.

🌿 **Paradise palm.** This is the palm that no well-dressed foyer or parlor could be without. It is among the most agreeable of all the palms, tolerating lower light conditions than others. However, as with all living things, it responds handsomely to something beyond mere custodial care. Good indirect light, evenly moist soil, and full feeding once a month through the summer will keep these palms in tip-top shape with nary a brown tip to a leaf.

Paradise grows more vertically than horizontally and will reach 5 to 7 feet indoors. Plant several to a pot for a full effect. Use a pot on the small side; an 8-inch one will do nicely. Make it a heavy pot, however—of clay, for example, rather than plastic—to add stability at the base.

🌿 **Parlor palm.** Long, thin leaves from wide, arching fronds, growing spiral fashion from base to top, produce a round, thick, full effect. Used in pairs, parlor palms assume the formal air of statuary.

🌿 **Bamboo palm.** Named for its stem, which resembles bamboo, this plant has a distinct Oriental look. Several canes to a pot produce slim columns of graceful greenery.

For elegance, no plant surpasses the palm.

Paradise palm.

Parlor palm.

Bamboo palm.

AND SOME OTHER TREES

🌿 The umbrella tree is widely available, reasonably priced, and fills space horizontally about as fast as it does vertically. It is not a plant you'd choose for small foyers or along traffic patterns in a house, but it fills up corners or room-divides in an unassuming, luxuriantly green way.

🌿 Japanese aralia has long, five-fingered leaves that stretch up and out, somewhat like

Japanese aralia.

giant ivy leaves, on long, stiff stems. It can start off as a table or pedestal plant and graduate to floor tree as it grows.

🌿 The Ming tree, with delicate, lacy foliage, is as Oriental-looking as its name implies. It can go from bonsai size to 5 feet or more in only a few years.

🌿 Norfolk Island pine, a true evergreen, is widely available in plant shops. It is tree-shaped from the very beginning, even at the 2-inch size, and can move from the front of a dollhouse onto a table and then to the floor as it grows. It fits comfortably into smaller rooms, even those with not-so-high ceilings, while still looking every inch a tree. Its Christmas-tree shape and easy care requirements make it a good choice for children, who love having a tree of their own for their own room. A plus: the Norfolk Island pine serves beautifully as a small Christmas tree for the child's room and later can emerge as the family tree when both are grown.

🌿 The monkey puzzle, or bunya bunya, tree is related to the Norfolk Island pine, but its general size and dark-green color are about all they have in common. Where the pine branches out in perfect symmetry, the monkey puzzle zigs and zags with a growth habit so irregular that apparently a monkey would have a hard time figuring out how to climb it. If you like abstract art, and if your house and other furnishings reflect that taste, then you will like this tree. Don't choose this one for a small child's room; the newly emerged needles are sharp and spiky, another contrast to the Norfolk Island pine with its soft-needled, draping branches.

🌿 The dragon tree's look is contemporary, but its asymmetrical lines also have an Oriental touch. You're best off acquiring this plant at near maturity, else you will have to wait years for it to assume the line and rhythm you want.

🌿 Southern yew is a slow, slow grower; so unless you plan to make a family pet of it, you will want to buy this one at a specimen size of 4 or 5 feet. Its soft, narrow leaves, and irregular, somewhat narrow form make it a tree for places where small scale is important. (As a family pet, southern yew can begin as a tiny terrarium plant.)

🌿 Chinese holly grape is for the person seeking something different in a big tree. The twisting, curving shape and glossy, stiff green leaves convey the sturdiness of a holly; the fernlike arrangement of leaves along the long branches suggest the delicacy of fern. If your walls are white and you like vivid graphics, you'll find the holly grape hard to beat.

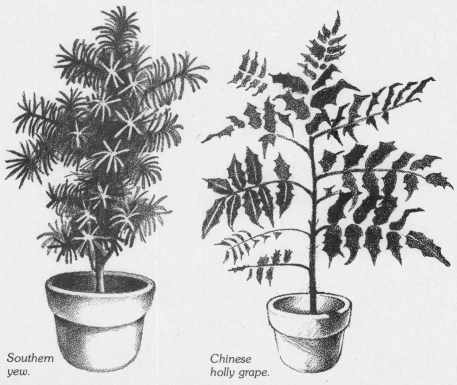

Southern yew.

Chinese holly grape.

Living and Dining

Plants up against the wall

Once a year, a spectacular happening—the Festival of the Patios—overtakes the city of Córdoba, Spain. Throughout the town, people decorate their patios and the façades of their homes with pots and pots full of flowering plants. Each home is more sumptuous than the one before, and should you find yourself in Spain some May, stop and see.

One such traveler created a living souvenir of the trip by moving this enchanting flower idea indoors and onto a living-room wall. Painted white and with enough strong afternoon light from a huge window, the wall literally comes alive with cascading petunias. They are actually the *pièce de résistance* of a year-round series of plants that follow one another onto the wall. This innovative plant lover selected a mixture of bright crimson and pure white petunias and has them ready for wall-hanging from December into February. When the bloom is done and the show is over (petunias are annuals, and when their time is up, that's all there is), they are replaced by pots of wax begonias that have been rooted and groomed while awaiting their turn on the wall. (For rooting, see page 287.) For yet another change, pots of browallia go up in October to take their turn until it's petunia time again.

If you have a good sunny spot, cascade petunias are an especially rewarding effort for the indoor winter garden. Even a single basket hung at a window repays with beautiful giant-size blooms. Colors range from delicate pastels to brilliant scarlets and purples, often with a throat of contrasting color. Add to this a delicious fragrance, and what more could you ask? George W. Park Seed Co. offers a wide selection of seeds.

Cascading petunias in bloom.

PETUNIAS FROM SEED

Plant seeds in late July or early August, in individual peat pots, two or three seeds to a pot. Keep moist and out of direct sun. After the seedlings are up and growing (three pairs of leaves), thin to one plant per pot. Move outdoors if possible, gradually acclimatizing them to the sun. Otherwise, place in a window where they can get at least four to five hours of sun, a bit at a time at first until they get used to it. Pinch out the tip ends of the plants' stems occasionally to encourage bushiness. When the plants reach about 4 inches in height, combine three or four of the peat pots in a single container. Peel away the peat if it's still heavy and intact, and fill the container with additional potting soil as needed.

If your plants summer outdoors, bring them inside to a sunny spot several weeks before frost. Flower buds should be setting now, if they have not already done so, and as soon as the full, beautiful blooms begin to show, move the plants onto the wall to brighten the whole room.

To keep petunias blooming at their best, remove flowers as soon as they begin to fade. (Annuals, such as petunias, flower, form seed, and die in one season. By removing the fading flowers, you remove the seed-making function, and the energy of the plant is channeled into more flower making.) Since petunias like long summer days for flowering, plan on giving them supplemental lighting after dark. They'll bloom best with sixteen to eighteen hours of light. In this room, the containers closer to the light are alternated every so often with those lower down to keep the whole wall abloom.

If you do not have a whole wall to devote to a flower fling, you can still create quite a scene with part of a wall. The dead-end wall of a long, narrow pullman kitchen (pictured opposite) has been greened up with plants that share space with various kitchen accouterments. Small-scale plants were chosen: small-leaved wandering Jews, miniature peperomia, creeping Charlie, prostrate peperomia. The pegboard, spray-painted a light lemon-yellow, covers a cracked, patched, and hopeless-looking wall. (Because white and light backgrounds will reflect more light for your plants, it makes sense to either paint the pegboard, rather than leave it dark natural brown, or select the prepainted type.) Pegboard comes in sheets up to 4 by 8 feet and ⅛ and ¼ inch thick. Choose the latter thickness if your paneling is to support the heavy load of a wallful of hanging plants. Nail the pegboard to furring (1-by-3-inch wood

Plants up against the kitchen wall.

This upstairs hall turned out to be another natural place for plants against the wall, with pots of green-and-white variegated pothos hanging from decorative wrought-iron brackets. The fluorescent tubes behind the cornice (built with a deep 12-inch facing and carefully matched and covered with the brick-patterned vinyl) provide light not only for the plants but for the hallway itself which had once been a plain and rather gloomy stretch of space.

Pothos in an upstairs hall, now turned gallery.

strips) attached to the wall not more than 2 feet apart.

All kinds of hooks, brackets, and holders are available to hang almost anything from pegboard. When choosing hangers for your plants, make sure the extension out from the wall is at least a bit more than half the diameter of the container, to give it room to hang neatly and cleanly away from the wall.

OTHER PLACES, LESS LIGHT, DIFFERENT PLANTS

🌿 **For your dining spot.** An airy green-and-white fern-print wallpaper becomes three-dimensional when real ferns move onto the wall, too. Crisp white wicker or woven rattan containers can show off a variety of the real thing: fluffy ruffles, rabbit's foot, and Boston fern.

🌿 **In the bedroom.** Panels of mirror stretched floor to ceiling, alternating with narrow strips of plain wall, provide an easy and economical way to stretch a room and double up with green at the same time. Install mirror tiles in 2- or 3-foot widths, leaving an 8- to 10-inch strip of wall between, where brackets for plants will go. From any angle, you'll see lots more plants than there actually are.

🌿 **Down in the basement.** Save one of those cinder-block walls, and instead of consigning it to oblivion behind plasterboard or paneling, give it a couple of coats of whitewash, and with the help of track lighting make yourself an illuminated living mural. Round up all those baskets you've acquired, and hang them on the wall with plants tumbling out of them. Line the baskets with polyethylene, and put drip catchers in the bottom. Aluminum tins from frozen foods are good for this use; they can be easily shaped to fit. Add a shallow layer of pebbles, then the potted plant. Prop the plant up if necessary so that the foliage is high enough in the basket to tumble over the side. Mushroom baskets, creels (fishermen's baskets), bread baskets, picnic baskets, all kinds of baskets look great with plants and great against the wall. Think about other containers for other rooms. What about old mustache cups, filled with small plants, in the bathroom?

MOUNTING FLOWERPOTS

While mounting a flowerpot on the wall is not a formidable project, there resides deep in most of us a terrible unease about sinking holes into our walls. Multiply the number of holes needed, as in the case of a wallful of flowers, and the project could well overwhelm all but the sturdiest soul.

There are, however, so many types of brackets, clip-ons, collars, hangers, trophy trays, and platforms available today, as well as a wide choice of ways to mount them, that with a bit of investigation at hardware stores and the like, you can easily come up with a hanger and a method that will do minimum damage to your psyche, the wall, and the landlord's well-being.

So, before pounding any hole in the wall, decide on the type of hanger or bracket you want to use, the kind of container it will hold, its approximate weight, and then settle on the right method for attaching it to the wall. The result will be minimum hassle in putting the plant containers up and minimum repair if and when they need to be removed. As a matter of fact, some of the new extra-strong adhesives might do the job for you, avoiding the trauma of drilling altogether.

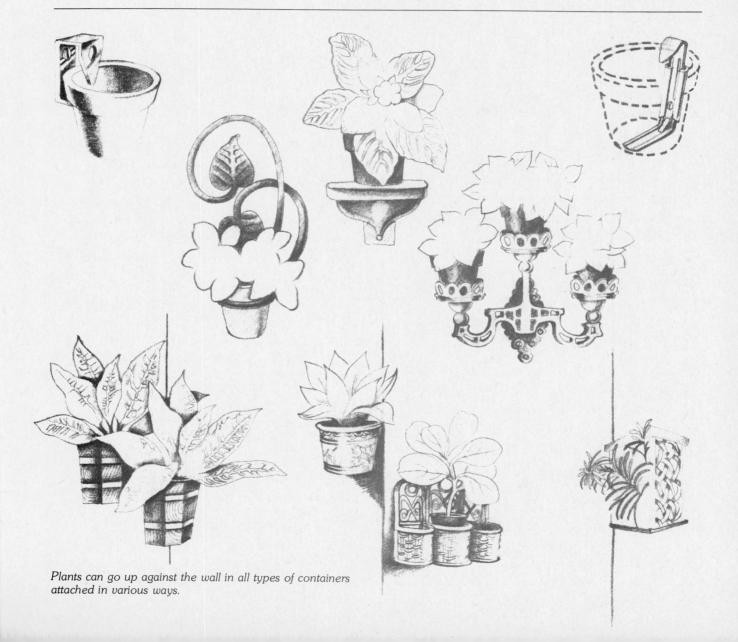

*Plants can go up against the wall in all types of containers
attached in various ways.*

WALL-HANGING HARDWARE

Here are some general guides to hanging the hardware needed for substantial jobs:

🌿 **For plaster walls.** Use a fiber or lead plug, which is a cylinder you insert into the wall to hold the screw tightly in place. First, you drill the hole. It should be the same width as the plug and slightly longer. Tap the plug into the hole all the way. Now put your bracket or planter mount or whatever support you are using in place, and then turn the screw firmly through the plant support and into the plug. Plugs, along with screws to fit, come in different sizes to suit the weight of the object to be hung.

Fiber or lead plug.

🌿 **For plasterboard walls.** Use a Molly bolt (unless you position your container over a stud, in which case use a wood screw). Drill your hole the exact size of the bolt. Insert the bolt; then tighten the screw (this pulls the wings of the bolt up to lie flat against the back of the plasterboard). Now remove the screw, put the bracket or mount in place, and twist the screw back through it and into the bolt.

Molly bolt.

If at some point you need to remove the brackets or mounts, the screw can be removed and the mounts taken down. The Molly bolt remains in the wall, but its rim is small, and it can be filled in and painted or papered over and won't show that much. If for some reason it *has* to be removed, it can be knocked out, but the wall will need a patch job.

🌿 **For hollow-core doors** or thin wood paneling. Use a jack nut, which works on the same principle as the Molly bolt and provides good support. Removal is bound to leave some scars; so on paneling, if possible, it's preferable to thump around to find the studs and then use a wood screw that's heavy and long enough

Jack nut.

to support the weight of the container. If you want to hang plants on the wall between the studs, consider bridging the studs with a piece of wood. Use wood screws to fasten the board to the studs and also to fasten the brackets or mounts to the board. You can stain or paint the boards to match the wall and position them so that they become a part of the wall-of-plants design.

Wood bridge between two studs.

🌿 **A word on drills** and such. Any household of any size should count among its possessions a power drill. They are not expensive (from $10 to $30) and worth every penny for the occasional jobs needed around the house: putting up a curtain rod, pictures, a shelf, and of course, hangers for plants. They are easy to use, and every boy and girl over the age of sixteen ought to know, or be taught, how to handle one. (Practically nothing can make a female feel more self-sufficient for less cost.) If you are just setting up a household, then after you acquire a can opener and subscribe to the newspaper, buy yourself a power drill. Next, look into power jigsaws; they are just about as inexpensive as drills and almost as liberating.

Garniture de cheminée

Many people can live with their fireplaces and mantels for years and never really see them. Take a look at yours. Have you turned it into a a dumping ground for assorted figurines, ashtrays, and yesterday's, last week's, last *month's* mail?

Don't do this. Stop right now and consider ways to dress your mantel for the important role it plays in the room. Classical treatments for mantels span the centuries, and there's one—*garniture de cheminée*—that is particularly lovely. The arrangement consists of five pieces—traditionally, two trumpet-shaped porcelain beakers and three covered porcelain vases. This asymmetrical composition, Chinese in inspiration, was introduced to the Western world by European porcelain manufacturers in the seventeenth century. In contrast with the paired arrangements of the day, it was a welcome change. The porcelain garniture set became particularly popular in the eighteenth century, so much so that today five of anything on a mantel says "eighteenth century" to a design eye.

Here, for the indoor gardener, the idea is translated into five emerald ripple peperomias on an eighteenth-century mantel. The plants have been carefully potted and groomed for the garniture. Their dark-green leaves, beautifully rippled and ridged, grow tightly together, especially when there is more than one plant to a pot. For a full, compact look, plant three or four to a 4-inch pot.

By growing in good, strong light, but not direct sun, and turning the pots regularly so that

Five emerald ripple peperomias on a mantel.

all sides develop symmetrically, you can produce plants that will almost pass for majolica, an Italian earthenware dating back to the Renaissance.

When large enough to move onto the mantel for a garniture, these robust, compact plants assume a formal, elegant air in their French-reproduction cachepots. Long, thin catkin flower spikes are allowed to grow on plants in three of the pots; the other two are clipped off to add to the garniture design. The plants can be kept in good condition on the mantel with judicious use of water and food, meaning not too much of either.

Track lights also help keep the plants in top shape. You can enjoy these plants in such a setting for months, but eventually, as the peperomias grow older, their leaves begin to sag. Before they show definite signs of going over the hill, take leaf cuttings for rootings. Later, when you want to repeat this stunning mantel treatment, you will have new plants waiting for you. What an opulent look emerald ripple can bring to a room!

An arrangement of Mexican clay pots filled with Christmas cactus in full bloom can also

Christmas cactus in bloom.

make a garniture, amusing and informal. Ordinarily, Christmas cactus should spend most of its time in one of the sunniest spots in your house. However, once you have them blooming (around Christmastime, as their name implies), they can suffer excursions into darker areas. Land them on the mantel, where they'll do fine through the holiday season; then return them to their place in the sun.

For the small, squat cottage fireplace, come summertime, try a mantel arrangement of seafans and coral—those incredibly beautiful structures from the sea. Then consider arranging, in one large, round container, a truly fabulous display of bunny ears cactus (*Opuntia microdasys*), that you can move into the empty fireplace for an improbable delight. Cacti are among the most agreeable of the portable plants and are particularly enjoyable found in unlikely places. They can occupy the fireplace for a few days at a time or for an evening solo, but then put them back in their sunshine spot. The cacti can be called on for return engagements off and on all summer, as often as you enjoy showing them off.

Any traditional fireplace comes off well-dressed with pairs of green trailing plants in matched cachepots. Position a plant on either side of a center mirror or painting. English ivy is as traditional as you can get. Other lovely trailers you can use, depending on the light you have and the size of the mantel, are columneas, pileas, and cissus.

Bring a touch of the Oriental to a French mantel with a Ming aralia in bonsai on one side (see page 211) and a handsome ginger jar for the other. For the center, hang a large Chinese Chippendale mirror.

For another French mantel, try espaliering two dwarf citrus trees or training ivy in a candelabra shape for either end of the mantel. This makes a beautiful Christmas decoration.

A random-width or knotty pine fireplace wall calls for a primitive or country look. Use cachepots that are utilitarian—from bean pots and salt jars to spice boxes and tinware. Fieldstone fireplaces also are informal and usually have large hearths. Larger plants in larger containers can move in here. Copper pots and cast-iron kettles can go on the hearth, and large-leaved trailers from the cissus genus, such a kangaroo vine and grape ivy, will suit them fine.

If not on the mantel, plants can go under the mantel. But make a choice—don't have both at the same time. And avoid the grottolike, slightly chilling look that a single plant on the hearth often conveys. Mass several containers

A plant grouping graces a bare fireplace during the summer months.

of plants. Philodendron, mock orange, and Boston fern make a nice combination housed in baskets of different sizes and weaves. They are particularly nice in front of a white fireplace for the summer months.

The dragon tree claims undisputed stardom alongside any hearth where there is no mantel. In fact, the dragon tree has waited patiently in the wings for who knows how many hundreds of years until this contemporary look came

A dragon tree perched on a hearth.

along. Its curving lines add welcome contrast to the straight ones that predominate in contemporary rooms, where no-mantel fireplaces are often found. Other no-mantel treatments: hang a lavabo or mount a good-sized trophy shelf

above the fireplace, and use this important place to put important plants. Important plants, in this case, are those that have leaves large enough to hold their own with the scale of the fireplace and that are in mint condition—and kept that way.

FIREPLACE FACE-LIFT

If the facing around your fireplace needs a face-lift—cracked plaster, sooty bricks, just blah—look into ceramic tiles. Shop around for the size you need; they are much easier to find today in sizes other than the usual 4-inch and not quite 6-inch squares. If you can't find tiles in the precise size you need, remember that you can make adjustments by closing up the space between tiles to as little as ⅛ inch or widening the space up to ⅜ inch.

Spread a ceramic-tile adhesive over the clean, dry surface, using a ⅛-inch sawtooth trowel. Be careful not to leave any bare spots. Tiles can usually be applied to the wet adhesive up to three hours after spreading, so you have plenty of time to work without panic. Press each tile firmly into the adhesive. Try to get it in place without sliding it around too much, so that the adhesive doesn't squeeze up through the tile joints. Don't use too much adhesive. (You can remove adhesive from tiles with a damp cloth before it sets; for smears that have set, use a petroleum solvent.)

After the tile has set in the adhesive a good twenty-four hours, apply grout to the spaces between the tiles. Mix the grout with water to make a thick paste. Allow it to stand for fifteen minutes, and then stir it often while using. Dampen the joints with water. Press the grout into place with a putty knife, a popsicle stick, or your finger, smoothing it out while it is still wet. Wipe off any excess promptly with a damp cloth. With your fingertip, smooth water lightly over the grout to "cure" the grouting so that it will dry without cracking. Repeat a few times at intervals of several hours.

(When you're through with the fireplace, think about stair risers—another charming, practical place for tiles.)

Plants on pedestals

Striking out on your own? Setting up your first apartment? Hesitant about sinking money into a lot of furniture when you're still not certain what you want? Yet your place looks so empty?

The solution: plants and pedestals. The young marrieds who designed this room decided to leave it leanly furnished and to fill the space with plants. They made three white pedestals and topped each with a lacy tree philodendron. The lacy tree philodendrons probably cost less per square foot of space filled than plants of any other kind and certainly a good deal less than a piece of furniture. (Two other easy-to-find, relatively low-cost space fillers are the splitleaf philodendron, and the umbrella tree).

Note that the pedestal arrangement is in the Oriental asymmetrical style. In a grouping of pedestals, three can be more interesting than two; likewise, five is better than four. Block out one of the pedestals in this room, and you can see for yourself.

A linear pedestal effect can be created by the use of small, inexpensive glass and chrome étagères—the type you assemble yourself. Buy a pair of four-shelf étagères like the ones pictured on the next page. Leave out the top glass shelf of one of the étagères, and stage a feather fern on each of the remaining three: smaller plants for the two lower shelves, a larger plant above. On the second étagère, leave out the

Up-lights add shadowy drama at night; experiment with placement to get the effect you like.

Five feather ferns.

top two shelves to make room for another really large fern. Place one more smaller plant on the floor. Then add it up—five plants (two large, three small), two étagères, and a million bucks' worth of elegance.

The feather fern is multidimensional in both color and form. The group of fronds in the center grow straight up, while the outer ones grow out. The tips of the leaves are curly, feathery, and bright, while the rest of the fronds are dark. The contrasts make for a colorful, lively composition.

OTHER PEDESTALS, OTHER ROOMS

Flip through catalogs in furniture stores; browse in flea markets, antique stores, and junk shops—there are pedestals of all types available. If you want something more traditional, think about carved, ribbed, and spiraled col-

umns. They come in marble, wood, porcelain; they are lacquered, stained, gold-leafed. The search for the right pedestal for the right plant for the right place can be an enormous amount of fun with no pressure attached. It can be one of those things you "keep your eyes open for."

Think about a Victorian pedestal for a huge Boston fern in your dining room; a spiraled column of pickled pine for heartleaf philodendron in the bedroom; a pair of Adam pedestals with sago palm in urns for the entrance hall; a glass and chrome pedestal for piggy-back in the bath-

From left to right: Jacobean (seventeenth century), Adams (eighteenth century), Regency (early nineteenth century), Victorian (late nineteenth century), contemporary (twentieth century).

room; an English Regency with forced paper-white narcissus for the living room; a satin-enameled metal sculpture holding Japanese aralia. Pedestals were made for plants!

DO-IT-YOURSELF PEDESTAL 1

Decide on the height for your pedestal. Figure out how many feet of lumber will be needed. If you don't have a saw, ask the lumber dealer to cut the pieces to size. This sometimes involves an extra charge. (Don't demand quick service on a busy Saturday afternoon.)

To build: Spread glue (white household type is okay) along the cut edges of two sides; lap one over the other. Nail the pieces together with six-penny finishing nails (these have no heads and can be sunk into the wood and then covered up with putty). Start nailing at one end and work down, making certain the edges are butted evenly as you go. Glue and nail the third side, then the fourth.

The top can be cut to fit flush with the sides or to have a slight overhang. Finish the edges of the top with screen-reed (also called bead molding; it's a flat molding). Glue and nail in place with small finishing nails or brads.

If you plan to paint the pedestal (alternatives are covering it with wallpaper, fabric, mirror tiles, decoupage, and so on), make sure the wood is well prepared first. Sand the sides, top, and seams. Putty over the nail holes and seams. Let dry. Sand again. Then put on a good grade of paint. You will love the sleek, gleaming results.

If the back side of the pedestal will not be seen, why not leave it off and use the inside space to store extra pots. Or perhaps tuck an up-light in there where it can't be seen. If you go backless, provide a bottom for the pedestal for extra strength and stability, and fit it within the sides as shown. The pedestal, by the way, looks super at the base of the stairs if you don't have a newel post. Top it with a dumb cane plant.

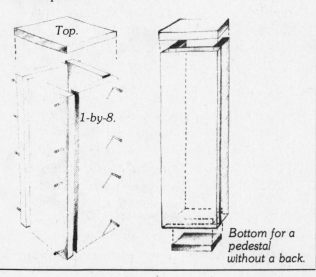

Top.

1-by-8.

Bottom for a pedestal without a back.

DO-IT-YOURSELF PEDESTAL 2

Terra-cotta drainpipes make great plant pedestals for rustic settings—summer cottages, country kitchens, porches, and such. Pipes that are 8 inches in diameter are particularly nice—rough-textured and natural in tone. You have a ready-made pedestal by simply fitting a large terra-cotta pot within the top so that the lip catches on the rim of the drain pipe.

The 8-inch size, however, is not so easy to come by these days. If you can't find this size through a building supplier (many of whom now stock only plastic drain pipes), it's worth trying to wangle one from a wholesale construction supplier or from a construction site. The length of the pipes varies—usually 18 to 36 inches—and you settle for what you can find.

Four-inch-diameter terra-cotta drainpipes are easier to come across; regular building supply and hardware stores often stock them. They are most often found in the traditional red clay color, sometimes as smooth, round cylinders, sometimes with angled sides, and usually in 1-foot lengths. You can group and glue the 1-foot pipes together in three-pipe units, then stack and glue them, unit on unit, until a desirable

height is reached. Cut pieces of 2-by-2 the height of the stack, and place a piece down the center of each of the three columns to add stability. Cap with a terra-cotta saucer.

If you have a sunny spot for your terra-cotta pedestal, try a burro's tail, a beautifully draping plant with small, thick leaves of pale gray-green that overlap each other and trail down in braidlike tails. A burro's tail is easy enough to grow, asking only for good bright light. Don't overwater it; don't repot it. Leave it mostly alone, watch it grow, marvel at the geometry and beauty of the leaf arrangement, and try for a long-term relationship. You can start out with a small plant and wind up, some years hence, with a large specimen-sized plant that you couldn't easily find on the market.

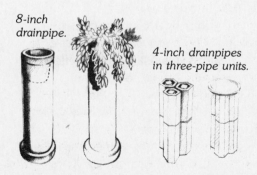

8-inch drainpipe.

4-inch drainpipes in three-pipe units.

Plants with punch

There are some plants whose color or texture or shape conveys an enormous sense of energy and which do wonders for an otherwise blah setting. Empty, this room is really just a box; it has no distinguishing architectural features. It is the kind of room you find in hundreds of high-rise apartments: two plain walls with a window wall between. But add an imposing line-up of pony-tails, an enormously vital tree, and it becomes a room of another color.

There are four plants in this room—on purpose. A handsome Navaho rug that hangs on the wall was acquired firsthand by the owner, along with the knowledge that four is a dominant number in Navaho craft and culture.

Just standing still, the pony-tail somehow looks in motion. Its trunk swells up out of the soil in a huge, wrinkled brown bulb. Then it slims out to a narrow trunk topped with a fountain of long, narrow green leaves. Very exciting.

Pony-tail makes a good long-term investment. It accomodates well to indoor life and is easy to care for. It does best where it can get some direct sunlight a few hours a day. If you have only artificial light, get the most out of it by placing the plants against a highly reflective setting—a glossy white wall, for example.

Although the large, swollen base of the pony-tail's trunk might lead you to believe that the plant requires a lot of growing space, such is not the case. It will get along fine in a relatively small container and can go for years without repotting. Allow your plant to dry out

Four pony-tails carry on.

between waterings. Full-feed it when growth begins in the spring and a couple of times more through the summer.

VARIATIONS ON A THEME

In another setting for the same sort of room, a grouping of caladiums lifts the whole

Caladiums on a French bread rack.

scene out of the ordinary. A French bread rack (reproduction or a real one) against one wall holds white ironstone bowls—the perfect cachepots for brilliant shocking pink and green caladiums. (During the winter months when the caladiums are dormant, bowls of forced paperwhite narcissus can be moved in to take their place; these can be followed by pots of yellow crocus and a few pink hyacinths. For the how-to, see page 281.)

Caladiums are started from tubers, which can be bought for about $1 apiece, and will provide bright, colorful foilage for eight or nine months of the year—year after year. Choose from the brilliant pinks, the deep reds outlined in green, or the snow whites etched with lacy green veinwork, and plant more than one tuber to a pot. Allow at least three for a 6-inch pot; more for bigger pots.

Caladiums are easy to start and easy to grow. The tubers begin showing up in florist and garden shops in January. They can be started anytime from late January through June. If ordering from a catalog, order early so the tubers will be on hand for planting in time to give you some bright color in the house while the days are still gloomy outside.

Plant the tubers about 1 inch deep in a regular potting mix; water them thoroughly; let them drain well; keep them in the warmest part of the house (maybe on top of the refrigerator); and don't water again until the tops have come through the soil.

Once they're up, you can move the plants to wherever you want them. Somewhere near a north window would be ideal. They have to be kept out of the sun (direct sun will burn their leaves), and yet if you give them too little light, you prevent the beautiful strong colors from developing fully. If the leaf color seems anemic or lacks vigor and the stems grow too tall and rangy, then shift to a stronger but still indirect light, or boost the natural light with an artificial source.

Caladiums need to be kept moist but not soggy, and never dry. Dilute-feed each time you water until dormancy begins, or full-feed every three weeks until dormancy begins.

Along about mid-September or early October the foliage will begin to droop. This is the signal that dormancy is beginning, that the plant is getting ready for its rest period. Eliminate fertilizer, and hold off on water, gradually decreasing it until all of the leaves have withered. You

Caladium.

can keep the plant looking in fairly good shape for a while by removing the first few leaves as they wither, but don't cut them off before they have definitely passed their peak. They'll fade fairly fast at the end, anyway.

Now no more water. Store the pot in a dry place (a closet shelf will do) for a three- to four-month rest until the following January or February. Then bring the pot out, water thoroughly, let drain well, then put on the top of the refrigerator, and the tubers begin life all over again.

The dull high-rise living room pictured opposite—this one with a shorter window—is transformed with the help of a natural bamboo roll-up blind. In front of the blind, a Parsons table and a couple of stools make a basically good but plain setting until a collection of crotons arrive to add plenty of punch. Five table-sized plants in basket containers are ranged along the back edge of the table; a big floor-size croton, also in a basket, ties the whole thing together.

Whether you recognize its name or not, you undoubtedly know the croton. It has exotic, leathery-looking leaves of varied color. Some varieties have leaves shaped like large, twisted oak leaves; others are long, thin, and curled; still others are broad and pointed. Choose the color you want for your room. Some plants are accented with green, while others are yellow, pink, orange, or deep red; some plants combine

two or three of these colors, and you might even find them all in one.

A good rule with crotons: Don't buy the first plant you see unless you absolutely love its color and form. There are so many to choose from; check around first.

Crotons deliver a lot of design interest for a minimum amount of care. A sunny window is best, especially in winter, when bright light will produce the brightest-colored leaves. The plants should be kept moist in summer, but never soggy, and watered less in winter. Fertilize on a three-week schedule through the growing season. Crotons like high humidity. Misting helps; so does a saucer full of pebbles.

The croton is an obliging rooter, which makes building a collection easy on your pocketbook. Buy two plants. Use one as is, and cannibalize the other for the five table plants you need for this setting.

Crotons are obliging rooters. They can be rooted in water (for instructions, see page 287).

Croton.

Coffee-table plants

Seated on the sofa with this coffee table before you, consider the delights that await the eye. A collection of *millefiori* (thousand flowers) paperweights are arranged for maximum viewing. Nestled among them in a porcelain demitasse cup is a small blooming beauty—a miniature gloxinia—totally unexpected, totally beautiful, totally in place with the jewellike flowers encased in the paperweights.

Another day the paperweights are elsewhere, replaced by a small wooden drawer salvaged from an old sewing machine cabinet and holding a slab of earth brought in from the outdoors. It is mostly covered with moss, with a twig or two, and a few small pebbles. To this piece of nature-in-the-raw has been added a small planting of partridge berry. Nearby on the table is a hand magnifying glass, the better to see closely the micro world in the drawer. A brass mister is also at hand, used often by owner and guests alike, helping to keep this small piece of the outdoors green and growing.

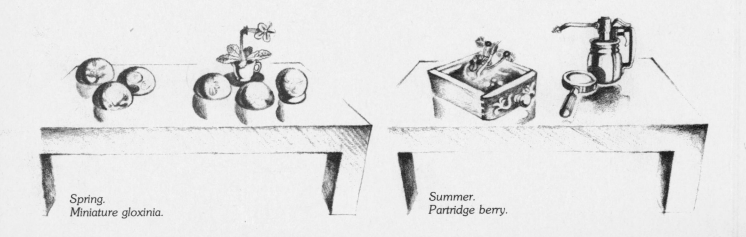

Spring.
Miniature gloxinia.

Summer.
Partridge berry.

Fall arrives, and apples come to the table—on a small plate with a fruit knife. A clay pot of prayer plant is nearby, its exotic markings of deep wine-red echoing the coloring of the apples.

January calls for a lift, and now a tall glass cylinder filled with tangerines takes its place on the table along with a bright yellow ceramic pot filled with nerve plant, its intricate white vein-work and lively upward tilt of green leaves making it an upbeat plant for any coffee table.

Fall.
Prayer plant.

Winter.
Nerve plant.

While a coffee-table book doesn't necessarily reveal the owner's acquaintance with its contents, a coffee-table plant is something else. It states loud and clear the relationship between it and the owner at first glance. An ailing plant or one that is barely hanging on will not do. Coffee-table plants are subject to close scrutiny, so first of all choose plants that are in top condition, and plan to keep them that way. Remember, too, that your coffee table is a small stage where plants from other parts of the house can take turns getting in on the act. No one plant should have to play a long-term engagement on the coffee table.

Coffee-table plants will be viewed mostly from above. While most plants are pretty from that perspective, some are more so than others, in particular the low-growing rosette forms—earth stars from the bromeliad family, for example, and hens and chicks and other rosettes from the sempervivums and echeverias. Plants with intricate pattern and texture, such as the rex begonias, also make strong coffee-table candidates, while most of the ferns and philodendrons and ivies (often seen on coffee tables) pale in comparison—their foliage and growth habit simply do not offer the feast for the eyes that many other plants do when viewed at leisure and close up.

Many of the ferns are too tall, too thick and untidy for coffee-table duty. Part of their foliage is almost constantly in the process of browning, and the beauty of their grace and drift is usually lost when anchored to a table. Notable exceptions are the small, entrancing button fern, and the lively birdsnest fern (which may eventually grow too large but will be lovely to look down upon for a long time).

Then there are the seemingly ordinary plants that turn out not so ordinary after all. Consider creeping fig, for example, with its tiny new leaves of bright lime green. Look down on creeping fig, and you see these small heart-shaped leaves in among the older dark-green foliage; look across the plant, and you miss them altogether.

Baby plants of almost any kind are good to look down on, which makes the $.88 plant counter a good spot for coffee-table plant shopping. The appeal of new growth and de-

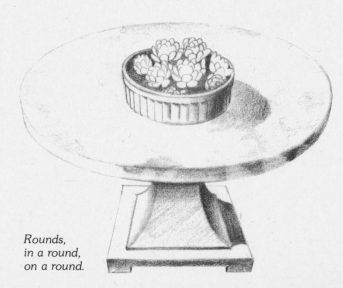

Rounds,
in a round,
on a round.

velopment is as fascinating to observe in plants as in any other young living thing.

Even the large-size plants are bargains as babies. You can enjoy them when young on the coffee table, on a side table when they're older, and eventually as floor plants. A 5- to 6-inch tricolor dragon tree will present you with a lovely pink, green, and cream fountain effect on a coffee table and move on later to become a tree. Baby pony-tails, staghorn ferns, or Japanese aralia all make fascinating, inexpensive coffee-table plants.

Other coffee-table babies can come from plants-in-the-making. Float an offshoot from a spider plant in a wineglass filled with water for a lovely miniature aquarium in a goblet, with or without a goldfish. Rootings and cuttings, rather than

being stashed in an out-of-the-way place, can produce daily drama as they grow, right out where everyone can watch. A collection of small bottles on a glass tray can hold a small forest of cuttings for water rooting; all kinds of decorative dishes and boxes can house cuttings for soil rooting.

The size, shape, and height of a coffee table also has a lot to do with the size, shape, and height of the plant you will want to put on it. A round of white marble inspired the choice of a round white soufflé dish filled with the round rosettes of Mexican snowball. Plant, container, and table are all saying round.

Watch out for plants that are too tall. They may look all right when you're standing, but once seated, you'll be moving them out of the way for conversation. If you need mass and

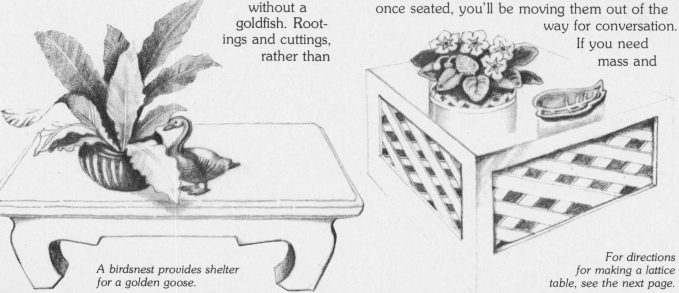

A birdsnest provides shelter for a golden goose.

For directions for making a lattice table, see the next page.

DO-IT-YOURSELF COFFEE TABLES

Making a lattice table. Start with a wood Parsons table—either an old one you are recycling or a new unpainted one. Turn the table upside down. Nail 1½-by-¾-inch shoe molding along the inside of each leg and across the underside of the top. Place the molding slightly back from the front edge of the leg to allow for the thickness of the lattice and the brace between the legs at the bottom. Cut the latticework or filigree paneling to fit the opening. If you don't have the tools, have it cut to size when you buy it. Fasten the lattice to the shoe molding with small finishing nails or brads. Add a brace between the legs on each side. Trim the sides and top of the lattice with screen molding.

Sand the table satin-smooth. Cloak in a coating of a shiny white or sherbet-colored paint. Paint a large basket to match. Line the bottom of the basket with heavy-duty foil; fill with pots of African violets, each with its own drip catcher.

For a low-cost garden look. Start with an outdoor redwood table—round or square or rectangular. If necessary, shorten the legs to the desired height. Sand carefully before applying paint. High-gloss paint in white or bright sherbet colors will produce a crisp, refreshing look, a place where plants will sparkle. A flat-finish paint that is rubbed into the wood will produce a muted, natural look where bowls or baskets of green foliage are eminently at home.

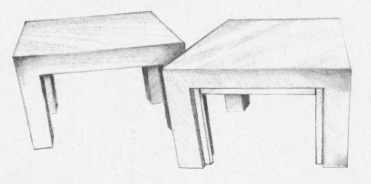

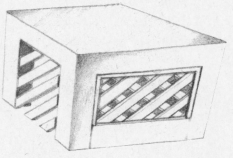

large size, get something large-leaved but which grows out, not up; maybe a plant that drapes over the side of the table. The cissus—grape ivy and kangaroo vine, for example—are not often seen on coffee tables, but on a large one they can look great because of their good strong horizontal lines.

A low coffee table obviously gives you the opportunity to use plants that would be too tall on other tables. A low chow table, for example, accommodates with ease a large birdsnest fern.

For the high tea table, flowers are traditional. Move in a blooming violet or small-sized begonia from another part of the house, and enjoy the color for an afternoon, an evening, a week or so. Nothing is more likely to make you seem rich and idle (when you are neither, but would like to be for an afternoon) than a tea table replete with some delicious fattening treats and a flowering plant for cheer.

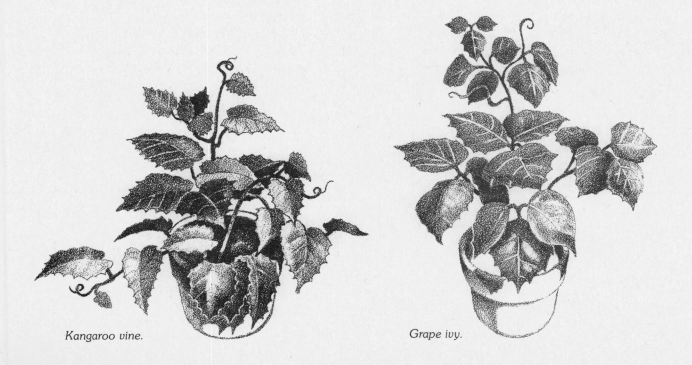

Kangaroo vine.

Grape ivy.

A commanding stage for plenty of plants.

Window stretchers

One of the most wasted spaces for plants is the space that is most treasured: right in front of the window. A plant platform built under your window can enlarge this prime gardening spot and interfere not at all with furniture arrangements, traffic patterns, and such, or at least far less than you might think. If you have two windows together or a wide window, you ought especially to give this suggestion a thought. Built as a three-sided box (open side down), the platform doesn't need to be attached to the wall and can be easily removed if necessary. If it's impossible to hedge the fact that if you've got a radiator or air conditioner at your window, this gorgeous treatment is not for you. (See pages 241–243 for an idea that is for you.)

With such a commanding stage, resist the temptation to fill the space with lots and lots of little plants. Go for the important size in plants, the ultimate in containers. On the opposite page, the lover of blue and white displays a collection of jardinières (reproductions!) that house mostly palms whose simple leaf and symmetry enhance the whole. And just to show that he is not all that opposed to the simple things of life, there are a few large clay pots.

OTHER SPACE MAKERS

Sill-height window shelves are another easy space stretcher. In this case the shelf runs wall to wall, but it obviously can be made to fit any window size. The information on page 49 on how to make a frame for plant trays applies here. First, select the trays that will act as liners for the shelf, and then build the shelf to fit their dimensions. The shelf bed can be made of ½- or ¾-inch plywood; 1-by-2s ought to do for the rim, which is used to conceal the sides of the trays. A back rim is not necessary, since the shelf is attached to the wall.

To mount the shelf against the wall, use decorative wall brackets or angle irons. For extra support, rest the back edge of the shelf on a 1-by-2 nailed to the wall. If you like, you can space the angle irons out of sight away from the

Wall-hung plant shelf.

ends of the shelf for a cantilevered look; or you can use a length of chain at each end of the shelf, stretched from the window molding to the front edge of the shelf for a suspended effect.

Old brownstones, with their grand ceiling heights and fine architectural details, often come equipped with narrow rooms that have two windows on the short wall and perhaps a va-

Typical brownstone windows.

grant, but essential, pipe or two running up the wall. The woodwork around the windows is often lovely; a shame to cover it up. While the view may not be grand, there is usually a tree or two to be seen and a bit of sky. (The view from the outside looking in is not critical here because the room is up off the street.)

You can leave these windows undressed, so to speak, and use them to join the small piece of outdoors with the green inside. Relate floor plants to the windows and use the wide sills for several more plants. With a hanging basket, you can also trail green from the top of the window down. You are not after a jungle effect, though, so use restraint, and don't crowd a lot of plants in here. (Paint the pipe away into the wall.)

The same sort of room is pictured on the opposite page, but in this case, draperies were needed, and hanging plants and windowsill plants wouldn't do. So, instead, a shelf for plant trays was stretched across the floor from wall to wall. Tall plants at the sides and low plants along the front of the windows join the view to the outside when the draperies are open and create a strong center of interest when they are drawn.

Be choosy about plants for this setting, too. Nothing small or cluttery will look right here. Palms, dracaenas, and bromeliads are all good choices and go well together. They all have leaves with strong lines, and they all have

Plant platform

leaved bush), or a huge African violet, or a purple passion plant, or a lemon vine cactus.

A window with a nothing view—in the kitchen, the bathroom, or anywhere—can also be draped with green from top to bottom. Glass, Lucite, and Plexiglas were all invented with window shelves in mind to make it easy for you to green up a view of your own.

If your window has reveals (the inside wall of the window), use small shelf supports from the hardware store especially designed for the purpose. They're easy to install; you drill a hole and push the support in place.

If you don't have reveals, use adjustable shelving strips on the window molding if it's flat enough, or on the wall next to the window if it's not. Or hang shelves from four chains suspended from the ceiling.

There are all sorts of flowerpot fixtures made expressly for windows.

well-defined shapes. For contrast, add one soft, curvy creature—a big jade plant maybe (they don't look soft and curvy when they are young, but as they grow, lovely undulating lines appear as their branches and leaves develop into a sort of carefree, free-form small, thick-

Keep in mind the type of plants you are going to use when constructing your shelves. For example, if the window receives full summer sun, you'll have to choose plants that will not curl up and die from that much heat and light. Geraniums and a number of other flowering plants would love that spot; ivy and a number of other foliage plants would not.

Houses with high horizontal strip windows (ranch windows they're called) are designed by architects who don't care or, worse, don't think about houseplants. To reach up for a place in the sun, try stacking a sawbuck set against the wall. Of course, this is outdoor furniture, but

even for use indoors they're a good buy. They can be given whatever finish suits the room— from a soft weathered-wood patina to a lacquer look in brilliant yellow or parrot green or whitest white.

One bench goes on top of the table, pushed back against the wall, and the other bench goes in front of the table—so you have three tiers, which makes for lots of garden space. The top bench will be about 48 inches off the floor, the table top about 30 inches, and the bottom bench about 18 inches.

Pick your sunniest winter window for this space maker, and use it to coax blooms from violets, begonias, Christmas cactus, and other flowering plants. These can then be carried off to brighten other rooms in the house. With this much space, you can have lots of extras— plants that can shuttle back and forth where and when you want them, plants for gift giving, plants to root to increase your own collection.

Akin to the sawbuck idea is a pair of library stairs flanking a window to widen it out and stretch it up. Be sure to select left- and right-facing stairs. If library stairs seem extravagant on your budget, use wooden step stools. Turn them at right angles to the window, and if you like, stretch a shelf between the bottom steps.

Space at the window can be pushed out as well as in. Prefabricated window greenhouses are available to fit a wide range of window sizes—in fact, adjustable to fit almost any window—and are easy to install. If you decide to invest in a window greenhouse, plan to capitalize on it as a major design asset as well as a place to grow plants. For example, use a wall covering that has a garden "feel," or mount a pair of shutters on either side of the window to showcase the greenhouse. The latter is especially effective when the greenhouse is to be installed in a kitchen, laundry, or basement window, where a household appliance of some sort may be in place below the window, or where there is not much flexibility available to add design interest with wall coverings or furniture arrangement or additional shelves or such.

P.S. One more window stretcher: When building shelves around windows, don't shut out the light for plants by boxing in the sides nearest the window. Leave them open and use wall brackets to support them. You'll get much more light and consequently much more space where plants can perch and be happy.

Prefabricated window greenhouse.

Textures and textiles

In this room the plants themselves inspired the furnishings. One look at a shelfful of Moon Valley in a plant shop, and oak furniture and patchwork quilts were not far behind. Moon Valley is one plant that really looks "quilted." To keep it company, a crib quilt became a tapestry for one wall, and another quilt was used to drape a round table. Secondhand shops yielded the kitchen chairs, which were

*Moon Valley
has a quilted look.*

stripped of paint and returned to their soft golden wood tones.

A low milk-glass cake stand in the center of the table holds small patchwork-covered cachepots full of the brilliant emerald-green and pink Moon Valleys. More plants fill a long shelf in front of the two north windows.

Moon Valley is relatively new to the houseplant scene, having been patented in 1967. (Yes, plants can be patented.) The original Moon Valley was discovered in an Ohio greenhouse growing as a vegetative "sport." A sport in the world of horticulture is usually a part of a plant that differs sharply from the rest of the plant: for example, a branch of a rose bush that bears pink flowers while the rest of the plant's blooms are red. Many new varieties of plants have been discovered in this way.

When shopping for Moon Valley by mail order, you may find it listed under the genus name *Bertolonia* in some catalogs and under *Pilea* in others. Apparently some confusion arose when Moon Valley was first classified; it is now generally accepted as a species of *Pilea*. The confusion is understandable. Taxonomists, whose work it is to group and classify all living things, have a task that approaches the impossible.

Now that you know Moon Valley is a species of *Pilea*, you might like to become acquainted with some of its relatives. Among them are the small, charming miniature peperomia and the energetic creeping Charlie, mentioned often in

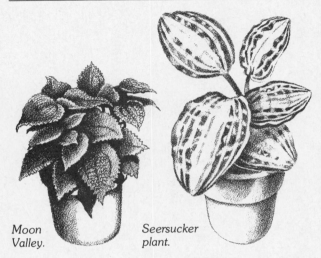

Moon
Valley.

Seersucker
plant.

these pages, and which no houseplant grower should miss having about. Like Moon Valley, these two pileas need bright light but not direct sun. They wouldn't survive the direct rays of the hot summer sun in a southern exposure. These plants like humidity, so pebble-filled trays where water can drain and frequent misting are in order. They also love life in a terrarium. A large glass salad bowl planted with Moon Valley would be a stunner, too.

Other plants whose leaves are particularly interesting in texture are the seersucker plant and the emerald ripple and watermelon peperomias.

A graceful fabriclike plant deserves for its setting a graceful, skirted table. Quilts make lovely cloths, all are agreed, and so do bedspreads, such as an Indian crinkly cotton

bedspread from one of the import stores, or a tailored jacquard throw.

Top a large round cloth with a square, and the layered look comes to the table. Or use a series of rounds in tiers. Skirts can be gathered to the top edge of the cloth for a country look; beautiful printed sheets and scarves and fabrics, as well as treasured old quilts, offer endless possibilities for draping tables for beauty, for fun, for something different.

When buying or making a to-the-floor cloth, allow for 1 extra inch or so, so that the cloth lies on the floor in the French manner. Some directions tell you the cloth should end

A coffee table dressed for dinner. Note that the tablecloth rests on the floor.

about 1 inch from the floor or barely skim it. Pay them no mind; the pouf is better, whether for country or formal surroundings.

No matter how or with what you drape a table, always plan for foliage or flowers atop it.

TO HANG A QUILT

Method 1: Cut two 2-inch-wide strips of sturdy muslin the width of the quilt. Slip-stitch each strip by hand across the back of the quilt, one at the top and one at the bottom. Slide a round drapery pole through the top strip so that the quilt can be hung banner style. Slide a smaller round curtain rod through the bottom so that the quilt will hang flat.

Method 2: Make decorative loops, sew them to the top of the quilt, and hang the quilt by slipping the loops on a drapery rod.

Tapestries and other hangings can also be mounted in either of these ways, but light-weight fabrics such as scarves or beautiful silk or cotton prints should be mounted on canvas stretchers available at art supply stores. Handling the material gently, tack it to the stretcher, keeping it taut so that the corners will finish off neatly. To hang the stretcher frame simply rest its top edge on two small nails inserted into the wall several inches apart.

COVERING CONTAINERS

Coffee cans and cottage-cheese containers (and the world of household receptacles in between) turn into flowerpots and cachepots (like those shown opposite) with the help of a little fabric, ribbon, yarn, leather, rope, or string.

To make patchwork pots. Use pinking shears to cut 1-by-3-inch pieces of gingham, polka dot, or small flower print fabric remnants. Choose a container that is nonporous. (Porous clay or wood containers should be coated with polyurethane varnish, allowed to dry, and given a second coat to moistureproof.)

Spread white glue on the pot, starting at the top, and apply the fabric patches, overlapping each slightly and arranging in an irregular pattern. Press and smooth each piece of fabric with your fingers as you go. If the pot has a rim, arrange the patches so that the edges meet evenly under the rim. Allow enough fabric at top and bottom to overlap the edges of the pot. Apply rickrack or braid as desired. When dry, apply a coat of polyurethane varnish.

If you wish to cover the pot with one piece of fabric, measure the amount you will need, and add a bit extra on both length and width for overlap. Cut the material on the bias. If the container has a rim, cut a separate strip for that on the straight grain.

Coat the flowerpot below the rim with glue and apply the fabric, pressing it into place and smoothing out air bubbles as you go. Work the fabric so that it stretches taut at the top and angles smoothly at the bottom; lap under and seal down with glue, or allow to dry and trim off with a sharp razor blade. If there is too much material at the base to fit smoothly, make several short slashes from the bottom up, and overlap the material to fit. Glue the straight strip of fabric to the rim, pressing the lower edge of the fabric under rim. When the glue dries, coat fabric with polyurethane, or apply a coat of shellac followed by a coat of varnish.

Any can, any size—from tuna fish to potato chip—can be covered. Coat the can with an acrylic polymer medium from the art supply store. Apply the material, let dry. Apply an overcoat of polymer medium, and let dry for a sturdy, moistureproof container.

Paint cans with a rust-retardant metal primer, let dry. (If the container is not metal, you can, obviously, skip this step.) Apply two coats of water-soluble flat paint, letting each coat dry. Sand lightly with fine steel wool (4-0) after the second coat. Seal with a thin coat of clear,

Remember to provide drainage holes. (If you can't punch holes through the bottom of your container, use it as a cachepot instead of a flowerpot.)

nonyellowing, satin-finish varnish; let dry, and sand lightly with the steel wool.

Carefully cut out the picture or illustration you have chosen for the decoupage. Mount it on the can with a thin coat of all-purpose household glue. Now comes the patience part. Apply five coats of the varnish, letting it dry after each coat. After the five coats are on, sand lightly and carefully with the 4-0 steel wool until the surface is absolutely smooth and flat. Repeat with five more coats of varnish and an additional sanding, until the cutout is embedded smoothly under the finish. A minimum of ten to fifteen coats of varnish is usually required. Final step: Use a small amount of paste wax to rub a good sheen, and polish into the dry finish.

Centerpiece show-offs

Good centerpieces are never the forever kind. The most memorable ones are usually the most fleeting, created for the mood and the moment. For a little pure eighteenth century on a bare wood table, you can make yourself a parterre, or knot garden. To capture the feel of a formal, geometrically arranged outdoor garden in an indoor centerpiece, you need several yards of wide grass-green ribbon, eight very small boxwoods, and one boxwood that's a bit larger. English boxwoods are available at plant nurseries and are not expensive in small size. In fact, they are often on sale. Though they can be grown indoors, they do appreciate a little outdoors in the summer, as do most house-plants. Keep them away from the heat in the winter, don't let them get too dry, and they will do fine inside. They are very slow growers and won't outgrow this assignment for several years.

The arrangement (shown opposite) consists of two ribbon squares, one positioned within the other. Substituting string for ribbon, figure out how much yardage you will need for your table. Grosgrain ribbon is heavier than satin, it lies better on the table, and has more texture to it, so get yourself some of that.

The larger—outside—ribbon square is positioned on the diagonal, like a diamond. The smaller—inside—square is positioned on the square. The ribbons can be simply overlapped at corners, or they can be sewn, stapled, or glued. Station a small boxwood on each corner of each square, and the larger boxwood in the center of the small square. The whole takes no more time to assemble than it does to round up the plants and roll out the ribbon.

The perfect parterre container should have that classic wrought-iron garden-furniture look, a look of old, oxidized metal. To give plastic pots a weathered look, spray them with a flat black paint, and while still wet, spray with a coat of moss green. Then rub the pot gently with cheesecloth, mixing the paints to a pleasing blend before they dry. (This is quite an improvement over the colors plastic pots usually come in and a good idea in general, no matter how or where the pot is used.)

If you have small clay pots that have attained a weathered look naturally, use those. (Scrub well to remove any accumulated salts.) If you're starting with new ones, try a commercial finish. One of the products available that works well is called Authentique Weathered Bronze Finish (made by Tichacek Finishes, Inc. P.O. Box 7064, Richmond, Virginia). It makes ordinary cement pieces such as urns, statuary, and birdbaths look as though they were cast in metal. Glass and ceramic containers also come out with an outdoor-garden air. A base coat of dark brown is applied and allowed to dry, and a second coat is put on. After it is dried, a glaze of Verde (green) Patina is applied and then wiped off gently for the desired effect.

Spring and fall are convenient times to go a bit giddy about centerpieces because the

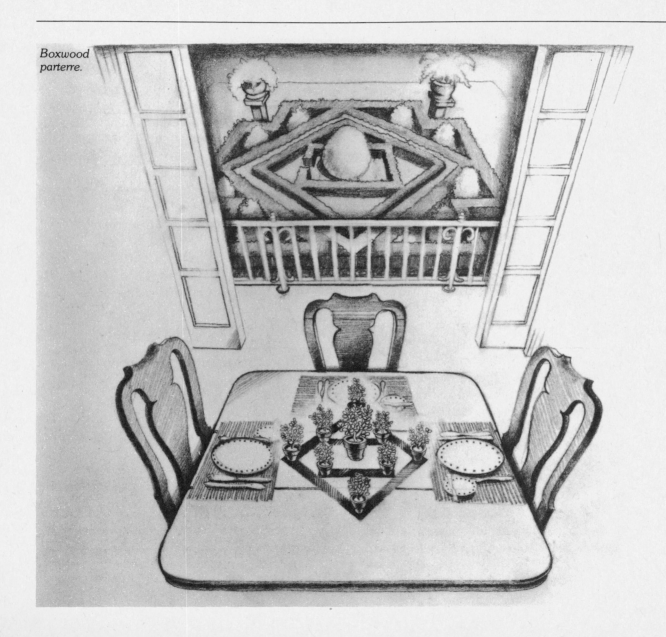

Boxwood parterre.

choices in plant shops are at their best then. Also, bedding plants begin to appear even before winter's gloom is gone. You see flats upon flats of them in front of drugstores and supermarkets and roadside stands.

Bedding plants are overlooked by some houseplant gardeners who may simply assume that they are destined only for outdoor flower beds. But these flats (in the past, usually low wooden boxes; today, usually plastic trays holding anywhere from four to a dozen flowering annuals, perennials, herbs, and other outdoor garden goodies) are one of the best buys the indoor gardener can find. For a dollar or so (often less), you can buy perhaps a dozen small plants of any one kind. These can provide cuttings for lots more plants; or they can be repotted and used in fresh, upbeat centerpieces; or they can live happily on a sunny windowsill; or they can go outdoors, where they'll bloom all summer. For a few dollars you have all this.

A super centerpiece arrangement could be marigolds that you've bought in flats, yellow squash, and long, scrubbed-clean carrots. Work a brown glazed pottery casserole into this pretty picture.

For a deep-purple mood, try eggplants, turnips, and ageratum in a white porcelain quiche dish. For something on the cheery side, what about a spry wire chicken egg basket to hold candytuft and painted Shasta daisies? A smaller chick could trail along carrying fresh fat brown eggs, hard-cooked for eating on the spot

or for use in the next meal—curried, creamed, or stuffed. Should it happen to be Easter, the eggs, quite naturally, would be white ones—decorated to a T.

And what about pansies? They seldom receive the close-up treatment their beautiful faces deserve. Correct this oversight next spring; look for the French blues—they're irresistible. Line long, narrow French bread baskets with foil; arrange the plants in the baskets, filling in with more potting soil (already dampened) as needed to firm plants in place. Plan on enough plants to fill each basket so that the leaves and blooms flow over and cover the sides. Place the baskets end to end for a long, narrow runner of upturned flower faces.

In the nineteenth century, a decorative

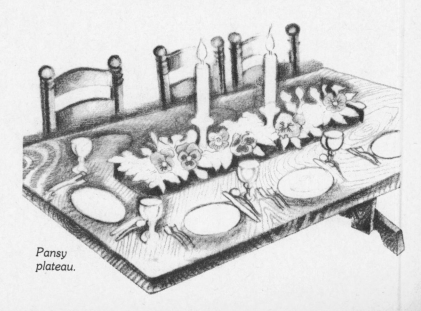

Pansy plateau.

footed tray called a plateau was used to elevate centerpieces on the table. Often it was quite long, taking up more than half the table, though it was centered, of course. For a flower version of the traditional plateau, fill long, shallow, foil-lined roasting pans with the pansies or other bedding plants, and stretch them across the middle of the table. A good-sized oblong or oval gallery tray would do nicely, too. Prop the tray or pan up about 1 inch off the table with something small but sturdy—a small book, for example. The propper-upper won't show if placed under the center of the tray; just make certain it is large enough to provide the sturdy support and elevation of an authentic table plateau. Of course, should you be lucky enough to own the real thing, use it! It will never look lovelier than when covered with flowers.

Houseplants have a natural affinity for other familiar and hospitable objects and the possibilities for go-togethers become endless. Candles and plants are an obvious match. Not far behind are the edibles—fruits and vegetables and nuts. Small individual treasures or parts of collections can also become part of the center-piece scene, from seashells to onyx eggs to small lacquer boxes to baskets. And there are baskets and baskets and baskets.

Then there is kitchenware. All kinds of kitchenware—its usefulness reflecting its beauty—can join up with houseplants for cen-terpieces that are unpretentious classics. On a cutting board, a loaf of crusty black bread, a crock of butter, and a pot of chives get together at a hearty, plain-fare dinner party. At a late breakfast, Tiny Tim tomato shows off its bumper crop alongside a clear glass pitcher of Bloody Marys.

Limes and green grapes and spearmint pile up and out of a white enamel colander at a summer supper on the porch, or in the center of a ring mold a fat, squat chrysanthemum shades a rimful of nuts and kumquats.

You can also marry your houseplants to your menu for some stunning centerpieces and table settings: for instance, a coeur à la crème surrounded by fresh strawberries on a cut-glass cake stand in the center of the table, while at each place a small white wicker coeur mold holds a miniature African violet or gloxinia in full bloom. As long as it's hearts and flowers, and if you want to be especially sentimental,

A miniature African violet keeps company with a coeur à la crème.

COEUR À LA CRÈME

5 ounces cream cheese at
    room temperature
1 1½-inch piece vanilla bean or ½ tea-
    spoon pure vanilla extract
¼ cup sifted confectioners' sugar
1 cup heavy cream
1 pint (2 cups) strawberries
¼ cup sherry
¾ cup currant jelly

1. Place the cream cheese in a bowl, and beat with an electric beater until smooth and soft. Split the vanilla bean and scrape the seeds into the cheese, or add the vanilla extract. Continue beating, adding the sugar gradually. Whip the cream until it holds a firm shape. Then fold into the cheese mixture.

2. Rinse out a piece of cheesecloth in cold water, and line a coeur à la crème mold (six-serving size). Spoon the cream mixture into the mold. Bring up the overlapping ends of the cheesecloth, and fold lightly over the top of the mold.

3. Refrigerate and chill thoroughly, about two hours. Meanwhile, wash and hull the strawberries. Combine the wine and jelly in a small saucepan, place over low heat, and beat with a wire whip until smooth. Mix with the strawberries.

4. To serve, unmold the cheese onto a chilled serving plate, and surround with strawberries. Have a bowl of confectioners' sugar at hand for those who wish it.

Serves 8 to 10

place a doily under each basket, just large enough so that its lacy edge can be seen all around, and fold one napkin into a rose.

If you decide to buy violets for the occasion, look for the new tiny-leaved semi-trailers. They can make an African violet convert out of the hardest holdout and provide you with a continuing resource for many more centerpieces. (Lyon's Pixie Pink was made for a coeur à la crème table.) If you are moving some of your own violets in from their regular station, be sure to trim and groom them and have them at their blooming best. (See pages 304–305.)

Other good plants to keep about the house if you want to have the makings of a centerpiece always close at hand are ivy, piggy-back, begonia, baby's tears, fluffy ruffles, creeping Charlie, miniature peperomia, and the rosettes of the sempervivum or echeveria genus.

Should you happen to own or acquire a candle-burning chandelier, don't have it electrified. Hang it, as is, from a ceiling hook, and enjoy the charm of candlelight from above. And for another charming change, try a canopy centerpiece. Unhook the chandelier, and replace it with a bower of flowers and foliage. A graceful, arching, opulently flowering fuchsia would be one beautiful choice. Hang by a wide satin ribbon, and cluster candlesticks in the center of the table.

A Christmas centerpiece for the kids has to begin with a gingerbread house. Do a little landscaping with cuttings of small-leaved plants, such as boxwood, miniature peperomia, and 'Minima' ivy, slipped into small moistened hunks of florist's Oasis. Place on small butter dishes or painted bottle caps.

If you love fresh cut-flower centerpieces and find the prices out of sight, remember that a green houseplant or two can stretch a cut-flower budget. Three daffodils or daisies along

Boxwood.

Piggy-back.

with pots of small trailing ivy can form the makings of a great centerpiece. How about a single rose circled with ruffly ferns in small silver-washed pots?

FOLDING NAPKINS

A napkin by any other name can turn out to be a rose or a lily or a tulip, depending on how you fold it. If you love beautiful or amusing or different table settings, and all their accompaniments, you'll love the art of napkin folding, too.

To make a napkin "rose," fold a square napkin in half, and then in half again to make a square. Crease along the fold lines with fingers. Open the napkin back out, and with the fold lines as a guide, fold each corner in toward the center so that the four points meet. Holding these corners in place, fold in the new corners so that their points also meet in the center. Repeat once more. Holding the three layers of corners firmly in the center, turn the napkin over and place face down on a flat surface. Now fold the present four corners in so that their points meet at the center. Hold these in place with one hand, and with the other, reach in under the napkin and carefully pull the previously folded-in corners, one by one and one complete layer at a time, out from beneath the napkin and up and over the top corner points. The three layers of folded corners on the underside will form the petals of the rose as they are pulled up and over the corners to the top.

Permanent-press napkins do not hold creases well and are best used for the simple "rolled" folds, For good, crisp folds, use freshly starched and smoothly ironed napkins. Practice the fold on a piece of paper first before you tackle a freshly ironed napkin.

For directions for eleven additional napkin folds, including the tulip and the lily, write to the Belgian Linen Association, 280 Madison Avenue, New York, New York 10016.

Sideboard savvy

Though buffets, sideboards, and serving shelves make beautiful homes for houseplants, they are not often found there—or at least not for very long—because this is one of the places in the home where the light is often a bit less than adequate for plants. Fortunately this gloomy situation is entirely remediable. With all of the good design available in lighting today, plants "on the side" can make it, too.

Here, a single row of track lighting takes care of a number of lighting needs: it provides general room illumination, highlights the art on the wall, and lights the plants beneath. The lights are 150-watt reflector floods, spaced 3 feet apart to provide even illumination across the plants.

While track lighting provides the answer for some plant needs; others can only make it with fluorescent. In its earlier incarnation, the wall of this dining ell was one of the least likely places

The healthy plants on this sideboard owe it all to the track lights.

Fluorescents keep these plants in bloom.

in the whole house for the growing of plants. The light was simply not there. The first decision—installing cornice lighting—led to the second: lowering the lights. The cornice, made to hold two 96-inch fluorescent tubes, was set 2 feet down from the 8-foot-high ceiling. The wide 12-inch faceboard was installed to direct the light down on the plants and conceal the tubes from persons seated in the room. The Formica top has a soft, matte finish (to cut down on glare). It spans a combination of cabinets and drawers, prebuilt but chosen to fit wall-to-wall—11 feet in all. (A space board was added to fill out an inch or so on either side of the cabinets for a built-in look.)

One end of the sideboard stores gardening gear; the rest is allocated for tableware and other storage needs. Plants are housed in separate trays, each of which can be easily moved out at a moment's notice, if and when the shelf is called upon for other purposes. The trays themselves are sleek, handsome darkroom trays from a photographic supply store.

The sideboard often appears covered with bloom because the owner now experiments with a wide range of plants that can be brought into bloom under the lights and then sent off to brighten other rooms for a time. But, the owner says, regardless of what is under the lights, "even if it's a tray of tomato seedlings getting ready to be put out by the patio in the spring, the buffet still looks beautiful. It's much more interesting for anyone to look at than the silver-plated tea service I once thought was what belonged on a sideboard. There's always something growing, something new and green going on here, and people love it."

Where sideboards and buffets can't fit, a wall-hung serving shelf often can. The shelf should be higher than the dining table, which is usually 29 inches high. Locate a serving shelf anywhere from 31 to 34 inches off the floor. The lower the shelf within this range, the more modern the look. Anything higher than 36 inches begins to put you into the bar or kitchen look, so watch out for too much height where it's not wanted.

For a contemporary look, think about using a thick 1½- to 2-inch butcher-block shelf. Or a shelf covered in Formica, metal tile, or mirror. For the traditionalist, marble, travertine, slate, old wood, new wood, or painted wood would be appropriate.

Make the shelf as long as you need, wall-to-wall if you choose (which will also make the room appear wider). If you are an apartment dweller, check out elevator accommodations before buying long hunks of lumber. An 11-foot shelf may not fit, and you will have to be prepared to do some stair climbing and board juggling. Any shelf that's more than 4 feet long should have additional support besides the braces at the two ends.

Consider how plants-on-the-side might help you when searching for ways to "do some-

*Plant shelves show off
in the bathroom.*

(Remember that if you're painting or papering the wall, a light color, high-gloss enamel or a shiny, wet-look vinyl will increase the room's reflectivity and, therefore, the amount of light getting to your plants.)

A bright, inviting entryway was fashioned out of this narrow front hall with the help of track lighting and a shelf of houseplants. Track lighting demonstrates its versatility here. Two of the lights are swiveled to flood the plants; another angles to provide good lighting for the stairway. The brightness index also took a healthy climb when the old floors were sanded smooth and painted glossy white.

thing'' about other trouble spots around the house. Look what happened to a plain, stripped-down, bare-essentials bathroom when shelves were put up so that plants could move in. Track lights replaced the old over-the-mirror light; two for good task lighting and two to focus on the plants. The new shelves hold the plants, plus towels and other oddments, and help pull the whole wall and its fixtures together in a bright, inviting, alive way.

A little bit of light and life in a narrow front hall.

TO PAINT WOOD FLOORS

If the floor you are about to tackle has any kind of finish—varnish, wax, or shellac—it must be removed first. Do not consider trying to cheat or cut corners on this part of the job, for if you do, your later painting efforts will crack, peel, and/or chip away; possibly the paint will never dry. Any of the foregoing consequences should convince you that proper preparation of the floor is a must.

Ideally the floor should be sanded by a professional. You can, however, do a good job of removing the old finish yourself by using a liquid sander—*if* you have patience, time, and energy.

Work a small area at a time. Pour the liquid sander over an area of about 2 square feet and wait thirty to sixty seconds for it to penetrate. Then wipe slowly with a fine steel wool until the old surface is dissolved. Remove with a clean cloth. Continue doing small sections until the old finish is completely removed. Let the floor dry for twelve to twenty-four hours before applying a new finish.

Though the above project took only five sentences to describe and a do-it-yourselfer will probably be happy with the results, don't let anyone tell you that it is not a *big* job. It is.

After the floor is free of all old finish, vacuum it carefully to remove any loose particles of steel wool. Now come the layers of deck enamel.

Choose a high-quality enamel, and use a roller to apply it. It will take at least two coats of deck enamel to produce a smooth-looking painted finish. Let each coat dry for twenty-four hours before applying the next coat. Some designers use as many as five coats of deck enamel to get a slick, lacquer look, sanding each coat lightly after it is dry and wiping lightly with a cloth moistened with denatured alcohol to remove dust. Not a difficult job, definitely a time-consuming one. Results: beautiful.

Some floor refinishers also follow with coats of polyurethane varnish for a diamond-hard surface. Choose a combination of number of coats of paint and varnish that will perform the best for the type of traffic the floor will have.

Plant Gallery and Guide

African violet

Saintpaulia (saint-PAUL-ee-uh)

African violets belong to the Gesneriaceae, a huge family of plants that numbers among its members some of the loveliest of houseplants, including flame violet *(Episcia)*, lipstick vine *(Aeschynanthus)*, and Cape primrose *(Streptocarpus)*.

Violets are good candidates for wicking (see page 33), which minimizes the work of watering and feeding. (Most gesneriads seem to like a constant water–feed routine.) Unfortunately, violets are fair game for a number of pests and diseases, so keep an eye out for trouble as you make your rounds. Isolate immediately any plant that seems in distress until you can diagnose the cause, and either cure or discard the plant. If you have a large collection or a prized plant, join the African Violet Society (for its address, see page 305). Their magazine publishes helpful advice on diagnosing problems. For extra insurance in safeguarding a favorite plant, have a couple of leaves always in the rooting stage. It's easy to do (see page 287).

African
violet

Aluminum plant

Pilea cadierei (pye-LEE-uh kad-ee-AIR-ee-eye)

Most people acquire this pilea as a baby plant—an appealing little foliage plant with silver-flecked leaves. With good care—bright light, regular feeding, even watering, and misting (which it loves)—the aluminum plant will grow into a tall, showy beauty. Terrarium conditions also suit it fine. (The dwarf variety 'Minima' is especially suitable for terrariums.)

Pinch out the growing tips of the aluminum plant, and it will bush; but without pinching and with bright light and enough humidity, it grows into a handsome erect shape, which makes it a good backup planting for lower, more spreading plants. Aluminum plant is also a good choice when you want the symmetry of a series of the same plant on a mantel or in a centerpiece.

Aluminum
plant

Amaryllis

Hippeastrum (hip-ee-ASS-trum)

What more to be said about this showstopping plant beyond its picture here and details for its care on page 279? Except maybe what happens *after* the bloom has gone. The long green foliage will flop around, taking up a lot of space in a bright spot that other sun-loving plants could use. (Amaryllis needs bright light and food after it has finished blooming, too, for the bulb will be storing energy for next year's flowers.)

If you can transplant amaryllis outside, do so; put it where it gets the morning sun, and bring it back in before frost. Otherwise, to keep within bounds, tie the leaves to a stake—loosely, though, so that as much foliage surface as possible will still be exposed to light.

The main thing to remember when growing amaryllis, before bloom, is to give it as much sun as you can. (If the flower stalk is too tall and spindly, if the foliage is a thin, wan green, then the plant did not get enough light.) Move it out of the sun while it is in bloom and then back again afterward for more of the rays.

Amaryllis

Arrowhead

Syngonium (sin-GOH-nee-um)

Syngonium appears on plant counters everywhere—a modest little green thing, almost nondescript except for its pronounced arrowheaded leaf shape. Don't let this unprepossessing appearance fool you. Syngonium is a highly ornamental plant, and if it weren't such an easy, fast-growing, long-lasting plant, it would no doubt be far more prized than it is. The young leaves are usually thin and pale-green, but they soon take on sharp green-toned patterns. As the plant grows larger, it enters a creeping stage and will begin to climb or trail, depending on where you place it. In its mature stage, the leaves lose their arrowhead shape by dividing into a number of long fingerlets. All this action comes from the least-expensive, least-promising-looking plant you can find on the dime-store counter. Keep it evenly moist and out of direct sun.

Arrowhead

Artillery plant

Pilea microphylla (pye-LEE-uh mye-KROFF-ill-uh)

This old favorite is not as popular today as it deserves to be. Its name implies a sturdy, bulky plant, but actually it is soft and feathery in appearance, with tiny, thick leaves that make up fernlike sprays. Its common name comes from the way in which the pollen explodes in a fine dust when it ripens.

This pilea likes to be kept evenly moist and will do well in moderate light. It mixes well with a fern collection; as a single, it makes a more attractive coffee table plant than many a fern.

Baby's tears

Helxine soleirolii (hell-ZYE-nee soh-lee-ROH-lee-eye)

Expect an unpredictable performance from baby's tears. It will appear to be thriving and growing vigorously; then suddenly it will go into a rapid decline, with foliage yellowing and drying out at an alarming rate. You will be left with a tangle of branches and stems that once were covered with thick, lush mounds of tiny leaves. If you can bear with baby's tears while it is in this disreputable stage and be careful not to kill it by trying to "cure" it, the plant will simply rest for a while and then begin to put out new leaves. Give bright light but no direct sun. Keep evenly moist except when resting; and let it dry out between waterings.

Artillery plant

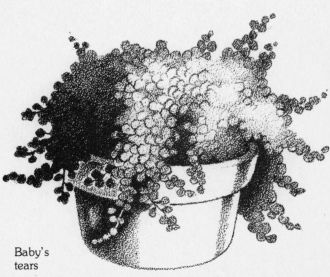

Baby's tears

Banana

Musa (MEW-zuh)

Given bright light, warmth, and lots of water and food, the banana makes superfast growth and can reach 5 to 6 feet in a summer—a smashing green winner.

Musa ensete and *M. amoldiana* produce the largest amount of green imaginable for the price because both can be started from seed. (The first sells at five seeds for $1.00, and the second at three seeds for $.65 at George W. Park Seed Co., Greenwood, South Carolina 29647.)

Ornamental dwarf bananas can be found in some nursery and plant shops. They can be expensive, too, depending on the type. However, if you want the satisfaction of growing your very own, start a banana from seed. (For how-to, see page 56.) While seeds can be started indoors at any time of year, if you start banana seed in early spring, the plant will have all the long days of summer for making fast growth. In winter, growth slows down, and the plant maintains more or less a holding action.

Bead cactus

Senecio herreianus (suh-NEE-see-oh hair-uh-ee-AY-nus)

Everyone ought to own one of these plants. Of course, if everyone did, some of the fun of having such an unusual-looking plant might be lost. Its green beads form along thin, threadlike strands, beginning as the tiniest pinheads and developing into shiny marblelike beads. To encourage fullness in the pot you can cut the strands back a bit as they grow. (Plants also put out new roots where the strands come in contact with the soil.)

Treat the bead cactus as you do most succulents: give the plant a sunny spot; let it dry out between waterings—bone-dry in winter. Mealybug can attack it, so keep a close watch, and clean scrupulously with alcohol or water.

S. rowleyanus is a slightly smaller, more rounded version of *S. herreianus*.

Banana

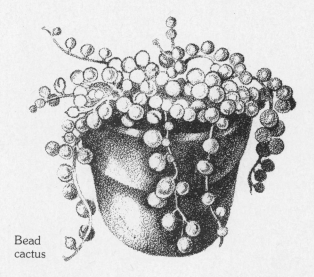

Bead cactus

Begonias

Probably no plant genus offers more by way of diversity and beauty for indoor gardeners than does the begonia. From delicate miniatures to large tree types, from plants covered with blooms to plants with foliage prettier than flowers, begonias offer something for every plant fancier.

There are the rex begonias, with their colorful, dramatic foliage. *B. rex* 'Merry Christmas,' with its beautiful red-and-green patterned leaves, is understandably one of the most popular of the species.

There are the angel-wings, with their lobed leaves and beautiful flowers. Many of these and other cane-stemmed begonias grow tall enough to become house trees.

There are the new Riegers, covered with blossoms, in compact, sturdy bush form or full, lush hanging-basket types. (See page 314.)

Most of the well-known, widely available begonias (and there are dozens of these) are easy-to-grow plants. Some like more humidity and water than others; some like more light than others; but almost all of them can accommodate themselves to your environment if you give them proper care.

Fernleaf begonia *Begonia foliosa* (bee-GOH-nee-uh foh-lee-OH-suh). The special appeal of this hanging-basket begonia is the fernlike foliage and showers of delicate flowers. Fernleaf begonia doesn't like direct sun and will benefit from pruning back. (Use the cuttings to make new plants.)

Fernleaf begonia

Iron cross begonia *B. masoniana* (bee-GOH-nee-uh may-soh-nee-AY-nuh). Iron cross is one of the most popular of the begonias that are grown more for their foliage than their flowers. The brown iron cross pattern shows up dramatically against a green puckered background. The plant likes bright light but not direct sun. Keep it evenly moist, and mist often.

Rex begonia *B. rex* (bee-GOH-nee-uh REX). These begonias are loved for their beautiful leaves. There are dozens of varieties to claim your attention, with wide differences in leaf shape, texture, and color.

While some of the rexes are more demanding about their care than other begonias, many can be grown under home conditions. The main thing to know about rex is that it likes humidity. Keep your plant on a pebble tray where water can collect, and mist the plant often. At the same time, be careful not to overwater; let the soil dry out after each watering. Give rex bright light but not direct sun.

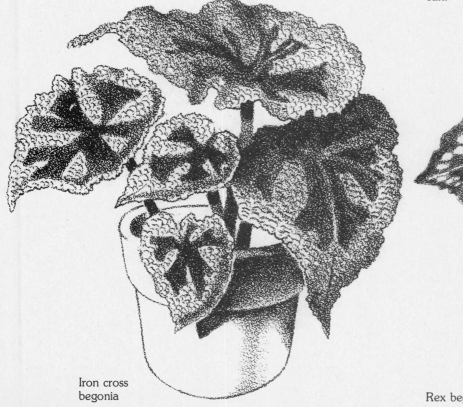

Iron cross
begonia

Rex begonia

Wax or everblooming begonia *B. semperflorens*
(bee-GOH-nee-uh semp-er-FLOH-renz). There are dozens of varieties to choose from among these everblooming beauties—foliage ranging from bright green to deep bronze-red, with flowers of white, pink, or red and shadings in between. Pinch this spirited, indomitable plant back to make it bushy and shaped to suit your fancy.

Bright light and winter sun will produce the best blooms. Let it dry out between waterings.

Boxwood

Buxus microphylla japonica (BUX-us mye-KROFF-ill-uh jap-ON-ick-uh)

Boxwood can introduce to your houseplant scene a look totally different from that created by most of the tropical foliage plants so widely grown indoors. Boxwood is a disciplined little bush from the very beginning, with small, firm leaves and sturdy little branches.

Boxwood will take full sun; a row of these small bushes on a sunny windowsill makes a charmingly prim lineup. Keep plants evenly moist.

Wax or everblooming begonia

Boxwood

Bromeliads

Bromeliaceae (broh-mee-lee-AY-see-ee)

The care and feeding of the beautiful, fascinating bromeliads are described in the chapter on bromeliads (page 293). Ten species for the beginner are also described there. Among them are beauties from the following genera:

Aechmea (ECK-mee-uh). These are the best known of all the bromeliads (unless people are aware that the pineapple, *Ananas comosus*, is also a member of the same family). The plant forms a rosette, as do most of the bromeliads; its shape is more vase- or urnlike than that of the other bromeliads. The broad, stiff leaves, often banded in a striking, constrasting color, make aechmeas handsome foliage plants. The brilliant berry-and flower-bearing stalk that rises above the foliage is an added dividend. Aechmeas are generally easy-care plants, adapting to light conditions from low to bright.

Billbergia (bill-BERJ-ee-uh). These bromeliads grow taller and slimmer than most others, forming a tall, slender vase. The foliage is often a standout. *B.* 'Fantasia,' for example, displays pink and cream-yellow markings against a green background, earning it the name of rainbow plant. Billbergias are easygoing; they adjust readily to almost any sort of light situation from low to bright. Water when dry.

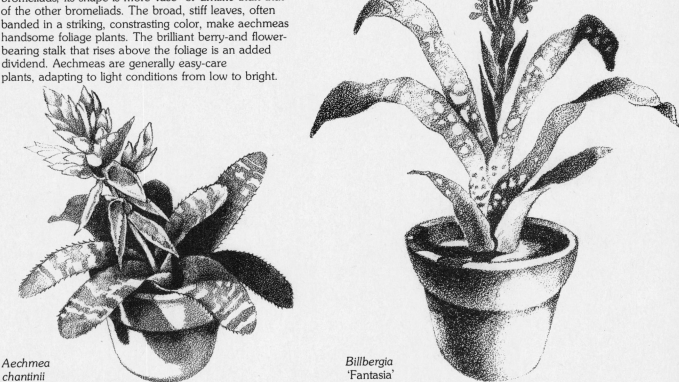

Aechmea chantinii

Billbergia 'Fantasia'

Cryptanthus (krip-TANTH-us). The plants of this genus are the earth stars, as lovely as their name implies, with rosettes that flatten out in a star shape. Although the leaves are stiff, their rippling edges impart a softness to the plant, and their often striking banding or striping adds drama. Earth stars are easy to grow and make ideal plants to look down on. Brighter light (not hot summer sun) produces brighter coloration.

Guzmania (guz-MAY-nee-uh). While this genus retains the rosette shape, it is generally more that of a low, open fountain. The leaves are thinner and not so stiff as the aechmeas, and the plant has a looser, less strongly defined shape. The showy bracts and flowers make the guzmanias as beautiful as any of the bromeliads.

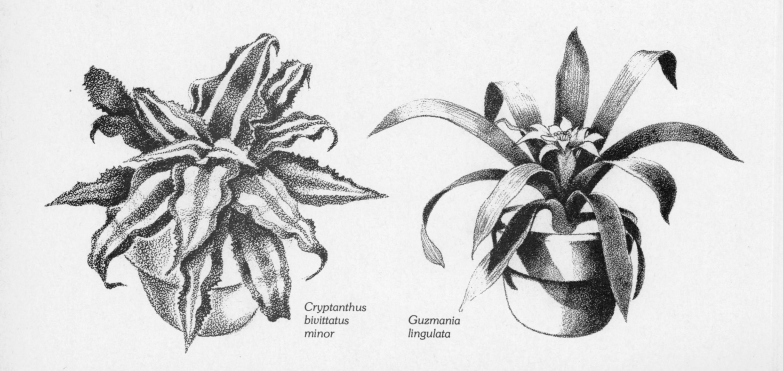

*Cryptanthus
bivittatus
minor*

*Guzmania
lingulata*

Neoregelia (nee-oh-ruh-JEE-lee-uh). Often called the blushing bromeliads, the neoregelia's rosette takes a bowl or basket shape. The showiest part of this plant is right in the center of the foliage, which develops a blush that deepens into bright red. This bromeliad needs brighter light than most of its relatives.

Nidularium (nid-yew-LAY-ree-um). These are the birdsnest bromeliads, which take their name from their beautiful, wide rosette shape. The foliage is lovely, with blushing centers like the neoregelia. The smaller species make handsome coffee table plants; *N. innocentii nana* forms a small lovely rosette with a center that blushes a bright burnt orange.

Grow nidularium in low to medium light; no direct sun. Water when dry; keep rosette center filled with water when plant is blooming.

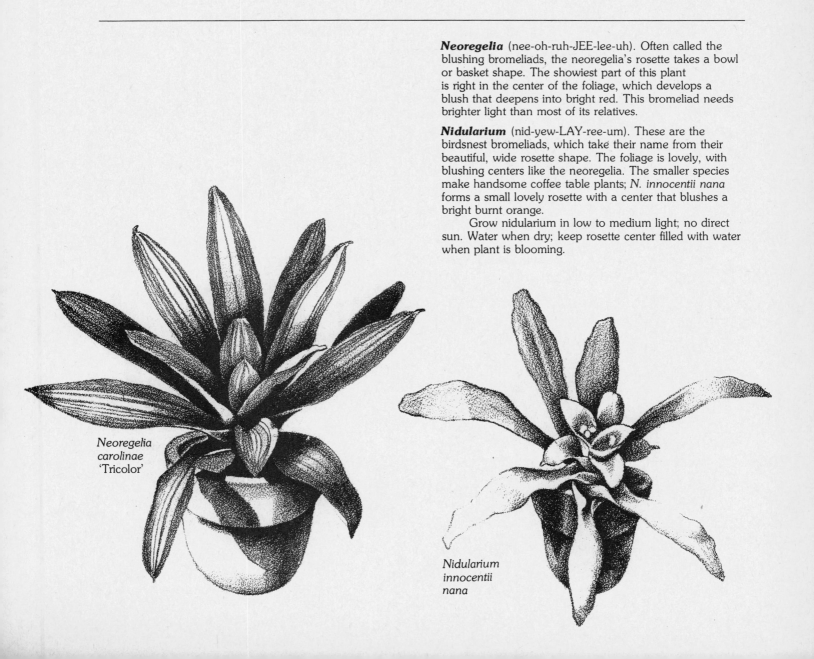

*Neoregelia
carolinae
'Tricolor'*

*Nidularium
innocentii
nana*

Tillandsia (till-AND-zee-uh). The tillandsias are a diverse lot; they include the stringy Spanish moss of the South *(Tillandsia usneoides)* and the tiny, enchanting skyplant *(T. ionantha)*, which can hang on a small piece of bark attached to a string and play spider in your living room. Some of the tillandsias are difficult to grow indoors; others, such as the skyplant, are not. Dunk them in water every couple of weeks, and mist them often.

Vriesia (VREE-zee-uh). Vriesias are called the painted feathers of the bromeliad family—a name easy to appreciate once you see the flower spike, with its showy shape and colors. Most of the vriesias prefer lower light than do other bromeliads, making them handsome plants for the "inside" parts of a room. Keep a mister nearby.

*Tillandsia
ionantha*

*Vriesia
carinata*

Browallia

Browallia (broh-WALL-ee-uh)

New varieties of browallia are increasing the popularity of this nonstop winter bloomer. If you can offer browallia, or sapphire flower, as it is sometimes called, a bright, cool place, you can enjoy its star-shaped flowers from fall through spring. Browallia needs to be pinched back often to keep it in shape and encourage a bushy, more attractive plant.

Browallia is an annual (it's also an herb), so one season's bloom is all you can expect. You can try rooting cuttings, but it is almost easier to grow from seeds. Plant seed any time from spring through midsummer for blooms during the drab days of winter. For spring–summer bloom, plant in the winter. Keep evenly moist.

Burro's tail

Sedum morganianum (SEE-dum more-gan-ee-AY-num)

Those who like geometric designs and orderly surroundings are invariably captivated by this plant. Its small, plump, petallike leaves overlap each other to form a tightly and beautifully organized pattern.

Be careful when tending this plant. Its stems and leaves are far more brittle than they appear and can be snapped off easily. Like most other succulents, burro's tail likes a bright, sunny spot (with enough sun, the plant will also produce bright scarlet flowers at the tips of the stems). Water the plant when dry in summer months; during the winter, let it go bone-dry between waterings.

Browallia

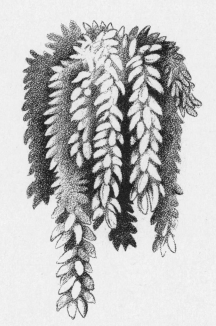

Burro's
tail

Cactus

Cactaceae (kack-TAY-see-ee)

The members of this family are risky to grow indoors only because they so often fall victim to overcare. Given sun or bright light and controlled amounts of water and food, the incredibly varied and beautiful cacti can make splendid indoor gardens. (See page 308 for detailed information about their care.) Among the easiest and most popular are:

Epiphyllum (epp-ee-FILL-um). *E. hybridus,* the orchid cactus, will grow large and heavy if given enough bright light. Less light will produce less plant and probably no blooms; nonetheless the small plants will put on as unpredictable and entertaining a show of growth in miniature as do the stronger, bigger plants growing in the sunlight. Provide for good drainage; let it dry out between waterings. (There are dozens of varieties of this flamboyant plant to choose from.)

Orchid
cactus

Mammillaria (mam-mil-LAY-ree-uh). This genus includes many of the tall, cylindrical cacti as well as the round, globular ones that many people think of when they think "cactus." Fluffy white hairs grow on many of the mammillarias.

Golden stars, *M. elongata,* is one of the most beautiful and easiest to grow of all the cacti. The light-green cylinders come up in clusters, each covered in a perfect geometric pattern of yellow spiny spirals.

Powder puff, *M. bocasana,* grows in fat rounds to fill a pot and resembles a spring bonnet, with lively green plants topped by a "veiling" of silky hair and small daisy-shaped flowers.

Old lady, *M. hahniana,* is a bright green globe, as round as it is high, sporting long, snow-white, curly hair. Its blooms are a purplish red.

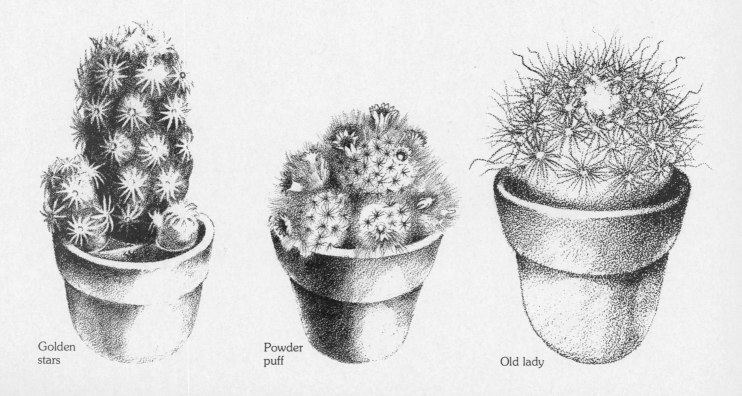

Golden stars

Powder puff

Old lady

Opuntia (oh-PUNT-ee-uh). These are the "prickly
pears," the kind of cactus seen so commonly on plant
counters. Many of them have flat oval or round pads that
produce "ears," which grow bigger and, in turn, produce
more appendages.

Bunny ears, *O. microdasys,* is an especially attractive
opuntia, with a lovely soft spring-green color, punctuated
with yellowish-brown bristles.

Teddy bear, *O. bigelovii,* is anything but soft and
cuddly, but it makes a handsome, fascinating cactus. It
sends out cylindrical offshoots; from a distance the bristly
"arms" and "legs" appear almost furry.

Bunny
ears

Teddy
bear

Pereskia (puh-RESK-ee-uh). Lemon vine cactus, *Pereskia,* looks nothing like most other cacti. Thin lemon-colored leaves are often tinged with purple, and the plant vines and stretches in a lovely arching manner. Sharp spikes run along the stem beneath the leaves. Lemon vine can be pruned back, encouraging more growth from the center for a full, bushy plant. It makes rapid growth if given a sunny spot but does well with indirect bright light or under artificial light. Water when dry; let it go bone-dry between waterings during winter months.

Schlumbergera (schlum-BERJ-er-uh). Active growth begins for this plant right after flowering, and that is the time to give it a bit more water and food than you might ordinarily offer to a member of the cactus family. Too much water will cause the stems to shrivel, and too little will do the same. The best way to tread the line between not enough and too much is to always be sure to let the plant go dry between waterings; when in active growth, let it go dry, but not the dusty dry usually recommended for cacti.

Keep the plant in a sunny window if you want flowers; buds will begin to set in the fall when days grow shorter and temperatures drop.

You can tell the Thanksgiving cactus *(Schlumbergera truncata)* from the Christmas cactus *(S. bridgesii)* by their "teeth." The edges around the joints of the stem on the Thanksgiving cactus are jagged and pointed, while those of the Christmas cactus are much more rounded and soft-looking.

Lemon vine
cactus

Christmas
cactus

Caladium

Caladium (kuh-LAY-dee-um)

Caladiums offer about the most dramatic punch for the price (see page 82). A wide range of colors and combinations lets you choose those that can deliver the particular accent you want, from a fragile, delicate tracery of either pink or green on huge white, arrow-shaped leaves to solid blood-red leaves, and infinite variations in between.

Caladiums are peak-summer plants; they die back and go dormant during the winter. They do not care much for air conditioning, so if you have a hot, muggy apartment, move some caladiums in with you. They'll thrive even if you don't.

Caladium

Calla lily

Zantedeschia (zant-uh-DEESH-ee-uh)

You need full sun to grow the calla lily. Most of the varieties are for winter or early spring flowering, and if you already know the pleasures of the usual bulbs—the crocus and hyacinth, the daffodils and tulips—then move on to the calla lily. (Notes on planting tubers appear on page 279.) Calla lilies can be found not only in the classic pure white but also in rich golden yellows and pale purplish pinks. Besides sunlight, try for high humidity for this plant, misting it often and keeping it evenly moist while in bloom.

Calla lily

Cape primrose

Streptocarpus (strep-toh-KARP-us)

Seeing this plant for the first time when it happens not to be in bloom, you might well pass it by. Its long, floppy, straplike leaves are almost ungainly; certainly there is nothing particularly beautiful or dramatic about them. But just wait; the streptocarpus in bloom is something else. Beautiful trumpet flowers stand up tall and proud above a flowing soft bed of green foliage.

 Streptocarpus is a member of the African violet family (Gesneriaceae). A long-lived plant, it blooms much of the year. It needs strong natural light for blooming (not direct sun), but it also does well under artificial light. Let it dry out between waterings.

Cast-iron plant

Aspidistra elatior (ass-pid-IST-ruh ee-LAY-shee-or)

A favorite of Victorian parlors, the aspidistra could be found doing fine in the shadiest corner of the room. It also prefers the cooler temperatures that were found in those Victorian rooms to the overheated suffiness of modern-day central heating. *Aspidistra elatior* has long, plain, shiny, dark-green leaves; *A. elatior* 'Variegata' has leaves striped green and white. Aspidistra's cast-iron constitution tolerates low light, low moisture, low feeding.

Cape primrose

Cast-iron plant

Chinese evergreen

Aglaonema (ag-loh-NEE-muh)

One of the low-light plants that can manage to hang on in the more remote corners of the house. Like most plants in the dim-light category, however, it will do better than merely exist if it gets more than minimum light and attention.

Chinese evergreen is a bit of a puzzle in its attitude toward water. It will survive and grow as a bottle plant in water only; yet when it is planted in soil, you must take care not to overwater it. Instead, let the soil dry thoroughly between drinks. There are several varieties of Chinese evergreen, from one with deep, waxy, solid green leaves to some with variegated green-and-cream or green-and-white foliage.

Chinese
evergreen

Chinese holly grape

Mahonia lomariifolia (muh-HOH-nee-uh loh-mare-ee-if-FOE-lee-uh)

If you want something different in the way of a house tree, the Chinese holly grape makes a good choice. It doesn't need as much bright light as some of the other house trees; it will grow in a narrow, vertical shape and take up little space, or it can be pruned to encourage branching. It will even bloom in early spring if you give it good bright light. Its leaves have the sharp, pointed shape of the American holly, so you'll need room to place the plant where it won't snag passersby.

Do not place it in direct sun. Keep it evenly moist.

Chinese
holly grape

Christmas kalanchoe

Christmas kalanchoe

Kalanchoe blossfeldiana (kal-an-KOH-ee bloss-feld-ee-AY-nuh)

This plant has more going for it than the blossoms seen so widely at Christmastime. The blooms do last a long time, but even before they are gone, new foliage growth begins. When the flower tops fade, cut them back so the new light-green foliage will show up more prominently.

This kalanchoe is just about as dependable as plants go if you give it a sunny spot and don't overwater; let it go bone-dry between waterings when not in bloom. Lots of new hybrids offer you a choice of blossom color besides the traditional red. Kalanchoe roots easily from cuttings.

Citrus

Citrus (SIT-truss)

Citrus trees offer foliage, flowers, fragrance, and fruit. As discussed on page 262, you can start almost any citrus tree from the seed of fruit; but if you want to be certain of flowering and fruiting, you're better off buying a plant from a nursery or catalog.

Give citrus a sunny place, and rotate it regularly so that all sides get exposure to the sun. Citrus hates blasts of dry heat, so keep it strictly out of the path of radiators or heat ducts. Full-feed once a month. When flowers appear, pollinate by using a soft brush and dabbing gently from one flower center to another. Provide extra humidity if you can; use a pebble tray filled with water, and mist often. A major pest of citrus is scale (see page 40 for treatment).

Calamondin orange *C. mitis* (SIT-truss MYE-tiss). This tree tends to grow tall and columnar. It produces an abundance of blossoms and fruit, often in different stages of maturity at the same time, and has small, waxy, green leaves and fruit measuring 1½ inches in diameter when fully developed.

Ponderosa lemon *C. limonia* 'Ponderosa' (SIT-truss lee-MOH-nee-uh pond-er-ROH-zuh). Its leaves are larger than those of the calamondin orange and lighter green in color; a single lemon is often 3 to 4 inches in diameter and can weigh more than three pounds (one is enough for a large pie); The fragrant trumpet-shaped blossoms are small, waxy, and grow in clusters.

Persian lime *C. aurantifolia* (SIT-truss aw-rant-if-FOH-lee-uh). The foliage is similar to that of the Ponderosa lemon; bears full-size, bright green fruit. A wonderful plant to have on display at holiday time.

Calamondin orange

Ponderosa
lemon

Persian
lime

Coleus

Coleus (KOH-lee-us)

Don't settle for just any coleus. There is such a wide variety of pattern available and a whole palette of colors—green, yellow, red, brown, pink, purple, bronze, cream, white, rust.

You can grow all the coleus you could wish for from one plant because it roots so easily from cuttings, and the more you pinch and cut your plant back, the bushier and better-looking it becomes. Consider cuttings old-age insurance for these plants, for they will eventually wear out. Give good bright light for good bright colors, and keep evenly moist.

Coleus

Columnea

Columnea (koh-LUM-nee-uh)

A beautiful candidate for a hanging basket, the columnea drapes gracefully down the sides of the basket and turns its stem ends upward in a most appealing way. Because of the shape of the flowers, the plant is sometimes called the goldfish plant.

Two discouraging signs—leaf drop and flowers failing to open—can usually be corrected by increasing the humidity for the plants. Mist them often. You can also prune back any branch that has suffered from leaf drop, and this will encourage the plant to put out new shoots. Cuttings from such a pinch-back session can be tucked in the potting mix right along with the plant. These will take root to give you a fuller and more beautiful plant.

Columneas do well under artificial light as well as in bright, natural light. Direct sun will scorch their leaves. Water when dry.

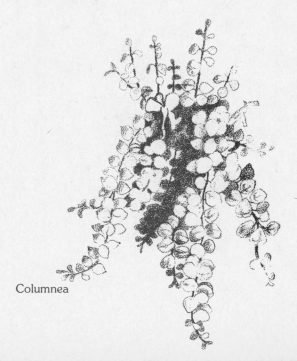

Columnea

Cornstalk plant

***Dracaena fragrans* 'Massangeana'** (druh-SEEN-uh
FRAY-granz mass-an-jee-AY-nuh)

This plant is enormously attractive in all its stages. When
young, it makes a good table or bench plant, with wide,
broad leaves that arch out from a rosette center. As it
grows, a stalklike stem develops that turns this dracaena
into a tree type. Too much water spells certain death (the
lower leaves yellow quickly). Water only when dry. The
cornstalk plant can survive in relatively low light, but the
lively yellow stripes that run through the center of the
leaves will show up more brightly if the plant receives
good light but not direct sun.

Creeping Charlie

Pilea nummulariifolia (pye-LEE-uh
num-mew-lay-ree-if-FOH-lee-uh)

Creeping Charlie is a bright, sprightly trailer with
apple-green, heart-shaped, quilted leaves. It can be
groomed for a solo performance anywhere from coffee
table to centerpiece. (Keep ends pinched back to
encourage bushiness; remove aging leaves at the first sign
of yellowing.) Creeping Charlie also fits obligingly into
almost any background of greenery; use it when you want
to highlight a flowering plant. Give it bright light, not sun;
let it dry out between waterings; mist often. It roots easily
from cuttings.

Cornstalk
plant

Creeping
Charlie

Creeping fig

Ficus pumila (FYE-kus PEW-mil-luh)

This plant starts off as a small-leaved, appealing little trailer producing a tangle of pointed, somewhat heart-shaped foliage. As it grows older, much, much larger leaves suddenly begin to appear on the fruit-bearing branches, though indoor plants are not likely to bear fruit. Creeping fig will climb and cling if you provide a suitable background for it (rough-surface paneling or a bark plank). Give it good light, even a place in the sun, but make certain to keep it evenly moist and the humidity around it as high as you can manage. A too-dry room is definitely a hostile environment for this fig.

Creeping fig

Crocus

Crocus (KROH-kuss)

There are autumn-flowering crocus as well as the beloved spring-flowering ones. The autumn crocus flowers readily indoors; in fact, they can scarcely wait to bloom. (Autumn-flowering varieties include *C. sativus, C. medius,* and *C. longiflorus.*) You can find these crocus on the market in late August and early September. Keep them in the refrigerator until you are ready to plant them. Once put in soil (barely covered and moistened), they're up and blooming in three weeks. Plan to stagger plantings for blooms through October and November. Don't delay planting for after that time; you will get leaves but no flowers. After blooming, these crocus can be planted outdoors to bloom there the following year.

The traditional spring-flowering crocus should be planted in October for blooms in mid-January (for how-to, see page 281). A crocus is not a true bulb, as is the tulip or hyacinth; it is a corm, a swollen underground stem that contains stored food for the plant that will emerge.

Crocus

Croton

Codiaeum (koh-DEE-um)

The croton defies any general description because individual plants can vary so widely. The leaves are large and leathery, but some are broad, and others are narrow, smooth, crinkled, twisted, or flat. The colors are as varied—green, red, orange, pink, or yellow; sometimes they all appear in splotches on a single leaf.

Give crotons bright light—sunlight in winter; good strong light brings out their color. Keep the plant evenly moist; let it dry out between waterings in winter. (For more about crotons, see page 84.)

Croton

Crown-of-thorns

Euphorbia splendens (yew-FOR-bee-uh SPLEN-denz)

This plant is as tough as it looks. It can be found widely on plant counters as a small specimen 4 or 5 inches high, which you can raise to a many-branched shrub as high as 3 feet. At this size, crown-of-thorns is positively wicked-looking, which no doubt accounts for much of its appeal; the branches are crowded with thorns interspersed here and there with a few bright green leaves. Small red flower bracts (the plant is a relative of the poinsettia) form at the ends of the branches.

Crown-of-thorns makes a handsome specimen plant, but for obvious reasons give it a place where it has plenty of room and is not likely to be bumped into or brushed across. It's a succulent, and it will want a sunny place and a dry period between drinks.

Crown-of-thorns

Dragon tree

Dracaena marginata (druh-SEEN-uh mar-jin-NAY-tuh)

This tree starts off as a small shrub, grows slowly into a tree with long, bare, angled stems that end in tufts of long, narrow leaves. Now that you know this, you will not be alarmed when the marginata you bought as a small plant begins to drop its leaves as it grows taller—this is a natural part of adolescence for this plant.

For some reason—perhaps the sparse foliage and angularity of the tree—many people think that marginatas are desert types. Not so. They don't like to dry out between waterings, and they don't care for direct sun, though they do like bright light. The tips of the leaves often turn brown no matter how careful you try to be about watering. Snip off the brown part if it's too noticeable, which usually isn't the case.

Tricolor dracaena, with pink, green, and cream-colored foliage, is a new sophisticated variety, and it is a winner.

Dragon tree

Dumb cane

Dieffenbachia (deef-fen-BOCK-ee-uh)

When young and full, these are beautiful plants with striking foliage patterns of green on green—ranging in color from palest celery to dark zucchini. If given enough humidity, they can grow quite old and large and still be beautiful plants.

As the plant grows taller, if the bottom leaves drop and the plant takes on a leggy look that you don't care for, you can make it more attractive by simply adding a new, smaller dieffenbachia to the container. Don't try to camouflage legginess with a different plant; dieffenbachia leaves are so big and distinct that dissimilar plantings will seem busy and distracting.

If you can bear it, you can cut the top off a leggy plant and root it in water for a new start. Cut the remaining stem off near the base, and you can encourage a new plant there, too.

Dieffenbachia gets along in low light but will do much better with moderate light, not direct sun. Let it dry out between waterings. Dieffenbachia makes a good, large-sized filler plant when you need a mass of greenery.

Dumb cane

False aralia

Dizygotheca elegantissima (dizzy-GOTH-ick-uh
el-leg-an-TISS-im-uh)

Here is a plant you can love or hate. To some people,
false aralia's foliage (long, thin, finely notched leaves) give
it the elegant air its Latin name indicates. To others, the
spidery effect makes the plant look "nervous." The foliage
color offends some plant shoppers, too, because it is not
the glossy or clear green of most indoor foliage plants.
Other plant lovers consider the dark reddish-brown cast of
the green leaves a distinct decorative asset (see page 229).

An undisputed virtue of the false aralia is its ability to
survive low-light situations. It likes warmth and humidity.
Mist often; water when dry.

False sea-onion

Ornithogalum caudatum (or-nith-OGG-uh-lum
kaw-DAY-tum)

This is not a plant you choose for foliage because there is
not much of it. There may be only two or three long,
drooping leaves—at most, maybe seven or eight.
Nonetheless, false sea-onion is a spectacular plant and can
easily become one of your favorites (see page 235). Give
it a sunny spot; let it dry out between waterings; after it
blooms, let it go bone-dry between waterings.

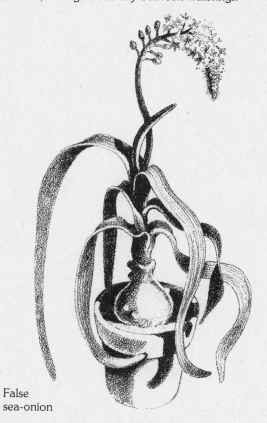

False
aralia

False
sea-onion

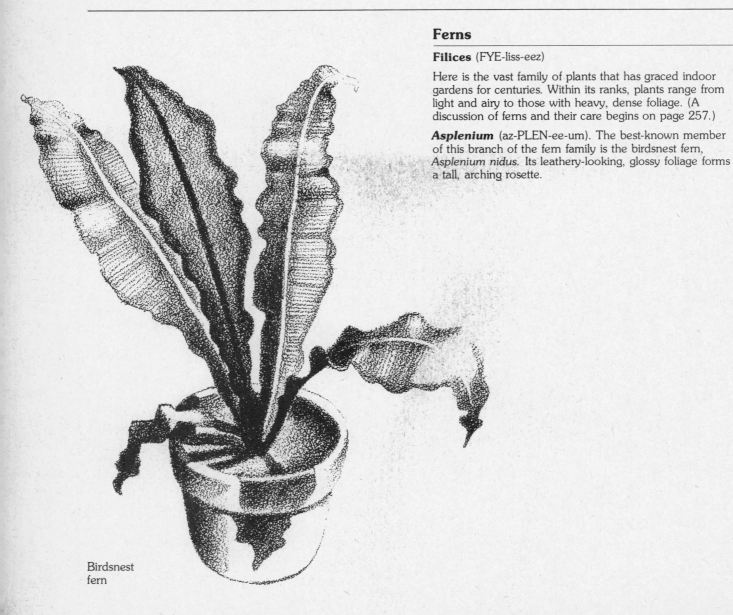

Birdsnest
fern

Ferns

Filices (FYE-liss-eez)

Here is the vast family of plants that has graced indoor gardens for centuries. Within its ranks, plants range from light and airy to those with heavy, dense foliage. (A discussion of ferns and their care begins on page 257.)

Asplenium (az-PLEN-ee-um). The best-known member of this branch of the fern family is the birdsnest fern, *Asplenium nidus.* Its leathery-looking, glossy foliage forms a tall, arching rosette.

Cyrtomium (sir-TOH-mee-um). These are the tough, sturdy members of the fern family; the holly fern (*Cyrtomium falcatum*) is a good example. Its dark-green foliage has a leathery texture, and the plant can take low light better than many other ferns.

Davallia (duh-VAL-lee-uh). These are the ferns with lacy, feathery foliage resembling that of carrot tops. Their furry "feet" are brown, woolly rhizomes that creep up over the edge of the pot and are fascinating to observe. Keep these ferns strictly out of direct sun.

Holly
fern

Rabbit's
foot

Nephrolepis (neff-roh-LEEP-iss). These are the ferns everyone knows—the classic shape of the long, pair-leaved fronds is exemplified in the Boston fern *(Nephrolepis exaltata bostoniensis)*. These ferns grow full and handsome in moderate, even bright light. Among the many varieties of *N. exaltata* are Boston fern *(N. exaltata bostoniensis)*, feather fern *(N. exaltata* 'Whitmanii'), and fluffy ruffles *(N. exaltata* 'Fluffy Ruffles').

Boston
fern

Feather
fern

Pellaea (pell-LAY-ee-uh). These tiny members of the fern family are known as the cliffbrakes. Among the smallest in both plant and leaf size is the button fern *(Pellaea rotundifolia),* a charming fern with round leaflets paired along narrow fronds.

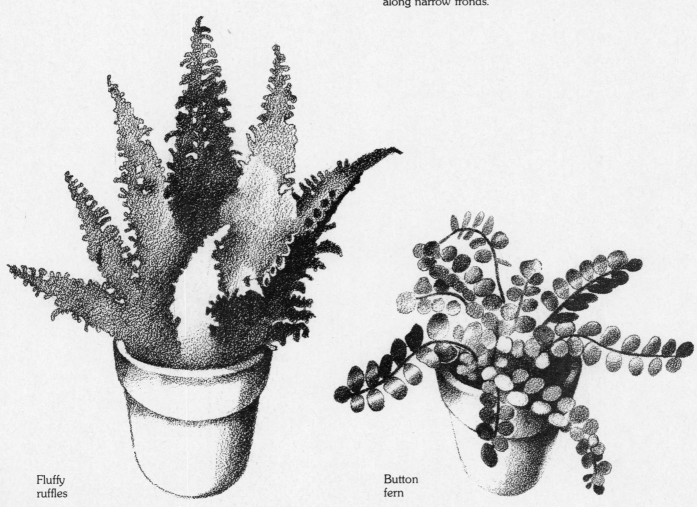

Fluffy
ruffles

Button
fern

Platycerium bifurcatum (platt-iss-SEAR-ee-um
bye-fur-KAY-tum). The exotic *Platycerium bifurcatum,*
commonly known as the staghorn fern, is easier to grow
than its appearance would indicate. It is expensive when
bought at maturity, so consider starting with a baby. It's a
slow grower (which is why the large plants are expensive),
but it makes for fascinating plant-watching. A thick spongy
base ("collar") forms that holds water for the roots of the
plant; as the plant grows, the decaying fronds at the base
add nutrients.

Staghorn likes it light and airy, neither in direct sun
nor in deep shade. Don't overdo the water; unlike many
other ferns that like to be evenly moist, it would rather dry
out before being rewatered. A half-dose of food about
once a month will help produce a vigorous, healthy plant.
A baby plant can start out in a small pot of coarse-ground
fir bark; larger specimens are usually mounted on a pad of
sphagnum moss and attached to a piece of fern bark or
slab of wood.

Polypodium (polly-POH-dee-um). A rich and varied
genus of the fern family, with some species resembling the
Boston fern of the *Nephrolepis* and others resembling the
rabbit's foot of the *Davallia*. The hare's foot fern
(Polypodium aureum) is a particularly handsome plant,
with a number of varieties to choose from, featuring
beautiful broad foliage and fat, creeping rhizomes.

Staghorn
fern

Hare's
foot

Pteris (TEHR-us). These are the table ferns, among the least-expensive and most widely available members of the fern family. They are worth buying in a small size because they make fairly rapid growth. Although their foliage is substantial-looking, the *Pteris* have the characteristic airy, arching, graceful growth habit of the classical fern. Some species have variegated foliage, such as silver brake *(Pteris quadriaurita* 'Argyraea'), in two-tone green and silver.

Fiddleleaf fig

Ficus lyrata (FYE-kuss lye-RAY-tuh)

Huge, lyre-shaped leaves make this fig plant distinctive. It grows tall without taking up too much room space and likes to be potbound, so it can get by for years in the same container.

Give the plant good light but not direct sun. Let it dry out between waterings.

Silver
brake

Fiddleleaf
fig

Flame violet

Episcia (ee-PISS-ee-uh)

The flame violet looks nothing at all like its relative the African violet. The flower face is a bit familiar, but the blooms themselves are trumpet-shaped, and the foliage is coppery green instead of the African violet's velvety deep green. Some varieties of *Episcia* are easier than others to grow. One of the most popular is 'Chocolate Soldier'; one of the most beautiful, 'Pink Brocade.'

The secret to growing flame violet successfully lies in providing enough humidity. If your room is hot and dry, do all you can to add moisture to the air: misting, using pebble trays and a humidifier. Give bright indirect light, and keep evenly moist.

Gardenia

Gardenia jasminoides 'Veitchii' (gar-DEE-nee-uh jazz-min-NOY-deez VYE-chee-eye)

While this gardenia may not produce flowers the size of the florist's variety, the velvety white petals, the gleaming green leaves, and the fragrance are all there.

Bud-drop is probably the major source of anxiety with gardenia. This is often the result of adjusting to its environment. Avoid shifting it about in the house once it has been put in a spot it likes. Yellowing leaves are also common; chelated iron (available in garden stores) is the recommended treatment.

Provide a sunny spot; keep evenly moist; mist often; and for more information, see page 235.

Flame violet

Gardenia

German
ivy

German ivy

Senecio mikanioides (suh-NEE-see-oh
mick-in-NOY-deez)

Also called parlor ivy, this old-time favorite is now making
a comeback. One wonders why the plant ever fell out of
favor in the first place. German ivy is easier to grow than
many of the "real" ivies of the *Hedera* genus. It does not
resent heat and dryness, as do some of the English ivies
(Hedera helix).

The leaves are fresh green and ivy-shaped—not so
delicately defined as those of the English ivies. It responds
enthusiastically to pinching back and will develop into a
full, vigorous plant that can perform as a climber, a trailer,
or a rambling ground cover.

German ivy gets along fine in moderate to bright
light but not in direct sun; water when dry. Cuttings root
easily in soil or water.

Gloxinia

Sinningia (sin-NIN-jee-uh)

If you can grow an African violet, you can grow its flamboyant relative the gloxinia. The large, bell-shaped flowers range in color from deep, dramatic reds and purples to pastels and pure white, with vivid combinations that are probably the most dramatic of all. The miniature gloxinia *(Sinningia pusilla* and *S. concinna)* probably boasts more beauty for its size (2 inches high) than any other plant.

Gloxinias grow from tubers; usually the larger the size of the tuber, the more flowers there will be for a longer period of time. Plant the tuber rounded side down. Give bright light but not direct sun. Keep warm and evenly moist, mist often, and keep on a pebble tray filled with water for extra humidity. Once a plant comes into bloom (three to four months after the first growth appears), new buds will unfold for weeks.

After flowering, keep leaves growing as long as possible—the tuber will be storing food for its next blooms. When leaves begin to yellow, reduce the watering gradually, and let the plant go dry as it dies back. Repot when new little gray mouse-ear leaves appear (resting time can vary from days to months). Gloxinia tubers don't multiply but do increase in size. Leaves can be rooted to make new plants.

If your gloxinia grows leggy, you can pinch it back, or you can whack off the stalk, leaving a stump of about 1 inch to send out new growth. Tuck the cutting into vermiculite or a rooting mix until it forms a tuber of its own. (For more information about gloxinias, see page 279.)

Grape ivy

Cissus rhombifolia (SISS-us rahm-biff-FOH-lee-uh)

A sturdy, large-scale climber or trailer, grape ivy seldom languishes, no matter what its treatment (short of total neglect). It will thrive in a sunny spot but will also adapt and grow in a low-light location. Give it moderate light, water when dry, and you will have it around for a long time. Wrap it round and round a moss pole for a tall, slender column of green; or repot it every couple of years, and separate the roots for new plants.

Gloxinia

Hens and chicks

Sempervivum tectorum (semp-er-VYE-vum teck-TOH-rum)

If you want lots of succulents fast, then this species of sempervivum is the one to choose. The rosettes grow in clusters which can be separated and potted on their own. (For instructions, see page 309.)

Hens and chicks grow 3 to 4 inches across. Each gray-green leaf is tipped with reddish brown.

Give warmth and sun; water when dry—bone-dry in winter.

Grape ivy

Hens and
chicks

Herbs

Herbs can be grown indoors year-round if they're provided with enough good strong light. Most herbs need twelve to fourteen hours of light to keep up active growth, which means, come winter, artificial light may be needed to supplement the sun's rays.

Dry hot air is a particular enemy of herbs. Use humidity-building techniques to keep moisture in the air around the plants: group plants together; place plants on pebble-filled trays; mist often.

Herbs that are annuals (complete their life cycle in a year) can be planted from seed in the spring or fall. Perennials generally benefit from being cut back in the fall for a rest before regrowth, particularly if their winter day length is not extended with artificial light. (Dry the herb cuttings in a barely warm oven with the door ajar. Store in jars for later use. Or use the fresh-cut green herbs to make herb butters—cream a stick of butter, and stir in 2 or 3 teaspoons of the minced fresh herb. Store in small covered jars or crocks.)

Provide excellent drainage for herbs, which means using loose, coarse potting mix, pots with adequate drain holes, and pebble-filled saucers or trays.

Most herbs like to be kept evenly moist and to be misted; most like somewhat cool temperatures and get along better without too much feeding—use a water-soluble fertilizer at intervals recommended, but cut to one-quarter strength.

Basil *Ocimum basilicum* (OH-sim-um bass-ILL-ick um). Grow in good, bright light but not direct summer sun. Keep flowers pinched off, and the plant will be bushier and last longer. When it begins to deteriorate, take cuttings, and start new plants. Definitely use your basil to make fresh pesto Genovese, that phenomenal sauce for pasta.

Borage *Borago officinalis* (boh-RAY-go off-iss-in-NAY-liss). Borage tastes a good deal like cucumber and is lovely in soups and stews as a substitute for parsley. It makes a good hanging-basket plant. After the pretty blue, star-shaped flowers bloom, the leaves begin to change in taste; and as they turn older and rougher, they become unpalatable.

Borage can be grown easily from seed and needs less light than most other herbs.

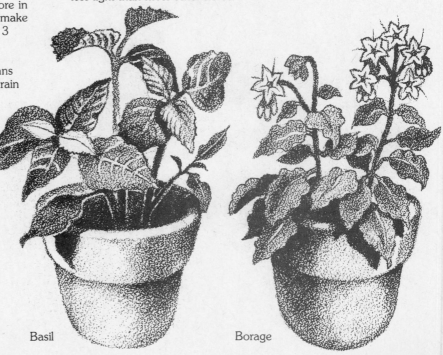

Basil   Borage

Catnip *Nepeta mussinii* (NEPP-uh-tuh muss-IN-*ee-eye*). Catnip does especially well under artificial light. It needs to be cut back to keep it from getting straggly. Kitty gets the trimmings.

Chives *Allium schoenoprasum* (AL-lee-um shane-oh-PRAY-zum). Chives like to be in full sun or close to lights. You can cut the grasslike leaves as often as there is regrowth; just be sure to let them grow out again before recutting. Like most other herbs, keep chives evenly moist.

Lavender *Lavandula dentata* (luh-VAN-dew-luh den-TAY-tuh). The gray-green leaves of this lavender are long and narrow and "toothed" (hence the Latin name "dentata"). It is probably the easiest of the various lavenders for growing indoors. With enough light, your lavender plant will bloom for you when it is two or three years old. Give it a place in the sun; let it dry out between waterings.

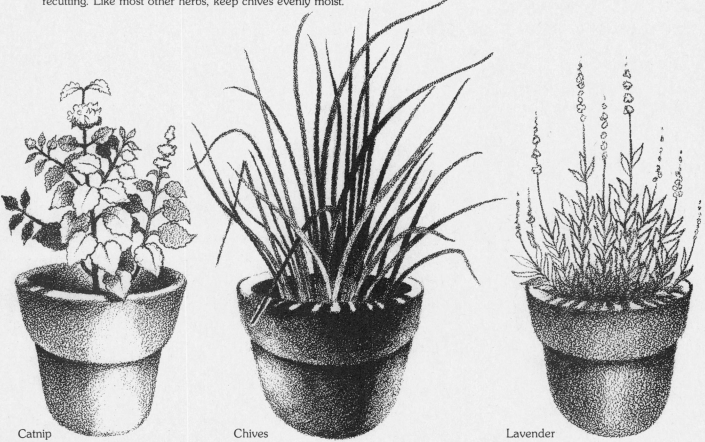

Catnip   Chives   Lavender

Lemon verbena *Aloysia triphylla* (al-LOY-zee-uh trye-FILL-uh). The scent of this fragrant long-lasting herb is stronger in mature plants. Come fall, put the plant out of the sun, prune its branches, cut back on water, and give it a resting period. It will leaf out again in a few weeks. Cuttings can be taken in midsummer for new plants. Lemon verbena does well under lights. Give it bright light but not direct summer sun. Lemon balm *(Melissa officinalis)* is another lemon-scented plant that can be grown indoors. Pinch it back to keep it compact.

Marjoram *Majorana hortensis* (may-jor-RAY-nuh hor-TEN-siss). Sweet marjoram thrives in a moist potting mix. Don't drown it, but don't let it dry out either. It likes more plant food than most other herbs, so feed it one-half the recommended dosage rather than the one-quarter suggested for most other herbs. Give it a sunny spot, or place it close to a light source.

Mint *Mentha* (MEN-thuh). There are many different kinds of mints. Try orange mint, spearmint, apple mint, peppermint. They are fast, sturdy growers that can be pinched back often and will bush more as cuttings are taken. Mint is a good herb for a hanging basket. Give it a larger pot than most other herbs to make space for its long roots. Mint needs to be kept out of the sun and likes to be evenly moist.

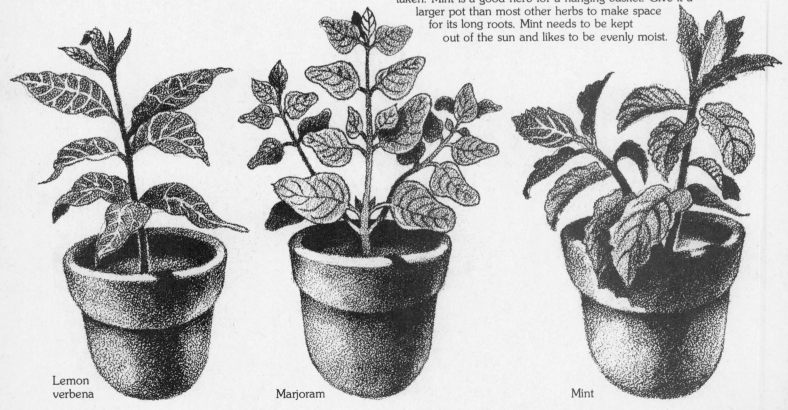

Lemon verbena

Marjoram

Mint

Parsley *Petroselinum crispum* (pet-troh-SELL-in-num KRISP-pum). Bright light (artificial, natural, or both) will do for parsley. Because parsley has long roots, it likes a larger container than most herbs. If it grows tall and spindly, give it more light. Keep it moist in a cool room.

Rosemary *Rosemarinus officinalis* (rose-muh-REYE-nuss off-fiss-in-NAY-liss) This fragrant, ornamental herb takes a larger pot, too, than most other herbs and will grow shrublike in form if you don't cut it too severely. If you start with a small plant, go easy on snipping the first year, and summer it outdoors if you can. Grow in the summer and snip in the winter is a good policy if you want to keep rosemary on hand year round.

Rosemary needs finely tuned watering. Provide perfect drainage; water the plant well; let the soil get barely dry to the touch before watering again. Keep in a sunny spot.

Sage *Salvia* (SAL-vee-uh). This herb is a heavy provider; you can snip away at it often and still have a large, handsome plant. Give sage the sunniest spot in the house. Golden sage has soft, long gray leaves edged in gold; pineapple sage has a heavenly aroma.

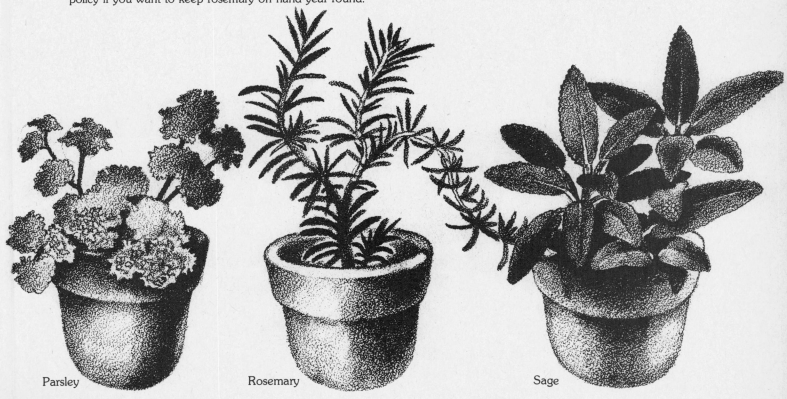

Parsley

Rosemary

Sage

Savory *Satureia* (sat-TOOR-ree-uh). Grow in full sun or under lights. Buy summer savory. *(Satureia hortensis)* for more delicate flavor; it also makes a more dependable container plant than winter savory *(S. montana).* Summer savory is easy to start from seed.

Southernwood *Artemisia abrotanum* (art-uh-MEEZ-ee-uh ab-roh-TAY-num). Plant this herb in a container that enhances the Oriental charm of its form and foliage. A miniature shrub, it can be clipped and trained for bogus bonsai (see page 211). It likes sun and should go dry between waterings.

Tarragon *Artemisia dracunculus* (art-uh-MEEZ-ee-uh druh-KUNK-yew-luss). Tarragon is one of the more difficult herbs to start from seed, so it's best to buy a small plant at a nursery. Give it a spot out of the direct sun; keep evenly moist.

Thyme *Thymus* (TYE-muss). Thyme is another of the longer-lasting herbs, and there are many species and varieties to choose from. Most varieties make charming occupants of hanging baskets. Give thyme sun and otherwise a good deal of neglect. It prefers less water than other herbs (let it go dry between waterings) and less food, too. Cut fertilizer application from one-quarter of the recommended dosage suggested for other herbs to one-eighth.

Savory   Southernwood   Tarragon   Thyme

Indian laurel

Ficus retusa nitida (FYE-kuss ruh-TOO-zuh KNIT-idd-uh)

Indian laurel is often confused with weeping fig because of the similarity in leaf shape and color. The way to tell the two trees apart instantly is to note their posture, for where *Ficus benjamina* droops (hence the name "weeping"), *F. retusa nitida* has an upright, confident air about it. This is the tree to choose if you wish to shape a formal effect. Standards are often made from this tree.

This member of the fig family likes as bright a spot as you can give it—full sun if you have it, perhaps screened with a thin curtain if it will be in the line of direct midday summer sun.

Let it dry out between waterings. As with all large potted plants, be especially careful to water thoroughly and make provision for good drainage.

Indian
laurel

Indoor grapevine

Cissus capensis (SISS-us kuh-PEN-siss)

The shape of the grape leaf is there, but the leaves of the indoor grapevine are small, thin, soft, and pale green. The whole plant has a soft, graceful, even shy air about it when left to trail as it pleases. Nonetheless, its leaves are large enough to put the plant on your list of strong, sturdy types that can hold their own in large-scale surroundings. Give the indoor grapevine bright light; water when dry; and you will have it around for a long, long time.

Indoor
grapevine

Ivy

Algerian ivy *Hedera canariensis* 'Variegata'

(HEAD-er-uh kuh-nay-ree-EN-siss vay-ree-eh-GAY-tuh). This is a dramatic ivy. The outer part of its leathery green leaves is splotched a rich creamy-white. It makes a handsome plant whether climbing, hanging, trailing, or rambling. It accommodates to moderate light but loves the bright spots. Keep evenly moist, and mist.

English ivy *Hedera helix* (HEAD-er-uh HEE-lix). There are enough varieties of English ivy alone to provide a real challenge for any plant collector. Some (such as heart ivy, *Hedera helix* 'Scutifolia') make good choices for training bonsai-fashion (see page 211); others (such as *H. helix* 'Itsy Bitsy' or 'Needlepoint') can make enchanting additions to arrangements of miniature plants; still others (such as *H. helix* 'Pittsburgh') are splendid candidates for hanging, trailing, or rambling plants. Some (such as *H. helix* 'Curlilocks') are easier to raise than others, not being too particular about humidity and heat. Most English ivies like a cool atmosphere. They also like humidity, will want misting, and generally like to be kept evenly moist.

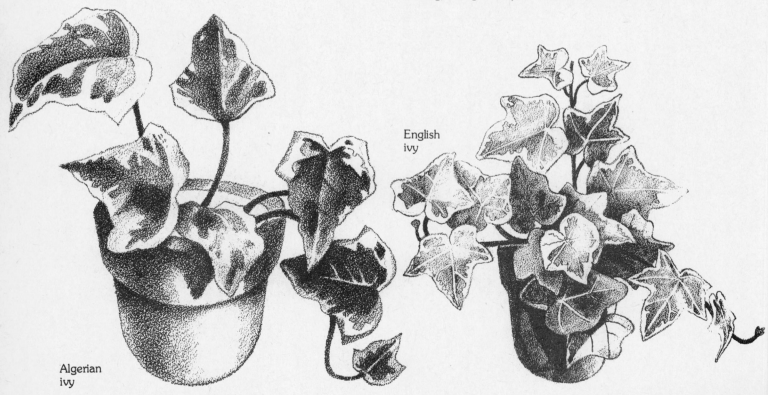

English ivy

Algerian ivy

Ivy tree

Fatshedera lizei (fat-SHED-er-uh LIZZ-ee-eye)

This strong, vigorous part-ivy plant is an obliging trainer. Start when the plant is young and the stem is still pliable, because it will grow thick and tough with age. Train the stem round and round for a large topiary. Or stake it straight up for a standard, pinching off all leaves except for those that can be trained to the fat pom-pom shape at the top.

The plant grows vigorously and looks its best in bright light without direct sun, but it can thrive in lower-light situations, too. It likes to be evenly moist, and it likes mistings. It will grow fast on a constant-feed program when it has adequate light.

Ivy
tree

Jade tree

Crassula argentea (KRASS-yew-luh ar-JENT-ee-uh)

The jade tree is a surprising performer, and its elegant, Oriental look belies how easy it is to grow and care for.

Jade tree does well in bright light and will survive in moderate light. Once potted, it can stay put for several years, preferring to be potbound.

With good light and good care, the jade tree will make full, fast growth. Good care includes being especially watchful for mealybug attack (see page 39) and being careful not to overwater.

Feed once a month through the summer growing time, and water when dry. In winter, let the plant go bone-dry between waterings.

Jade
tree

Japanese aralia

Fatsia japonica (FAT-zee-uh jap-ON-ick-uh)

If you don't care for the big-leaved philodendrons and want a large-scale plant, then consider *Fatsia japonica.* The plant itself can stretch as high as 5 feet indoors; its leaves can reach as much as 1 foot across in a beautiful palmate shape. Fatsia likes to be evenly watered and evenly fed from spring to fall, so tie the two together in a constant-feed program. Through the winter: less water, no food. Give the plant bright light but no sun.

Fatsia will not endure as much neglect without protest as philodendron might, so do not let it languish without proper light or watering, and don't take it for granted. Good, steady care will produce a plant you will love and will love to watch growing. The new leaves emerge as perfectly formed miniatures of the huge leaves they will become, which they do with amazing speed.

Jasmine

Jasminum polyanthum (JAZZ-min-um polly-ANTH-um)

Choose this pink jasmine for a delicate, arching vine and lacy, curling foliage. Prune it for a bushier effect. If you can give jasmine a sunny spot, you will also have deliciously fragrant flowers in late winter or early spring. Jasmine is one of those plants, like poinsettia, that need the short day length of winter to trigger their bloom. During the late fall and winter, keep the plant in a dark room at night, as even artificial room lighting can interfere with its bloom. Keep evenly moist.

Japanese
aralia

Jasmine

Kafir lily

***Clivia miniata* 'Grandiflora'** (KLIV-ee-uh
min-*ee*-AY-tuh grand-if-FLOH-ruh)

Give kafir lily bright light but not sun, and it will produce
brilliant orange-and-yellow flowers year after year. You
can leave it in the same container for five to six years
because it prefers not to be disturbed and likes being
potbound. It will, in fact, send up new clumps and flower
willingly as long as there is the tiniest space left in the
container.

Keep evenly moist when the plant is in bloom; let it
go bone-dry between waterings during winter, when it is
resting.

Kangaroo vine

Cissus antarctica (SISS-us ant-ARE-tick-uh)

Kangaroo vine is the most outgoing member of the *Cissus*
genus—as bold and shiny as its grapevine relative (*C.
capensis*) is shy and pale. Wherever it hangs or climbs, its
bright elm-shaped leaves reach out in a saucy, impudent
fashion. It is as tough as it looks and does well with
moderate light. Water when dry.

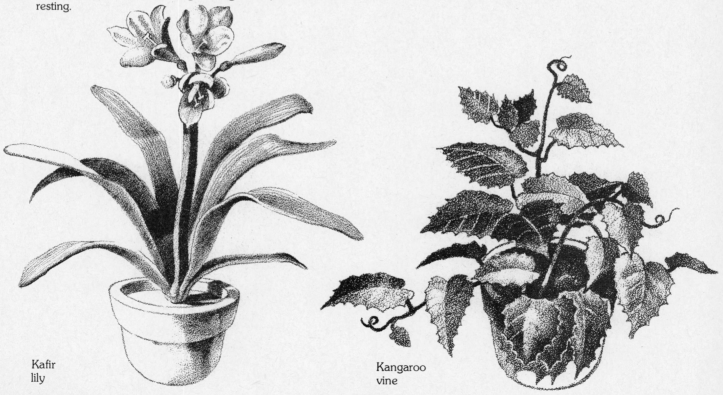

Kafir
lily

Kangaroo
vine

Lipstick vine

Aeschynanthus (esk-uh-NANTH-us)

Do not let this charming plant dry out completely while it is making good growth, and be careful not to give it too much water when it is resting. It needs good strong light in order to bloom, whether from a sunny window (watch out in summer that direct sun doesn't scorch leaves) or under artificial lights. If you cut back after bloom, you'll have a bushier plant and more flowers next time around. Humidity helps, too.

Scarlet basket vine *(Aeschynanthus pulcher)* produces bright scarlet flowers with yellow throats. This particular lipstick vine seems more willing to bloom in either summer or winter than do some of the other species. It also seems to bloom better if slightly potbound. It roots easily from cuttings.

Lipstick vine

Mexican snowball

Echeveria elegans (eck-uh-VEER-ee-uh EL-luh-ganz)

The classical rosette form of the Mexican snowball is typical of most echeverias; yet you can collect almost endlessly within this single genus and find enormous diversity. Some echeverias have a bluish cast to their leaves; others, a gray or pink blush. Some leaves have rounded tips; others are pointed. Some species are as small as ½ inch; others grow flat and can reach a width of nearly 1 foot. Plants send up a long, thin, curving flower spike which bears small, colorful blooms usually coral-red or orange.

The rosette of green jade *(Echeveria agavoides)* is almost star-shaped, with wide light-green leaves tapering into points. Plush plant *(E. pulvinata),* also called 'Chenille plant,' has thick, velvety leaves and a more open face than the closed noselike face of the Mexican snowball.

Provide excellent drainage and a sunny spot; water when dry in summer; keep bone-dry during winter. Echeverias are easily propagated (see page 309).

Echeveria elegans

E. agavoides

E. pulvinata

Ming aralia

Polyscias fruticosa (poh-liss-EE-us froo-tick-OH-zuh)

Here is another plant with an Eastern air that is
deceptively simple to grow. For all its lacy, delicate looks,
Ming aralia is, in fact, a sturdy plant not easily harmed,
even by an amateur gardener. It submits to bonsai
treatment (page 211), developing sinewy lines and draping
foliage of great charm. When allowed free growth, it puts
out new foliage rapidly. Mistreatment causes its foliage to
yellow and drop, but the plant can nearly always be
rescued, even at the stage where the stems are nearly
denuded.

Ming aralia grows well in moderate to bright light and
can take winter sun. It also does well under artificial light.
Provide for good drainage (especially important in bonsai
treatment); water when dry.

Polyscias balfouriana, a close relative of the Ming
aralia, has much the same sort of appealing growth habit
but quite different foliage. Its leaves are shiny, leathery,
crinkly green rounds. *P. balfouriana* is just as easy to grow
as Ming and just as beautiful to own.

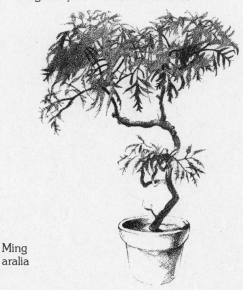

Ming
aralia

Miniature peperomia

Pilea depressa (pye-LEE-uh dee-PRESS-uh)

This plant is often confused with baby's tears *(Helxine soleirolii),* though about all the two plants have in common is miniature leaf size. *Pilea depressa* is the sturdier plant, with a stronger growth habit and more distinct foliage. It roots easily from cuttings. Give moderately bright light, not direct sun. Water when dry.

Mistletoe fig

Ficus diversifolia (FYE-kuss dye-verse-if-FOH-lee-uh)

Mistletoe fig is a handsome plant that adds a festive air at Christmastime. The foliage is not full, but the leaves are lovely—waxy, veined, and shaped like big teardrops. With bright light, long-lasting small red figs will form along the branches at the base of the leaves. Keep the plant evenly moist.

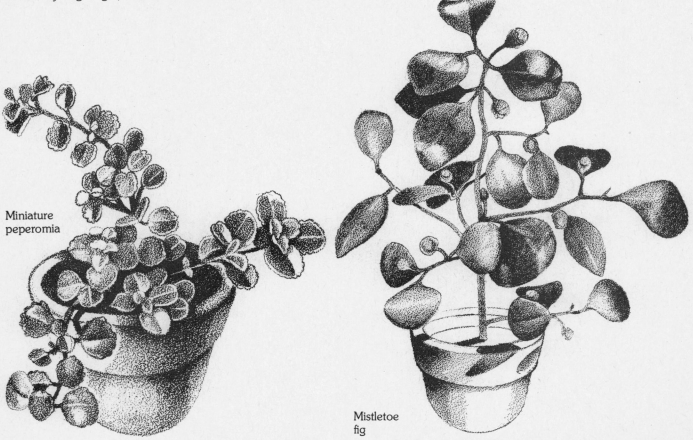

Miniature peperomia

Mistletoe fig

Mock orange

Pittosporum tobira (pit-toss-POH-rum toh-BYE-ruh)

This is another plant with an Oriental air. Its growth habit is asymmetrical, and the leaves form a sort of rosette on the ends of the branches, somewhat like a dark, waxy-green chrysanthemum. If you are acquainted with rhododendron, you might think mock orange a miniature relative.

Mock orange makes a good, tough indoor shrub, amenable to pruning and shaping, and would be high on anyone's list for a dependable floor plant. It does not need direct sun, though it doesn't object to it, either. A good bright spot will be fine for mock orange; let it dry out between waterings. Feed it twice a year (in spring and summer).

Monkey puzzle

Araucaria bidwillii (are-oh-KAY-ree-uh bid-WILL-ee-eye)

A true tree and a relative of the Norfolk Island pine, the monkey puzzle or bunya bunya makes a sturdy, unusual-looking houseplant. The foliage is thicker and denser than that of the Norfolk Island pine; its branching patterns more irregular and erratic. The shiny green leaves are sharp and pointed.

Monkey puzzle can make it in moderate light, but with bright light, it will grow faster and fuller. Let it dry out between waterings.

Mock
orange

Monkey
puzzle

Moon Valley

***Pilea* 'Moon Valley'** (pye-LEE-uh)

An upright, cheerful accent plant, Moon Valley has quilted leaves of apple green deeply veined in brown. It is a slow grower and will be content in a terrarium for a long time. Try a single plant under a clear glass dome.

The plant needs bright light but not direct sun. It does well under artificial light and likes humidity. Keep evenly moist, and mist often. (For more information on Moon Valley, see page 98.)

Natal plum

Carissa grandiflora horizontalis (kuh-RISS-uh grand-if-FLOH-ruh hor-iz-on-TAY-liss)

This plant's curving, stretching growth is markedly Oriental. Its dark-green leaves have a waxlike finish; the lovely star-shaped white flowers are striking against the foliage; and the small fruits (less than 1 inch in diameter) appear both green and ripe red through a good part of the year.

Carissa is an obvious candidate for the indoor bonsai artist and is easily grown. (See page 211.) Let it dry out between waterings, and give it a spot in a sunny window.

Moon
Valley

Natal
plum

Nerve plant

Fittonia verschaffeltii (fit-TOH-nee-uh
verse-shaff-FELT-ee-eye)

This plant reacts dramatically when you neglect watering
it. It collapses totally, sprawling limp and lifeless. But give
it a drink of water, and it makes an incredible comeback in
a matter of hours.

    Fittonia likes low to moderate light, as well as artificial
light. Keep it evenly moist.

Norfolk Island pine

Araucaria heterophylla (are-oh-KAY-ree-uh
hett-er-oh-FILL-uh) (also known as *A. excelsa*)

This plant (also known as *A. excelsa*) should never be
pruned or pinched back because the growth will not be
replaced and you will only ruin the shape of the tree. The
main enemy of the Norfolk Island pine indoors is a dry,
overheated room. Keep it evenly moist during its growing
season—spring through summer. Then begin to let it dry
out between waterings for the winter months. Give it a
spot with good bright light, but not direct sun. If you start
this miniature Christmas tree in a child's room, it can grow
up right along with him.

Nerve
plant

Norfolk
Island
pine

Ornamental grass

Acorus gramineus (ah-KOR-us gra-mah-NEE-us)

Ornamental grass can be a nice touch in plant arrangements and centerpieces. One of the prettiest of ornamental grasses is the little Japanese sweet flag. Its fanlike leaves are waxy and dark green. The variegated form mixes light green with white. Ornamental grass likes low to medium light. Keep it evenly moist.

Orchid

Orchidaceae (or-kid-DAY-see-ay-ee)

Many orchids are much easier to care for than their reputations might lead you to believe. You do not need a greenhouse. Filtered sunlight or bright light, a well-drained container (use shredded fir bark or a special orchid mix), and humidity are the essentials.

Ornamental grass

Lady-of-the-night

Lady-of-the-night *Brassavola nodosa*
(brass-AH-voh-luh no-DOH-suh). The foliage is plain: a
tall, thick blade grows out of each bulblike stem. Fragrant
white flowers form in the fall. Give this orchid perfect
drainage; water when dry. Let it rest after blooms fade.
    Provide bright light but not direct sun. Do not repot;
let the plant fill the container for full effect.

Lady slipper *Paphiopedilum* **'Maudiae'**
(paff-ee-oh-PEED-ill-um MAW-dee). 'Maudiae' is one of
the easiest orchids to grow in the home. It produces a
beautiful green-and-white flower on a tall, erect stalk. This
orchid likes bright light, no direct sun. Keep it warm and
evenly moist, and provide for extra humidity.

Vanilla orchid *Vanilla fragrans* (vuh-NILL-uh
FRAY-granz). This is a climbing orchid, and yes, it is the
plant from which comes the vanilla bean, from which
comes the extract. The vine itself is rather sparse-looking,
with its long, thick leaves growing in evenly spaced pairs
along the stem. The flowers are miniature renditions, in
light yellowish green and white, of the large classical
orchid. Vanilla orchid does not require sunlight to bloom;
bright light will do. Keep evenly moist. It likes humidity for
best flowering.

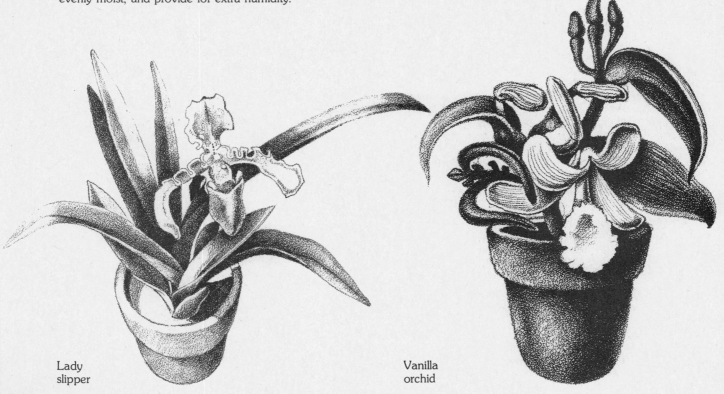

Lady
slipper

Vanilla
orchid

Palms

Palmae (PALM-ay-ee)

Palms are among the easiest plants to grow indoors. They do not require as much light as many other houseplants, and about the only thing that upsets them is a chill or draft. One of the nicest things about palms, aside from their graceful good looks, is their contentment; they do not have much of a root system, and they do not need—indeed, they do not like—to be repotted very often. Be certain not to give them too big a pot to begin with; provide good drainage; and let them stay put.

Palms should never be pruned or shaped with the mistaken idea that this will force new growth. Palms grow from the top only, and once any foliage is lost, it is not replaced.

Bamboo palm *Chamaedorea erumpens* (kam-ay-ee-DOH-ree-uh ee-RUMP-enz). This palm gets its name not for its foliage but for the long, thin bamboolike stems. The leaf is particularly interesting, the end segments being much broader than the rest of it and forming a split, fishtail effect at the tip of the frond. Bamboo palm is slow to get started, but after a few years, each frond it puts out can add another foot to the height of the plant. The plant can take low light but grows faster with moderate light. Keep evenly moist.

Lady palm *Rhapis excelsa* (RAY-piss egg-SELL-suh). Lady palm presents a graceful whirl of long, fanlike fronds from its slim main stems. It has less foliage and is more "see-through" than many other house palms, making it a good choice for a plant grouping. It contributes height but doesn't overwhelm. The lady palm likes bright light but not direct sun. Let it go dry between waterings.

Paradise palm *Howeia forsteriana* (HOW-ee-uh for-stir-RAY-nuh). Also called the kentia or fan palm, this plant conveys the very essence of a tropical island. It grows big and will need a large-size container. It drops its lower leaves as it grows and shows off a slender trunk. Paradise palm will make it in medium light. It likes to be misted and kept evenly moist.

Bamboo
palm

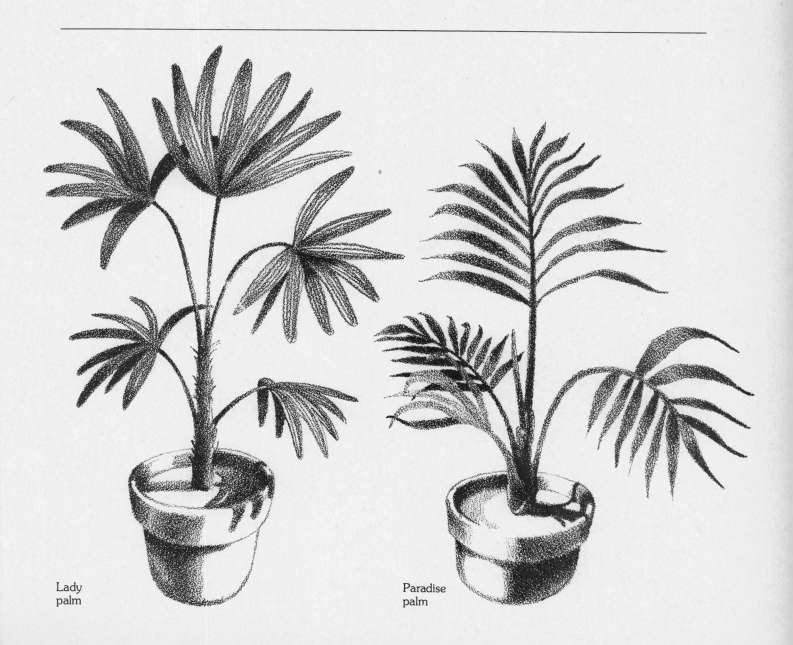

Lady
palm

Paradise
palm

Parlor palm *Chamaedorea elegans* **'Neanthe Bella'**
(kam-ay-*ee*-DOH-ree-uh EL-luh-ganz nee-ANTH-uh
BELL-uh). *Bella* describes this lovely parlor palm, a
member of the palm genus called "Kameys" by those
who know and love them. Parlor palm can survive
moderate light, but it thrives in bright light. It appreciates all
the misting you can provide. Water as soon as dry.

Sentry palm *Howeia belmoreana* (HOW-ee-uh
bell-moh-ree-AY-nuh). A cousin of the paradise palm, the
sentry palm is a wide-arching, graceful plant. It is much
more informal than the paradise palm, having long,
segmented leaves attached to much shorter stalks. Give
moderate light, and keep evenly moist.

Parlor
palm

Sentry
palm

Panda plant

Kalanchoe tomentosa (kal-an-KOH-ee
toh-men-TOH-zuh)

Children take to the panda, with its "fur" (the soft, fuzzy surface of the leaves) and its brown-tipped "ears." With one small panda plant you can make a whole trayful of new ones. Remove the leaves carefully, and place them in a shady place for two or three days until the ends are completely dry; then tuck the end of each leaf into a tray of sand or vermiculite, place in a bright place (not in direct sun), and water sparingly. The leaves will put out new roots of their own. Give panda plants good drainage, sun, and water only when dry.

Partridge berry

Mitchella repens (mitch-ELL-uh REE-penz)

Glossy, dark-green little leaves and bright red berries make this ground creeper a favorite terrarium plant. It loves humidity and the company of other plants, and the berries add a brilliant color accent through the glass. If partridge berry is used outside the high-humidity, indirect-light setting of a terrarium, then take pains to keep up the moisture around it with frequent misting. Keep out of direct sun.

Panda
plant

Partridge
berry

Patience plant

Impatiens (im-PAY-shenz)

Patience plants have been indoor and outdoor favorites for years, and the choices among varieties today are enormous, with one more tempting than the next. While some of the newer varieties are more difficult to grow in the warm, dry household than others, a number of them will get along well if you can give them bright filtered light (not direct sun) and keep the humidity around them as high as you can. The rewards are plants literally covered with blooms in almost any color you could choose—rose, fuchsia, scarlet, orange, white, pink, and variegated patterns, too.

Impatiens roots easily from cuttings. Pinch plants back to keep them from growing too leggy. Each pinch will help shape up the whole plant and give you compact growth and more bloom. Keep the plant evenly moist, and mist often. If you can provide enough light, natural or otherwise, patience plant will bloom year-around.

Peace lily

Spathiphyllum (spath-if-FILL-um)

This accommodating houseplant tolerates low light; as a matter of fact, it doesn't like sunlight. It does like to be well watered, so don't let it dry out completely. Keep it just moist, never soggy. It also likes warmth, so keep it away from chilly places. The reward: long, graceful dark-green leaves topped off nearly year-round with tall, lilylike white spathes resembling calla lilies.

Patience plant

Peace lily

Peacock plant

Calathea makoyana (kal-ul-THEE-uh
may-koh-YAY-nuh)

It's difficult to believe this plant beauty can survive an
indoor gardener's care, but it will if you mist it often and
keep it on the warm side. It likes bright natural or artificial
light. Keep evenly moist and away from chilly windows or
air conditioning. It prefers to be too warm than too cold
and enjoys as much humidity as you can provide.

Peacock
plant

Pencil cactus

Euphorbia tirucalli (yew-FOR-bee-uh
tee-roo-KAL-lee-eye)

If you have not yet moved beyond the concept of
houseplants as leafy green things, you might be at a loss
to understand why anyone would bother with this plant.
The pencil cactus, also known as milkbush, is a twiggy green
thing and a totally charming plant. You will be delighted with
its rapid growth, accomplished in spurts throughout the year.
Give bright light or sun in summer, and sun in winter, let it go
bone-dry between waterings. (See page 237 for more about
its many virtues.)

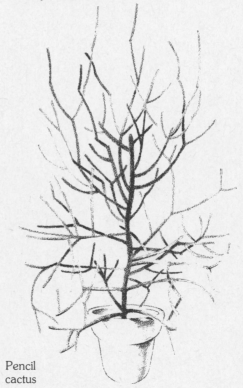

Pencil
cactus

Peperomias

Peperomias are so prevalent in dime-store dish-gardens that they've come to be taken for granted and vastly underrated as plants that can make it on their own. There are many kinds to choose from, offering great variety in growth habit and in leaf shape, texture, and coloring.

Peperomias generally flourish under a wide range of light conditions, doing well under an ordinary reading lamp and rewarding you with fast growth and full, handsome plants if given bright light but not direct sun. Do not let their fast growth tempt you into overwatering them. Their stems will rot with too much water. Provide good drainage, and let plants go dry between waterings.

Baby rubber plant *Peperomia obtusifolia* (pep-er-OH-mee-uh ob-too-siff-FOH-lee-uh). This charmer has the shiny good looks of the rubber tree (*Ficus elastica*) in miniature. It has smooth, waxy, dark-green leaves and a bowing, curving growth habit. It will grow well under an ordinary table lamp. Do not put it in the sun; water when dry.

Emerald ripple *Peperomia caperata* (pep-er-OH-mee-uh kay-per-RAY-tuh). For a full, compact look, plant several to a pot, and pinch back to keep in shape. The thin, catkinlike flower spikes that rise above the foliage are charming; put the plant where you can see it while it is in bloom. Give bright light, not direct sun; let it go dry between waterings.

Princess Astrid *Peperomia orba* (pep-er-OH-mee-uh OR-buh). A low, spreading, bushy little plant with narrow, pointed leaves. Good for terrariums. Give bright light, not direct sun; let it go dry between waterings.

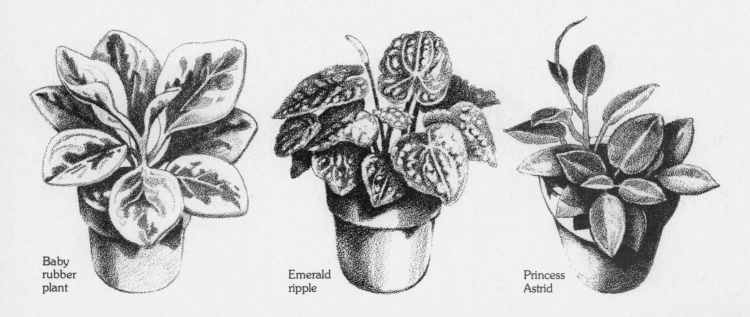

Baby
rubber
plant

Emerald
ripple

Princess
Astrid

Prostrate peperomia *Peperomia prostrata*
(pep-er-OH-mee-uh pross-TRAY-tuh). This creeping, trailing peperomia with tiny, two-toned, circular leaves makes a great terrarium ground-cover planting or a hanging plant for a confined space. Give bright light, not direct sun; let it go dry between waterings.

Watermelon plant *Peperomia sandersii*
(pep-er-OH-mee-uh SAND-er-see-eye). A beautifully patterned plant: silver and blue-green leaves, broad and round at the base and tapering gently at the tip. Pale-yellow catkins rise above the plant and carry tiny flowers. Pinch leaves back to encourage dense, compact growth and shape the plant for centerpiece or mantel use. The leaves can be rooted. This peperomia is easy to grow. It will adapt to moderate or bright light, but don't put it in direct sun. Let it dry out between waterings.

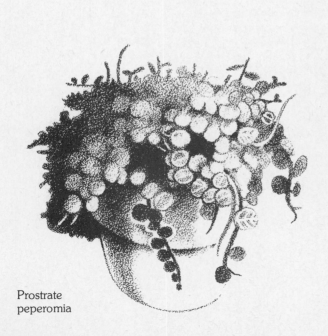

Prostrate
peperomia

Watermelon
peperomia

Petunia

Petunia (puh-TOO-nee-uh)

Petunias are easy to grow from seed and widely available as bedding plants. They thrive indoors in any sunny, bright-light spot (*see* page 65). New varieties offer huge flowers and sparkling colors. Sow in late winter for summer flowering and in summer for winter blooms. Give plants sun and bright light; let them dry out between waterings.

Petunia

Philodendrons

Heartleaf philodendron *Philodendron oxycardium* (fill-oh-DEN-dron ox-ee-KARD-ee-um). While this plant has a reputation as the most shade-loving of all houseplants, it really does not do as well in low-light situations as does pothos. The plant will survive, but the longer it remains in minimal light conditions, the smaller the new growth becomes, until the plant is putting out miniature leaves, if any.

The philodendron does not like direct sunlight, but it does thrive in good light. Let it go dry between waterings. It makes an excellent choice for a trellis, vining its way up, down, or crosswise, obedient to any wish.

Lacy tree philodendron *Philodendron selloum* (fill-oh-DEN-dron SELL-oh-um). This is the philodendron with the huge, deeply lobed leaves that thrust straight out or up on long branches. Lacy tree needs a great deal of space. The leaves often reach 2 feet in size, and as the plant grows older, its branches bend out more horizontally, thus making it as broad as, or broader than, it is tall. These plants do well standing on the floor or grouped in a pedestal arrangement for high drama in a large space (see page 77).

Lacy tree is a sturdy plant and will adapt itself to low-light, minimum-care situations. If you want top performance, give it moderate light, keep evenly moist, and feed full-dosage plant food once a month spring through fall.

Splitleaf philodendron (also called Swiss cheese, Mexican breadfruit, monstera) is often listed as *Philodendron pertusum*, but botanically the plant is classified as *Monstera deliciosa* and is therefore not a true philodendron. For its care, see Splitleaf philodendron (page 192).

Heartleaf
philodendron

Lacy
tree
philodendron

Piggy-back

Tolmiea menziesii (toll-MEE-uh men-ZEE-see-eye)

Piggy-back takes its name from the new plantlets that form on top and at the base of older leaves. A luxuriant foliage plant if treated right, piggy-back can also be temperamental in a too hot, too dry environment. It thrives in cooler temperatures, so don't put it anywhere near a radiator or other source of heat during the winter months. It likes bright light, but its thin, delicate leaves will not take hot sun. Keep evenly moist.

Pineapple

Ananas comosus (uh-NAN-us koh-MOH-sus)

A member of the bromeliad family, pineapple is an easy, attractive, inexpensive houseplant. Twist off the green-leaved top of a pineapple, pull off several of the lower leaves to expose 1½ to 2 inches of bare stalk (from which will come the roots). Put the stalk in water. When roots form, pot the plant in loose, fast-draining soil mix. Water only when bone-dry, but keep the rosette cup filled with water. Give bright light. For bloom: Place a ripe apple and the plant in a plastic bag. In a few weeks the center will turn crimson, and a flower spike will emerge. After several months a fruit will form at the top of the flower spike.

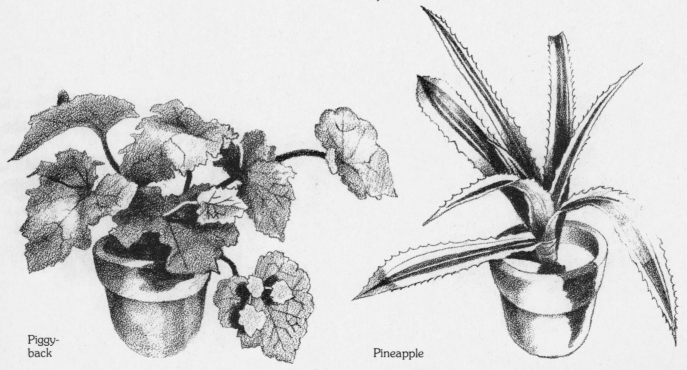

Piggy-back

Pineapple

Pomegranate

Punica granatum nana (PEW-nick-uh gran-NAY-tum NAY-nah)

This is the dwarf pomegranate, a delight to grow and a challenge for the bonsai fan (see page 211). The sturdy, substantial tree is perhaps no more than 18 inches high, with a fat, short trunk, branches rather sparsely adorned with bright green leaves, scarlet flowers, and maybe one or two pomegranates, small compared with the kind you buy, but large for the size of the tree. The plant is, in fact, a knockout. Give dwarf pomegranate a sunny spot, and keep evenly moist.

Pomegranate

Pony-tail

Beaucarnea recurvata (boh-KAR-nee-uh ree-kur-VAY-tuh)

A particularly vibrant plant with a carefree tangle of foliage and a swollen, wrinkled base. The pony-tail makes a long-lasting investment. It does best in a sunny spot but can get along with good, bright light. Let the plant dry out between waterings. (For more on the pony-tail, see page 87.)

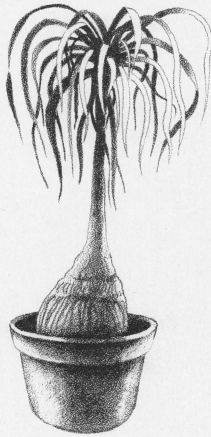

Pony-tail

Pothos

Scindapsus aureus (sin-DAP-suss OR-ee-us)

This plant, also known as devil's ivy, is often confused with philodendron. Their leaves look alike, and their vining habits are similar. It's as easy to grow as philodendron; in fact, it's a better performer in lower light. Its heart-shaped, waxy green leaves (splashed with creamy white) don't diminish in size as do the philodendron's in a low-light situation. The main thing to watch out for is overwatering. Let plant go dry between drinks; otherwise it is nearly indestructible.

Prayer plant

Maranta leuconeura (muh-RANT-uh loo-koh-NEW-ruh)

The small pots of prayer plant wasting away on dime-store counters don't do this handsome plant justice. Its simple needs, long life, and dramatic foliage (which becomes more dramatic as it grows) make it a most desirable houseplant. Prayer plant curls its leaves into slender, upright rolls at night; hence its name.

Provide bright light and as much humidity as you can. The plant loves frequent mistings and likes being kept evenly moist. Be sure to repot as the plant grows and requires more room.

Pothos

Prayer plant

Purple passion plant

Gynura 'Sarmentosa' (jye-NEW-ruh sar-men-TOH-zuh)

An easy-to-grow houseplant with soft, velvety, dark-green leaves tinged with purple. To keep this plant in top shape, prune to encourage bushiness, and root some of the cuttings to put back in the container to form new plants. Bright light encourages bright coloring; keep evenly moist.

Purple
passion
plant

Redwood burl

Sequoia sempervirens (see-QUOY-uh semp-er-VYE-renz)

The redwood burl is exactly that: a burl (knotlike lump) cut from a California redwood. Although a new burl grows in the place where one is cut, the taking of burls by unauthorized personnel is frowned upon, to say the least. The easiest way to obtain a burl is through gift shops associated with the various national parks. For example, the Ahwahnee Gift Shop, Yosemite National Park, California 95389, sells burls of coast redwoods from the Big Sur area.

To get a burl growing: Scrub the cut surface with a stiff brush, and then place, cut side down, in a shallow dish of water. Always keep water in the dish—about ¼ inch above the bottom of the burl. Lovely, lacy, bright green foliage grows out of the bark side in a miniature forest effect. Every few weeks, check for scum that may form on the cut side; clean off with a brush, and change water.

Redwood
burl

Rooting fig

Ficus radicans (FYE-kuss RAD-ick-anz)

This is a crawling fig, but it also hangs nicely from a basket. The foliage is thick, with long, pointed leaves. The variety 'Variegata' is often offered as a houseplant but is actually difficult to grow outside of a greenhouse. Stick with the sturdy, plain-green variety, and you'll have good success. Moderate or bright light suits this plant. It likes to be warm and evenly moist.

Rosary vine

Ceropegia woodii (see-roh-PEE-jee-uh WOOD-ee-eye)

This small-leaved trailer makes a big splash when several plants are potted together in a hanging container. Rosary vine is one succulent that can do without bright light or sunshine; it gets along with a moderate amount of light and does well with artificial light. Let it go bone-dry between waterings.

For making new plants, look along the stems of an older plant for small tubers. Poke these halfway into the soil, and keep slightly moist till new plants begin to grow.

Rooting
fig

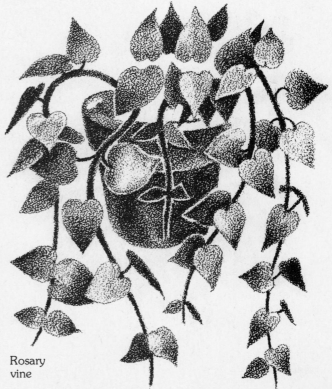

Rosary
vine

Rubber tree

Ficus elastica (FYE-kuss ee-LAST-ick-uh)

This familiar and durable house tree thrives in low-light rooms. It likes to be evenly moist while in active growth (spring and summer) and to dry out between waterings while it is resting. Do not put it on a constant-feeding system. Give it a dose of plant food only twice a year—spring and summer. Those broad green leaves demand routine dusting to keep the plant clean and shiny-looking. Don't try any leaf-shine products; you'll likely get leaf drop instead.

Sago palm

Cycas revoluta (SYE-kuss rev-oh-LEW-tuh)

Stiff, rigid, almost plastic-looking foliage with a patent-leather shine is part of the charm of the mature sago palm. And it grows more endearing as it grows more ungainly, developing a hugh, rough, oversized trunk. As a young plant with still-slender stems and curving fronds, it has more of the softness of a parlor palm about it.

The cycads, of which the sago palm is probably the best known, are making a comeback in popularity. They are sturdy, easy-to-grow plants. Sago palm does well in moderate to bright light but not direct sun. Let it dry out between waterings, and mist now and then.

Rubber
tree

Sago
palm

Screw-pine

Pandanus veitchii (pan-DAY-nuss VYE-chee-eye)

You'll enjoy watching this plant grow. Its leaves swirl around the stem in a spiral effect, and it produces offshoots near the base of the plant while above-ground roots grow from the stem, reaching straight down to sink like spikes into the soil.

Let the plant dry out between waterings, put it on a constant-feed program and in a sunny or bright-light place. Offshoots can be separated to make new plants.

Screw-pine

Seersucker plant

Geogenanthus undatus (jee-oh-juh-NANTH-us un-DAY-tuss)

Large, puckered, metallic-green leaves striped in a silver-gray make the relatively small-sized seersucker plant a standout as a "textured" plant. It likes humidity and does well as a terrarium plant or under a glass dome. It can be rooted from cuttings.

Give bright light, no direct sun, and keep evenly moist. Mist often.

Sensitive plant

Mimosa pudica (mim-OH-zuh PEW-dick-uh)

This is a short-lived plant, but it is easy to grow from seed, which can be ordered through catalogs. Plant several seeds together in a 4-inch pot to make a generous grouping; the seeds will be up and growing in a week or so. Sensitive plant is also widely available at plant counters because of its obvious appeal for children (touch the foliage, and the leaflets close up). Keep in mind that the plant won't last much longer than a few months so that you don't brand yourself as a non-green thumber when it goes into its decline. All perfectly normal. Sensitive plant likes sun, moist soil, and high humidity.

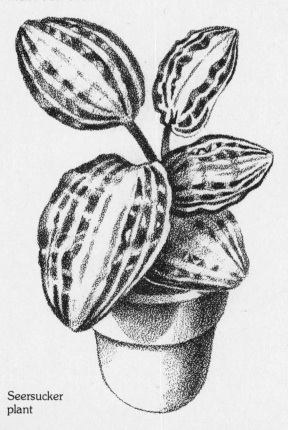

Seersucker
plant

Sensitive
plant

Snake plant

Sansevieria (sanz-uh-VEER-ee-uh)

Here is one of the most maligned, ill-treated, and ignored houseplants. It is known not only as snake plant but also as mother-in-law's tongue. For thirty years or more it has been snubbed by many indoor gardeners, mostly for the very reasons that once made it so popular—its sturdiness, loyalty, tolerance for near-total neglect. Now it is making its comeback, along with all the other greats of the Art Deco days.

If you don't neglect it, it grows into a large, handsome beauty with soft, sinuous lines built into the swordlike blades. Though it needs little water (let it go good and dry between drinks), it will develop its full beauty, color, and bloom (yes, and with a sweet night fragrance, too) with moderate light. Too much bright light or direct sun will cause the bold markings to fade.

Sansevieria trifasciata 'Laurentii' is a tall, handsome, yellow-striped variety. Birdsnest sansevieria *(Sansevieria trifasciata* 'Hahnii') is a low, rosette form. Both types can be increased by division: Separate new plantlets that form as the plant grows.

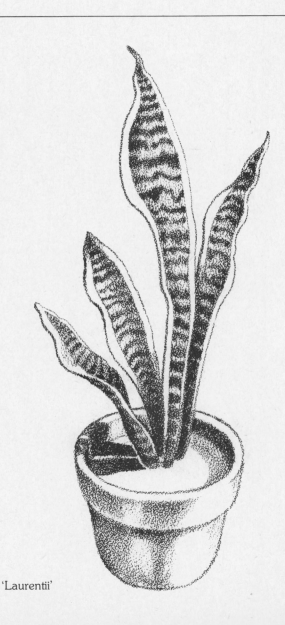

'Laurentii'

'Hahnii'

Southern yew

***Podocarpus macrophyllus* 'Maki'** (poh-doh-KARP-us
ma-KROFF-ill-us MAY-kye)

For a touch of chinoiserie, consider the southern yew, or
Maki, as it is also often called. This a true evergreen, but its
"needles" are broad enough and flat and soft enough to
look like long, narrow leaves. If you are buying a
specimen-size plant, 3 to 5 feet in height, be sure to buy
from a reputable plant shop because the plant should be
container grown and adapted, not yanked in from the
outside and potted up to be palmed off on an unsuspecting
plant lover. (Since southern yew grows outdoors in the
South as a shrub, the scenario described can sometimes
happen.) Southern yew does best in good bright light, a
sunny spot preferably, and should be kept evenly moist. Do
not fear that something is amiss if new leaves look anemic.
They will gradually take on the dark-green color of the
older leaves, and in the meantime you've got a two-tone
effect.

Southern
yew

Spider plant

Chlorophytum comosum (kloh-roh-FYE-tum koh-MOH-sum)

The mother plant forms a tall fountain of foliage with long stems arching down, from which new plantlets form at the ends and branch out from the sides. With still more plantlets emerging from the first set of plantlets, you will have whole tiers of spider, or airplane, plants.

If you resist the temptation to separate the plantlets to start other individual plants, you will have a most beautiful specimen, with plantlets hanging long and full all around the mother plant. A pedestal or plant stand is the best place to display *Chlorophytum comosum*. Varieties range from those with leaves of green-and-cream stripes to those of a uniform glossy green.

The plant has thick roots which store water, so let it dry out between waterings. Overwatering usually shows up first in browning of the tips of the leaves. These plants like humidity and light but not direct sun. They will also grow beautifully under fluorescent light, with plantlets forming thickly all around the mother. A vertical light setup (as shown on page 214) will give a spider plant all the encouragement it needs to be as beautiful as possible.

Splitleaf philodendron

Monstera deliciosa (mon-STAIR-uh duh-liss-ee-OH-zuh)

This plant is known by many names: Swiss cheese, Mexican breadfruit, monstera. It is not a philodendron, though it greatly resembles one. It, too, is a sturdy plant and can get along with little care. Give it bright light, water it when dry, feed it during growth time, and watch this plant flourish. If you like starting plants from seed, splitleaf makes a terrific choice. (Seeds are available at George W. Park Seed Co., Greenwood, S.C. 29647. Five seeds, $1.50.) The plant will be just a youngster for the first year, but see what happens in three years' time.

Splitleaf philodendron

Spider plant

Sprengeri

Asparagus densiflorus 'Sprengeri' (ass-PAIR-uh-gus denz-if-LOH-rus SPRENG-er-eye)

If you want a light, airy hanging plant then this is the ideal choice. Sprengeri, which is not a member of the fern family, grows quickly and produces a lovely green effect in a short time. Its long, flexible stems covered with delicate foliage can reach 6 to 7 feet; cutting them back will encourage fuller growth.

The plant's roots grow fast, too, and it will benefit from being divided every couple of years. To divide: Remove the plant from the pot, separate the clumps with a sharp knife, and repot. The new plantings will quickly put out new growth and lose their shorn look in a matter of a few weeks. Spring is the best time for dividing—the plant recuperates fastest then.

Sprengeri will get along in moderate light, but grows fuller and faster in bright light. Keep out of direct summer sun, and keep evenly moist.

Stephanotis

Stephanotis floribunda (steff-uh-NOH-tiss floh-rib-BUND-uh)

If you have a sunny bedroom window and an old-fashioned heart, make room for this one. The combination of waxen, white blooms, dark, glossy-green leaves, and a delicious fragrance proves irresistible. Stephanotis can be trained to a stake for a tall, vertical look or wrapped around a large wire loop for a wreath effect. Keep evenly moist while the plant is making growth; let it dry out between waterings during winter months.

Sprengeri

Stephanotis

Strawberry begonia

Saxifraga stolonifera (sax-IF-ruh-juh stoh-lon-IF-er-uh)

This plant is neither a strawberry nor a begonia, but it is as charming as both of them put together. Long runners like those of strawberry plants form; later, tiny new plantlets emerge and dangle from those stem ends. These plantlets can be rooted in smaller containers all around the mother plant or snipped off and potted up on their own.

Strawberry begonia does better in a cool room than in a warm one. Give it bright light, not direct sun; keep it evenly moist; and mist it often for as much humidity as you can provide.

String of buttons

Crassula perfossa (KRASS-yew-luh per-FOSS-uh)

This relative of the jade tree grows straight up, with thick leaves separated along seemingly stiff stems. As the plant grows older, however, the stems begin to arch, then bend, and eventually trail down the sides of the container. Elevate string of buttons on a special stand or small pedestal, or hang it low so that the intricacy of the foliage arrangement along the stems can be enjoyed.

String of buttons, or necklace vine, as it is sometimes called, is as easy to grow as the jade tree. Be especially watchful for mealybug attack. Though mealybugs are normally easy enough to control (see page 39), string of buttons has an endless number of crevices in which the insects can hide. You will be in for a time-consuming search-and-destroy mission unless you catch them early.

Provide it excellent drainage and lots of light, water it when dry in summer, in winter, let it go bone-dry.

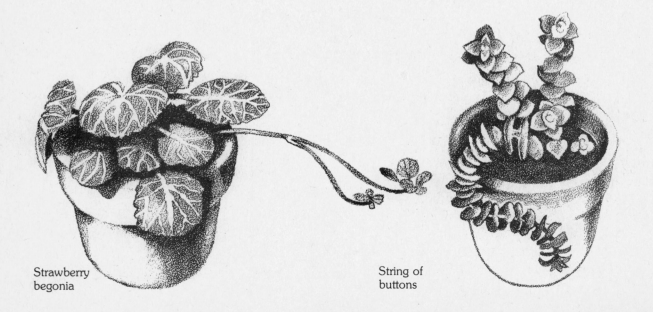

Strawberry
begonia

String of
buttons

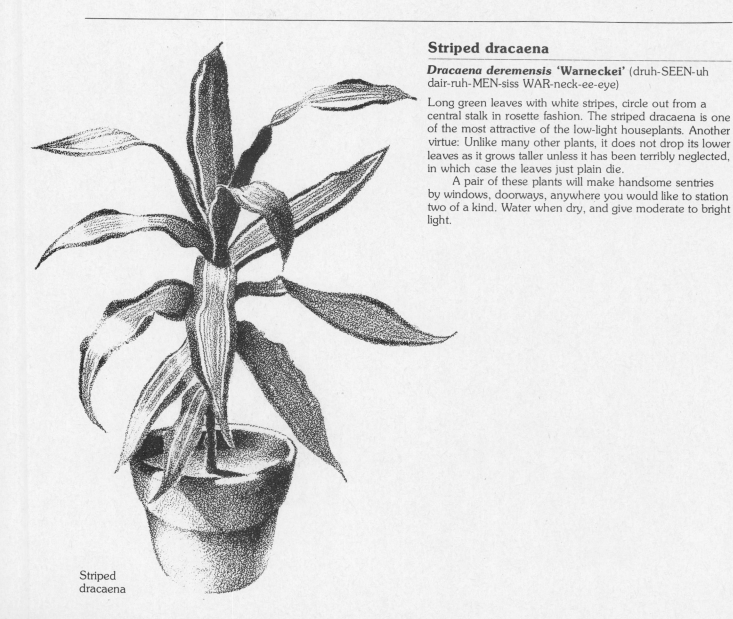

Striped
dracaena

Striped dracaena

Dracaena deremensis **'Warneckei'** (druh-SEEN-uh
dair-ruh-MEN-siss WAR-neck-ee-eye)

Long green leaves with white stripes, circle out from a
central stalk in rosette fashion. The striped dracaena is one
of the most attractive of the low-light houseplants. Another
virtue: Unlike many other plants, it does not drop its lower
leaves as it grows taller unless it has been terribly neglected,
in which case the leaves just plain die.

A pair of these plants will make handsome sentries
by windows, doorways, anywhere you would like to station
two of a kind. Water when dry, and give moderate to bright
light.

Swedish ivy

Plectranthus (pleck-TRANTH-us)

The best-known species *Plectranthus australis,* is also the most agreeable. It grows under almost any conditions: in a bottle of water or in soil, in sun or in shade. It roots practically overnight, grows rapidly; trails invitingly from a hanging basket; turns its stem ends upward for a cheerful effect when perched on a shelf, chest, or table edge. In other words, this is a great plant, from which many potfuls of new great plants can come. When planted in soil, let it dry out between waterings. After you become acquainted with *P. australis,* it will be only natural to wonder if other members of the genus are as pleasant. They are.

    P. purpuratus is a small-scale version of *P. australis,* with leaves of a grayer-green cast (sort of a lovely dusty green) and purplish undersides. It's a bit more particular about water and will not so readily forgive neglect, so do not let it wait for water. Let it barely dry out between drinks.

    P. oertendahlii is the show-off of the clan, with a network of silvery veining that stands out against bronzy-green leaves. It feels the same about water as does *P. purpuratus.*

Swedish ivy

Sweet potato

Ipomoea batatas (ipp-oh-MEE-uh buh-TAY-tuss)

A much more attractive plant than its origins might indicate. For inexpensive, quick green vining, sweet potato is hard to beat. Don't bother to plant the potato in soil; it is much easier to care for in water and actually does better there. (Instructions for how to grow it appear on page 43.)

    Purplish-red shoots appear first, unfolding into large apple-green leaves. Change water if and when scum appears.

Sweet potato

Temple bells

Smithiantha (smith-ee-ANTH-uh)

Smithiantha is another little-known and greatly underrated relative of the African violet. Any plant that produces long-lasting flowers and is easy to grow is worth making room for. Temple bells qualify on both counts: The bell-shaped flowers appear atop a tall central stalk, with bloom lasting over a period of two to three months.

This plant loves artificial light and will bloom under it nearly any time of year. With natural light (bright but not direct sun), it usually blooms in midwinter. Keep the plant evenly moist while it is putting out growth and blooming. After the flowering, let it go dry between waterings. When the foliage begins to die, withhold water. Cut dead foliage off, and dig up new rhizomes that have formed in the pot. Store in a plastic bag for a couple of months, and repot for new plants.

Temple
bells

Umbrella tree

Schefflera actinophylla (sheff-LEAR-uh
ack-tin-oh-FILL-uh)

If you want a large mass of green, choose this plant. The larger it grows, the larger its leaves become. The long, shiny leaflets form an umbrella at the end of the stems.

With good strong light, the stems will be short and the plant full and bushy. Lower light will produce longer stems and a stretched-out look that is more treelike, with the umbrella effect of the leaflets even more noticeable.

One thing to remember about this plant: It hates being moved once it has become accustomed to its environment. For example, don't plan to give it a summer vacation outdoors. It will repay you by dropping most of its leaves when you bring it back inside, no matter how carefully you try to prepare it for the adjustment. Keep the plant evenly moist.

Umbrella
tree

Wandering Jew

Trandescantia; Zebrina; Callisia; Setcreasea
(trad-ess-KANT-ee-uh; zuh-BRY-nuh; kal-LISS-ee-uh;
set-KREE-see-uh)

Dozens of plants go by the common name of wandering Jew or inch plant. Many of them belong botanically to the genera *Tradescantia* and *Zebrina;* others, to *Callisia* or *Setcreasea*. The choice of leaf size and coloration among these trailers and creepers is much larger and more interesting than most people realize. Some have large and boldly striped green-and-white leaves; others have tiny, plain-green leaves; still others have foliage showing tones of red, purple, yellow, pink, silver, or combinations—tricolors, as they're called.

All these plants are easy to propagate from cuttings in either soil or water. Most of these plants tend toward the straggly side as they grow older. Simply pinch them back and add new cuttings to the pot, and you can keep them always shaped up for a luxuriant hanging basket. Bright light generally means brighter colors, but direct sun will scald leaves. Let the plant dry out between waterings.

Wandering
Jew

Wax plant

Hoya (HOY-uh)

If you have good bright light and can choose only one vine, make your choice a hoya. The blooms are unforgettable: waxen, star-shaped blossoms with contrasting centers and an exotic fragrance. There are many varieties; a plant lover could specialize in hoyas and never have room for them all. Yet, surprisingly, hoyas seem not to be widely grown by indoor gardeners.

If you acquire a small plant, be patient with it. Hoyas are slow to get started, but once they begin, they make rapid growth. Besides providing good light, keep hoya on constant feed from spring through autumn. Let it dry out between waterings. The plant rests in winter months; be especially careful not to overwater it then.

Wax
plant

Weeping fig

Ficus benjamina (FYE-kuss ben-juh-MYE-nuh)

Here is *the* popular house-tree tree, with its truly treelike
leaves, its truly treelike trunk, and a drooping shape that is
not so treelike but seems more fitting for indoors, where the
ceiling would threaten a serious upward thrust. *Ficus
benjamina* can cost you a bundle at full tree size, but you
can also find it being sold as a youngster 2 or 3 feet tall. It
is a faster grower than many other house trees and can put
on close to 1 foot of growth a year if you give it enough
light and feed it well. Nonetheless, it takes some years for it
to grow up big and truly begin to weep.

This is one of those plants that may drop its leaves
when you first bring it home, particularly the larger
specimens. Don't panic; give your plant a few weeks to
adjust to a lower light level. Pick off dead and dying
leaves, watch for new growth, and don't be tempted into
overwatering because the plant is losing leaves. Use a large
spray bottle, and mist the tree as often as you can; it loves
the extra moisture. Let it dry out between waterings.

Weeping
fig

Cooks'
Corners

Indoor herb gardens

There are lots of plants in this kitchen, mostly herbs of one kind or another, for the cook is a serious one who appreciates fresh seasonings close at hand. The focal wall in this kitchen—once devoted to traditional counter-and-cupboards—was stripped down for more room and more action. Now, open storage shelves help to hold the equipment an involved cook would want, including an assortment of herbs growing in pebble-filled trays under two 48-inch fluorescent tubes.

The space above the counter is 28 inches, enough to accommodate taller-growing herbs. Smaller plants are staged atop empty up-turned pots to put them closer to the light. When seedlings occupy the space, a whole tray is propped up with two sturdy blocks of wood under each end. A 4-inch apron encloses the fixtures and directs the light on the plants and away from the eyes. Mirror tiles cover the wall behind the herbs, adding more light for the plants while reflecting their beauty, too.

Baskets of various shapes and sizes help organize kitchen clutter, keep utensils within reach, and create a design feature in themselves.

Some of the herbs here were started from seed; others were bought as small plants. The chives came from the grocery store. The golden sage (this cook's favorite herb, for its beauty as a plant), the tarragon (the favorite for house specials, winding up in wine vinegar for salads, in béarnaise sauce, in olive oil for lamb dishes,

The cook in this kitchen makes her own tarragon wine vinegar,

and in *poulet d'estragon*), the thyme, and the rosemary were all bought at a plant shop. (More and more plant shops are now carrying a good selection of herbs.)

Herbs that are annuals are usually easiest to grow from seed. That's how this cook starts pots of basil and summer savory, also parsley, which is actually a biennial, and sweet marjoram, which is a perennial.

Lemon balm and lemon verbena find their way onto this cook-gardener's list because of their fragrance and beauty. Their leaves combine with fresh fruit (blueberries and peaches, for example) to make a memorable salad or dessert, and their crushed leaves add zip to iced tea and other summer coolers.

SOWING SEED

Sprinkle seeds on the tops of pots filled with dampened potting mix. (Mix a regular potting mix with sharp sand, half and half, to ensure good drainage; herbs cannot stand wet feet.) Barely cover the seeds with a sprinkling of more dampened soil mix. Keep the pots moist but not wet and out of the direct light. When the plants are growing well (at least three sets of leaves), thin to two or three seedlings per pot and place under lights within 5 to 6 inches of the tubes or in a sunny window. Give seedlings only a few hours of light for the first few days, working up to sixteen hours. As the plants grow, lower the plants, or raise the lights to keep the light source 6 to 8 inches from the tops of the plants. Try to keep the soil evenly moist—never very dry, never very wet. Pinch out the tip ends of the plants as they grow to promote branching.

Problem: You have had success with a few herbs in the kitchen window—about the only sunny place you have—and you yearn for space to grow more, but there's no countertop space to spare. You have no basement, no garage, and not much space for, nor interest in, the bulky ready-made grow-light stands. You have even less courage to take on any build-it-from-scratch plans.

Consider this idea: On the market are two-tube, ready-to-plug-in grow lights that come complete with a hood to screen the light from eye view and to direct it onto the plants. These grow lights—24 inches long, 12 inches wide, and with a 3-inch facing on all four sides—are usually sold along with a set of detachable metal legs. You can leave off the legs and attach the hoods to the undersides of a tier of simple shelves and have yourself a light garden that runs from floor to ceiling, taking up only about 1 by 2 feet of space. For the highest shelf, add an additional piece of facing, 5 inches deep, to screen light.

A still more economical version can be made by buying ordinary fluorescent fixtures, attaching these to the undersides of the shelves and adding an apron of wood all around to screen the lights from view. Paint the undersides white for better reflectivity.

Consider turning the short end of this set of shelves to the wall to create a green peninsula. This way you can see more of the plants, with a view from both of the long sides as well

Front View.

5-inch apron for above-eye-level lights.

Plant tray.

3-inch metal hood or wood apron.

Two 20-watt tubes.

Side view.

shelves make room for nearly twenty pots of herbs and a couple of other small plants. Many herbs are quite content living in small pots; some can stay put for the duration of their life expectancy. Below the window, down where they're not expected at all, are four beautiful botanical prints—intricately rendered, taxonomically exact paintings of herbs. A small up-light

Because herbs appreciate fresh air, these shelves were positioned so that the window crank and latch could be easily operated.

as one end. A set of shelves and herbs have all the ingredients of a kitchen classic, but no one says you have to confine it to the kitchen or limit it to herb growing.

Herbs needn't take up a whole lot of space. In this casement window, 4-inch-wide highlights the prints and creates shadowy drama among the herbs when company comes.

When space is small, a common tray for the pots not only saves the space taken up by individual saucers, but provides a place for a pebble bed which creates a more humid environment for your plants. Trays generally eliminate clutter and provide a cleaner, sharper focus on the plants. The long, narrow trays shown on the preceding page are designed for use on windowsills and were ordered from a garden catalog.

This single's kitchen-and-dining area sports a small herb collection and, next to the table, a beautiful display of Swedish ivy rooted to a short totem pole so that it grows up as well as out and down. (To make a totem pole, see page 307.) You root the Swedish ivy by tucking pieces of stem into the moist moss of the totem pole. If you pull a leaf or two off the end of the stem that will be in contact with the moss, the roots will form more quickly.

An "L" track-light installation makes growing plants possible here. The herbs—borage, parsley, spearmint, and golden apple mint— were chosen because they get along with less light than most other herbs. (The chives and basil, which this cook cannot get along without, grow on a sunny windowsill in the bath.) Borage is an annual and can be started from seed, though that was not the case here. All of these herbs were purchased in the spring at a nursery selling bedding plants and herbs.

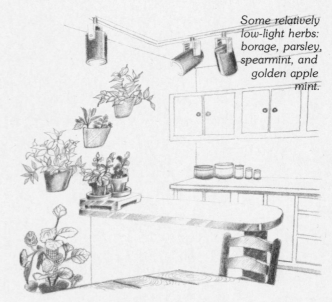

Some relatively low-light herbs: borage, parsley, spearmint, and golden apple mint.

The mints hang on the wall along with a green-and-white inch plant on either side. The parsley and borage are grouped under them on the high countertop on a teakwood stand of their own.

Two of the track lights focus on the plants; but, along with the third, they also serve the cooking and working space on the other side of the counter. They can be swiveled about for general and table lighting.

The herbs have been successful here. The borage even managed to produce a few flowers, which arrived quite unexpectedly and were greeted with great delight. The beautiful blue star-shaped blooms appeared at the tip ends of the stems growing closest to the light.

Plants to be close to

At family dining tables, houseplants don't just get seen; they get looked at up close and often. These are not fringe plants—passive backdrops for our furnishings and lives—but members of the household.

Choose them carefully, care for them properly, and they will be with you for a long, long time; their year-after-year growth and renewal will be part of the fond memories of family gatherings. Here are three that never wear out their welcome.

ORCHID CACTUS

Orchid cacti are still not well known in this country, which is odd because they're such incredibly appealing, zany-looking plants. They grow unpredictably—sending out new growth spurs and flower buds in improbable places up and down the leaf. The leaves of most hybrids are wide and flat with scalloped edges, and the new growth comes off these edges in long, thin, arching spurs. The flowers themselves are extraordinary in both color and size. There are orchid pinks, deep purples, salmon rose, vermilions, orange reds, clear yellows, and purest whites growing to 8 inches across.

What's more, the plants are not expensive, most ranging in price from $1.50 to $3.00 for a well-rooted cutting. For a wide variety, choose from a mail-order catalog. They're good travelers, arriving in good shape, even when simply wrapped in dampened newspaper.

Four orchid cacti.

For the dining table, plan to have several varieties because each does its own thing, and whatever it is, it's interesting. Containers should be on the small side, no more than 3 or 4 inches in diameter. Use a potting soil that drains fast and a low-nitrogen fertilizer. Let them go dry between waterings, but not for the extended periods as you would with cactus.

Orchid cacti will grow in a well-lighted room, but to bloom well, they will need a lot of strong reflected light or some sunshine. If your family dining table is close by a sunny window, you're in for a real treat.

In nature, orchid cacti grow high in the trees, and their branches hang down. As your plants grow, you could convert your pots to hanging baskets or elevate them on a small stand in the center of the table.

Plain clay pots are hard to improve upon for the orchid cactus, but if you want a cachepot that suits especially well, try berry boxes, stained or painted.

MINIATURE PEPEROMIA

No matter how small the dining spot, this charmer belongs on the table. It is tiny-leaved and trailing, and yet upright, too. It is bright green and sprightly and very "spring." It is cheerful and robust and, well, irresistible.

Miniature peperomia is a good plant for kids because it roots easily, and small sprigs from the parent plant can be popped into tiny cachepots, such as egg cups. Each child can have one by his or her own place at the table, with Mama or Papa in the center. The larger plant looks best elevated.

Miniature peperomia is happiest out of direct sunlight and not too close to artificial light. A good bright indirect light suits it fine. Water when soil is dry, and feed on a regular schedule during the rapid growing period of early spring and summer.

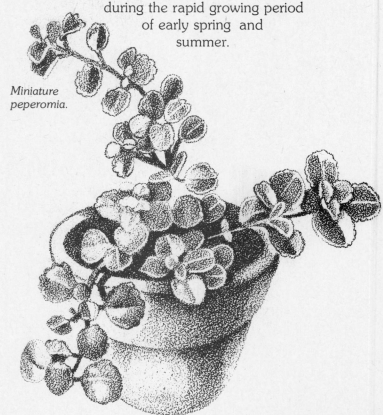

Miniature peperomia.

EPISCIA

Episcias are kissing cousins of the African violet and are endowed with all the family charm, particularly its beautiful foliage in a wide variety of colors and textures. You can choose from among smooth, green-leaved varieties and highly patterned, dramatically colored ones.

Dinner-table fun with episcias includes the propagation of new plants from the runners (stolons). The small bouquets of new plantlets can be rooted in smaller pots placed around the parent pot. Or episcias can be tucked into a wire egg basket lined with moss. Line, then fill with potting soil, and plant with two or three episcias. As the runners grow, root them back against the sides of the moss-filled basket.

Dozens of varieties of episcias are available now, mostly by mail order. The best known is probably the dark-leaved 'Chocolate Soldier.' Catalog listings will describe many, many more—leaf colors that include not only chocolate brown but dark mahogany, copper, silver, pink, kelly green; and flowers that are most often red or orange red, but also some in creamy yellow, pink, and lavender. 'Tropical Topaz' is a green-leaved variety; and 'Pink Brocade' a pink-leaved one.

Episcias like it warm, light, and humid; keep a mister on the table so that you can give them a spray often. Pot them in a light, porous, well-drained soil mix; African violet potting mix

is okay. Keep them nearly moist all the time, but never soggy.

Episcia.

P.S. Strawberry begonias are another appealing candidate for a dining table. They send out runners, as do the episcias. A whole ring of satellite plantlets still attached to the mother plant can be placed in small cachepots around it—a small soufflé dish for the mother, ramekins or individual custard cups for the plantlets.

SHEDDING LIGHT ON THE TABLE

No houseplant, regardless of location, need go without a share of light today. And you need not feel an extravagant energy user if the lamp you choose serves other needs while providing light for your plants. For those places where track or tube lighting just doesn't work out, consider some of the beautifully designed drop, floor, and table lamps available today.

Most of these fixtures are designed for incandescent bulbs. Choose from among those that have, or can be equipped with, a ceramic socket so that you can use one of the cool-type bulbs. These cool-type bulbs direct most of the heat through the back of the bulb, and a ceramic or porcelain socket is required to handle and disperse the heat. With one of these bulbs, plants can be positioned closer to the light, and they will love you for it.

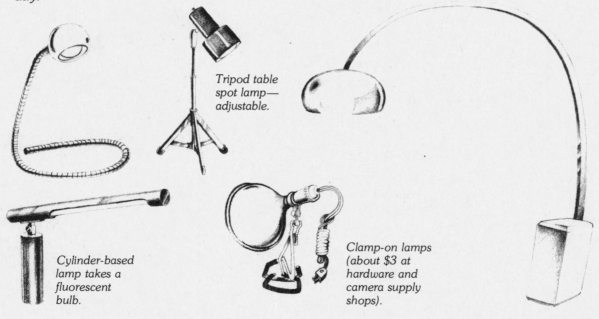

Tripod table spot lamp—adjustable.

Cylinder-based lamp takes a fluorescent bulb.

Clamp-on lamps (about $3 at hardware and camera supply shops).

Countertop bonsai

Often gardeners don't think of bonsai as houseplants. And it's true; the decades-old miniatures of forest gardens most certainly are not. Nonetheless, many houseplants make good candidates for the bonsai treatment. You might call it bogus bonsai, but it happens to be beautiful, especially in the kitchen, where meditation on the serene is often essential to survival.

Bonsai—real or bogus—produces an image of great age, of survival in the face of great stress, but always along with an aura of hope and tenacity. There is an air of restraint and containment about them. Bonsai is not for the Free Spirit; its beauty must be confined to be appreciated.

The main challenge in countertop bonsai is the surgery (pruning) that is necessary to keep the plants within bounds. You must be willing to set firm limits on size.

One of the most delightful candidates for indoor bonsai is the Ming aralia. It has a distinctly Oriental air about it, requires little if any wiring to produce the pleasing lines of bonsai, and grows rather quickly, so that you will not have to wait long for a full bonsai effect. However, it does require strict attention to pruning; you cannot afford to be unduly moved by the sight of new growth swelling along an existing stem, gathering energy to unfurl a new lacy fan of green. Nor can you afford to wonder what heights such an ebullient grower might attain if left unchecked. (Answer: small-tree size, 5 to 6 feet.) Another approach, obviously, is to own two Ming aralias, one for bonsai, one for tree.) If you have misgivings about extensive pruning, you might take up with some of the small-leaved English ivies. While ivy is a determined grower and pruning does not diminish its determination in the least, it can be pruned with less anguish than Ming aralia because of its smaller size and its more predictable growth. You can shape the ivy into beautiful forms, or you can train it around a piece of twisted, gnarled wood or up and over an interesting stone or rock. All in all, you can

Natal pum.

achieve a lovely bonsai illusion with ivy. There are dozens of small-leaved ivies to choose from: 'Minima' and 'Needlepoint' are two good ones.

Other candidates for indoor bonsai that already have an Oriental look about them: Natal plum, southern yew, and southernwood. Other choices: dwarf olive, pittosporum, pomegranate, calamondin orange.

The traditional evergreens—pines and junipers—so often seen in classical bonsai do not have much chance for long-term survival as houseplants. They need an outdoor environment, and while you might succeed in keeping them alive two or three years, it will be pressing your luck. What this means, of course, is that there's no harm trying. One of the most rewarding things about gardening is that any of us can prove the experts wrong, and frequently do.

CARING FOR BONSAI

The main thing to remember about a bonsai is that it is not just a potted plant kept in a small container in a state of semistarvation in the hope it will remain dwarf-sized. Bonsai must be fed and watered; judiciously pruned, both top and roots; and sometimes wired to gently pull branches into the desired position.

All bonsai *must* have perfect drainage, which means the container must have a drainage hole. And since saucers are not a part of the bonsai scene and cachepots and jardinières are the very antithesis of bonsai simplicity and understatement, you are going to wind up with leaky water problems unless you plan to move each plant to the sink, water it, and let it drain before returning it to its spot.

Furthermore, since the soil must be porous

Southernwood.

to allow for quick drainage, and since there is not much of it in the small container anyway, you will need to water your bonsai frequently—on an almost daily basis, in fact. This is an easy-enough routine for countertop bonsai housed in the kitchen. However, if your plants are elsewhere and not so convenient for sink watering, use some sort of inconspicuous small catch basin beneath the bonsai container—for example, a small plastic lid from a margarine carton. With practice, you can fine-tune your watering so that the lid will be sufficient to catch any excess water. Precision watering is much easier in the long run than either mopping up or carting plants back and forth to the sink from distant parts of the house.

For fertilizer, a regular houseplant type will do; use half strength and only once a month from spring to fall; none through the winter.

For training a tree-type bonsai, such as Ming aralia, use copper wire, which doesn't rust. Push the wire up through the drainage hole, and wrap it gently around the trunk and/or branches to force those that grow upward to bend outward and downward as you wish. Experiment by pulling branches into position by hand to see what it is you want the wire to accomplish. For a first bonsai effort, try the symbolic Japanese three-line design. The three lines represent Heaven, Man, and Earth. Heaven is always the longest line; Earth, the base, is the shortest line; Man, the joining or re-conciling line, is in between in length. This pat-

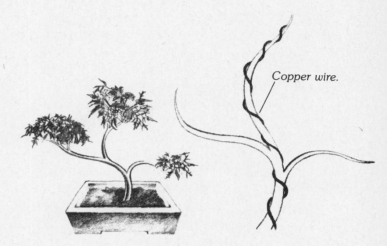

Copper wire.

tern forms the basis for *ikebana,* the beautiful, centuries-old Japanese art of arranging flowers. In *ikebana,* the flowers or branches representing Man and Earth are always placed so that the tips are turned toward Heaven. You can try for this same effect with your indoor bonsai, but in the case of the much-praised Ming aralia, the plant will not cooperate. No matter; its foliage produces a weeping, or cascade, effect that is equally Eastern in its beauty.

TIPS ON PRUNING

The lower part of the main trunk in bonsai should be exposed; any lower branches that are present or are beginning to form are eliminated.

Branches that cross to the inside should also be eliminated to open up the design. Branches that grow out, away from the center, are the ones to save. It may be, though, that you will want to work with a wayward branch, training it with wire to bend or twist for the eventual effect you want.

🌿 When pruning, cut off the branch, stem, or leaf close to its source, so that no stumps or protrusions are left showing. If necessary, use the edge of a small, sharp knife to carefully and *gently* scrape away at the pruning site, leaving a small indentation that will eventually scar over. Don't leave behind any rude protrusions that advertise "I was pruned!"

🌿 Roots will need to be inspected on a yearly basis. If they are heavy and matted, you will need to prune heavily. If there seems to be much more soil than roots, then go easy on the pruning. Cut back on longer, bigger roots to encourage fine feeder roots to grow. Be as gentle as possible with the tiny roots already there.

For the container itself, plain clay dishes in earthy browns, greens, grays, and off-white, and in the simplest of forms, are good for bonsai; the container should not detract from the plant. The container is part of the composition and should not be so big that it overpowers or so small that the visual balance is obviously out of whack. In terms of proportions, as a general guide, let about 80 percent of the composition go to the bonsai and about 20 percent to the container. If you have a low spreading bonsai, heavily foliaged, a 60-40 proportion may be more pleasing. By thinking in terms of propor-

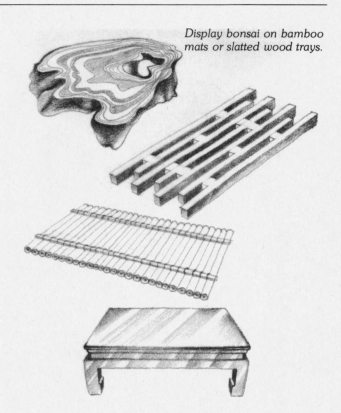

Display bonsai on bamboo mats or slatted wood trays.

tion, you begin to cast a more critical eye on what each part contributes to the total.

Bonsai are often displayed outside on slatted shelves. For indoors, you can adapt this idea with small slatted trays, bamboo mats, or thin slabs of wood. If you want more than one bonsai for your kitchen—and a real bonsai enthusiast could never stop with just one example—then consider displaying them on a long, narrow, slatted platform. These are easy

Before.

to make to size with lathing and need take no more than 8 inches or so of back-of-the-counter space.

Into the old, high-ceilinged kitchen pictured here moved a clean-counter cook who brought with her the Chinese kitchen god Tsao Wang, a

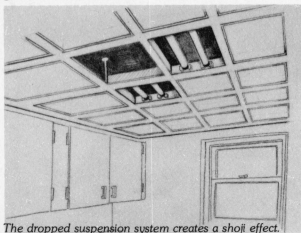

The dropped suspension system creates a shoji effect.

love of things Oriental, and a countertop bonsai collection that brings to the symmetrical room the asymmetrical lines of Eastern art.

The center light was banished and fluorescent lights installed under the cabinets for use by the plants as well as for task lighting. The ceiling was dropped, with panels that fit into a grid for a shojilike effect; fluorescent fixtures behind the luminous panels create a soft, diffused, shadow-free light. (High ceilings can also be brought down to a comfortable height with the use of strong color. A bold and inexpensive alternative for this kitchen pictured on the next page: paint the ceiling and soffit—the part of the wall that fills in the space between ceiling and cabinet tops—a lacquer red; use a Noguchi paper lantern over the old centered ceiling fixture.

The kitchen cabinets were stripped of their old light-pine finish and redone in a dark teak oil stain. The window over the sink was dressed with a space-stretching and light-loving lambrequin. Inexpensive matchstick blinds were stapled to the plywood frame and half-round bamboo molding glued over the edges and seams. (For making a lambrequin, see pages 251–252.)

A long, shallow tray filled with black pebbles stretches the length of the windowsill and holds pots of herbs—anise and fennel and coriander, in this case—and two larger pots of bok choy. This cook is serious about Oriental cuisine!

After.

Pots of anise, fennel, coriander, and bok choy keep company with a collection of bogus bonsai.

Among the Chinese vegetables tried in the sunny windowsill, bok choy, or Chinese cabbage, has been the most successful. Two pots produced enough stalks for a memorable meal of beef bok choy! Snow peas were also grown here one spring, and while the foliage was appealing, the seven-pod harvest was not enough to make a significant impact on any recipe the cook could come up with.

The seed of bok choy was sown the middle of July in 6-inch-deep containers; the plants were thinned to one to a pot in the middle of August; and by the first part of October, each plant had ten stalks, 7 inches tall and ready to harvest. (Source for seeds for Choy Chinese Cabbage: W. Atlee Burpee Co., Warminster, Pennsylvania 18974, *or* Riverside, California 92502, *or* Clinton, Iowa 52732.)

PAI TS'AI CH'AO NIU JO
(Beef Bok Choy)

Marinade

2 teaspoons cornstarch
2 tablespoons water
2 tablespoons sherry
1 teaspoon sugar
¼ teaspoon salt

Other ingredients

1 pound beef
2 heads Chinese cabbage
7 tablespoons oil
2 thin slices ginger
1 clove garlic
1 scallion, chopped fine
2 tablespoons oyster sauce

1. Make a paste of cornstarch and water; add sherry, sugar, and salt.
2. Slice the beef against the grain to make very thin slices, about ¾ inch wide and 1½ inches long. Pour the marinade over the meat, and let stand for about 30 minutes.
3. Cut Chinese cabbage into quarters, then into 1-inch sections. Heat 2 tablespoons of oil in a skillet, and when it's very hot, add the cabbage and sauté, stirring constantly, for 3 minutes. Set aside.
4. In a second pan, sauté beef in 5 tablespoons of very hot oil. Stir the beef quickly to barely coat with oil, and cook for 1 minute. Pour off excess oil.
5. Add the ginger, garlic, and scallion to the beef. Return the pan to the heat.
6. Stir in the oyster sauce. Add cabbage. Stir until cabbage is heated—a minute or two. Remove from heat and serve at once.

Serves four as a side dish.

ABOUT THOSE KITCHEN CABINETS

For a new stain finish. Apply a liquid or cream finish-remover with a paintbrush, wait, and wipe off. Follow directions regarding adequate room ventilation, and don't hurry the job. It's not a difficult one, but as with all good refinishing work, the secret begins with a clean, well-prepared surface. Follow up the remover by wiping the surface with turpentine; then rub with fine-grade steel wool.

Apply new oil stain with a soft, clean rag. Wait ten or fifteen minutes and then wipe off excess. If the stain is not dark enough, wait a few more minutes, wipe the surface again, and then let this first coat dry for twenty-four hours. Apply a second coat of stain in the manner above, wait a few minutes, and then wipe off again to get the shade and effect you want.

To paint wood kitchen cabinets.

Before you begin to paint, decide whether you will use the same hardware or if your new look deserves new hardware. A change, perhaps, from chrome-finish pulls to plain white porcelain knobs? If you do decide to make a change, now is the time to fill and sand any old hardware holes that won't be used for the new set.

If you choose to paint old wood-finish kitchen cabinets, prepare them first with a product that cleans and slightly roughs up the old surface. (Savogran PBC Deglosser is a good cleaning and bonding product.) You want a clean, dull surface that will provide a good bond for the new paint.

Choose a top-quality paint, one in a gloss (high-shine) or semigloss finish. These are easier to keep clean of finger smudges than a flat (no-shine) finish. Try one of the new mohair paint applicators instead of a brush for a smooth finish. Apply a thin even coat of paint, and let it dry thoroughly, at least twenty-four hours. Carefully apply a second coat, and wait another twenty-four hours. You can then help the paint harden by gently wiping the surface with a clean, damp sponge that has been dipped in very cold water (this is something on the order of setting nail polish). Put the hardware on, and for the next few days take extra care in using the pulls for opening and closing the cupboards and drawers in order to give the paint plenty of time to harden thoroughly.

Painting metal kitchen cabinets. Go over surfaces carefully with medium, then fine, sandpaper to rough up the old finish and give the new paint something to grab onto. A primer (first) coat of flat paint is a *must* before new enamel paint is applied. If there are any rust spots, use a special rustproof primer (De Rusto, for example); otherwise a plain flat paint will do. You can add a bit of your new color enamel to the flat-paint primer—only enough to barely tint it—to help the cover-up job along. Plan on two coats (might even take a third) of the new color enamel. Let each coat dry thoroughly before the next coat is applied. (Wait twenty-four hours beyond when you *think* the paint is dry.) A good dry base will make a big difference in how the next coat of paint goes on and in the final appearance. Sand each coat lightly after it is thoroughly dry to smooth out any bumps, specks, and ridges and to rough the coat just enough to help the next coat adhere well.

Kitchen crops

Naturally, edible houseplants are not only good to look at but good to eat. The easiest vegetables for strictly indoor growing are the leaf and root crops—lettuce and radishes, for example. Among the fruit-setting crops, the tomato is by far the most successful and is, in fact, rapidly becoming one of America's most popular houseplants.

The sunniest place in your house is where the vegetables ought to go. They can use all the sun they can get. You can plant vegetables in individual containers—hanging baskets for tomatoes or narrow containers for rows of radishes on the windowsill—or you can plant a miniature vegetable garden in one container. Any size and shape container will do as long as it is at least 4 inches deep. Round shapes offer some especially attractive planting possibilities. A round rubberware dishpan, for example, can be planted with a dozen or so green onions, or scallions, in the center and ringed with radishes. In three or four weeks the dark-green slender stalks will be up and surrounded with light-green rosettes.

When you have finished harvesting this crop, plant again. This time try a whole pan full of tiny carrots. Their lacy, fernlike foliage will be unrecognizable to anyone under thirty, since most carrots haven't come to market with their tops on in years. Tiny sweet carrots served with a hot lemon-butter sauce make a memorable dinner accompaniment.

For a final fall fling at farming, try baby

Carrots.

Scallions and radishes.

beets or spinach. Harvest the beets while still young. Their flavor is best then, and anyway, it is difficult to coax large size from beets when they are container-grown. Pull them when they are about 1½ inches in diameter. Plan to eat the tops, too—in salads or mixed with other cooked greens. Ruby queen is a good variety for container growing. It produces short tops and a round, smooth, bright red root.

Want a crop for the living room? Try ruby lettuce. Its bright green leaves are tinged with red. A row of ruby lettuce on a sunny bay window can bring the celebration of spring into your heart, your house, and your salad bowl.

Or park a toy wheelbarrow in front of the sunny window in your child's bedroom, where your young farmer can tend a crop of radishes and lettuce. A mat of artificial grass (this is about the only excuse you could ever find for using this stuff) makes the perfect antidote for the inevitable spills of soil and water that will likely accompany this adventure.

Line the wheelbarrow with a heavy plastic, add a thin layer of gravel, follow with potting soil, and then sow the seeds. You will probably have to help the young person who tends this crop tune up his senses of sight and touch for when to water and how much to apply. Since the wheelbarrow planter does not have drainage holes, accidental crop flooding or drowning can occur if an ebullient young caretaker gets carried away. For that reason it is a good idea to provide younger gardeners with a watering system suitable to their size. An empty plastic soap bottle, for example, holds less water and dispenses it more slowly than regular watering cans. What might seem to you a longer and more tedious process in tending the plants will be a satisfying accomplishment for the serious young gardener. Let your budding botanist do the craft bit with cutouts and whatever to decorate the water bottle, too. (Some ideas appear on pages 100–101). Helping him personalize his gardening accessories can only underline the importance you place on the love and care of

green and growing things and encourage him to do likewise.

Another container for use in planting crops that have high kid appeal is a mail-flyer wagon with removable sides. Line the bottom, and use individual containers grouped together in the wagon bed.

A toy truck can also carry a head of lettuce, three or four radishes, or a couple of beets and still provide one of the most interesting and entertaining loads your child can haul about. A three-year-old can faithfully truck the crop from one sunny window to another, if necessary, for the three weeks or so that it takes a radish seed to become a radish root, ready for eating.

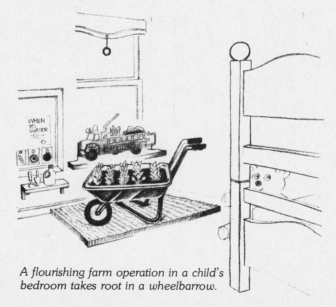

A flourishing farm operation in a child's bedroom takes root in a wheelbarrow.

PLANTING A MINIATURE FARM

Punch good-sized holes (¼ to ½ inch) in the sides of a dishpan container close to the bottom. About four holes evenly spaced around the bottom will do. Fill the container as you would pot any other plant (see pages 26–30), and use a large, round tray as a saucer to collect excess water.

Vegetable crops will need more sun, more water, and more fertilizer than most houseplants. Instead of a houseplant fertilizer, use tomato-plant food. The following are some midget vegetables that make good houseplants:

Tiny Tim Tomato. A true miniature tomato in size and fruit (about ¾ inch in diameter). Plants grow only about 15 inches tall and 14 inches across.

Tom Thumb Lettuce. Small, rosette-shaped plants that grow not much larger than 3 or 4 inches across. One plant makes an individual serving!

Tiny Sweet Carrot. Roots grow to 3 inches; tender, crisp, and sweet. These and other midget vegetables are available from George W. Park Seed Co., Inc., Greenwood, South Carolina 29647.

TOMATOES

The basics for tomatoes are sunlight and warm temperatures. If you have a window that receives at least four to six hours of sunlight, you're in business. This means a south or west exposure. The south side may actually make a better exposure during winter months than in summer. The sun is lower in the sky then, and the rays can slant in through the windows. You may even find that tomatoes do better indoors in the winter than they do in the summer if your house is air-conditioned. (Tomato plants don't like chills of any kind.)

Plan on starting your tomato plants from seed. (Several of the best varieties for indoor pot plants are listed on the next page.) Sow the seeds in individual compressed peat disks. When soaked in water, these disks expand to small, 1-inch pots complete with soil mix and plant nutrients; all you do is add the seed and water and care for them until the seedlings emerge. Plant three or four seeds to a pot, and snip off all but one of the seedlings after they're up and growing. When each seedling has acquired three or four sets of leaves, plant it, peat pot and all, into a larger pot—8 to 10 inch for the miniature or cherry tomato, a 1-gallon container for larger tomatoes.

Fertilize the plants at transplanting time, again in three weeks, and about once a week while they are producing fruit.

If you want homegrown cherry tomatoes

for the December holidays, start your seeds no later than the middle of October. Protect the plants from drafts. If necessary, rig up a small screen between the plant and the window to protect from drafts during the night.

Tomatoes raised indoors may need a substitute for the bees and breeze to accomplish pollination; otherwise, the plants may bloom but not set fruit. Each day while the plants are in blossom, give them a gentle shake to distribute the pollen. Remember, too, that new blossoms will be opening each day over quite a long period of time.

The following are recommended varieties.

Tiny Tim. An old-timer on a relatively new scene and still one of the best. True miniature in size and fruit (about ¾ inch in diameter). Looks great in a hanging basket. If it's potted in a nonhanging pot, provide a small stake for it to grow on (tie the plant loosely to the stake with a strip of soft fabric or nylon stocking). Takes about fifty-five days from seed to fruit.

Burpee's Pixie Hybrid. Especially developed for growing in containers; good in a hanging basket, otherwise stake. Bears bright red, smooth fruit larger than cherry tomato size. The plant grows up to 18 inches tall and takes about fifty-five days from seed to fruit.

Small Fry. This is a larger plant; too large to hang but smashing as a floor plant. It bears lovely bright crimson cherry-type fruit in clusters of seven or eight on a compact plant, which grows to a height of about 30 inches. Takes about sixty-five days from seed to fruit.

LETTUCE

Lettuce is a good nibble crop and an attractive houseplant, so whether you grow enough to make a full-scale salad every week is really irrelevant.

Choose a container wide enough to allow for two or three rows, and you can wind up with a real lettuce-bed look. Sprinkle the seeds on the surface of the dampened soil. Cover very lightly with more dampened soil mix. Lettuce likes lots of water, too—more than most houseplants. Prop your lettuce beds up close to the lights while the plants are still seedlings, but lower them as the plants grow so that the tops are 10 inches or so away from the lights. Fluorescent lights do not give off much heat, but even so, lettuce likes it on the cool side, and the leaves will tend to be limp if they are kept too close to the light.

You can thin out a few seedlings for eating within three weeks and then begin to take outer leaves by the following week or so. New leaves will put out for a couple of months, at which point they begin to toughen. If you are following a reseeding program, new plants will be coming along to take their place. The following are recommended varieties.

Oak Leaf. A small-leaved, deep, compact plant that forms more of a rosette than most other varieties of leaf lettuce.

Tom Thumb. A miniature butterhead which produces small, rosette-shaped plants.

Buttercrunch. A bit larger but more heat-resistant; makes very good eating, indeed.

Kitchen crops.

RADISHES

While these are good sunny-windowsill crops, they can also make it snuggled under the fluorescent lights with the lettuce. Sow radish seeds in the container in which they will grow. After the seedlings come up, thin them out to at least 1 inch apart so that each radish will have room to grow.

Radishes grow quickly. They also use up more water than ordinary houseplants because they are forming the crisp, tender roots that you will be eating in three to four weeks. Plant a new seed for each radish you harvest, and you can keep a sort of radish reforestation program going indefinitely.

Radish tops make attractive greenery, producing something between a rosette and a fountain effect. Grow the variety called Cherry Belli. It's a smooth, round, bright red radish, crisp and tender, with short tops that make it a good choice for a houseplant. The radishes take twenty-four days from seed to table.

Bathrooms

Plants for confined spaces

Space limitations are not necessarily negative attributes. Often they can help steer you clear of haphazard plant arrangements so that you come out with a design plus: a pleasing, controlled plant grouping. Take this bathroom as an example. A grouping of small-leaved plants has as much impact as any large-scale arrangement. Three creeping Charlies form a vertical grouping to one side (the lowest one hung closest to the window; the highest, farthest from the window) and bead cactus and a string-of-hearts hang to the other side.

Grouping together the creeping Charlies adds strength to their small size and scalloped, fuzzy foliage and sets off the distinctive foliage of the other two plants. The bead cactus, which resembles strands of small, round, shiny beads, and the gray-green string-of-hearts, an enormously interesting plant, are both shown to best advantage in the company of other plants with small foliage.

The bead cactus and string-of-hearts hang to the side of the window where they can bask in full sun. The creeping Charlies at the other side of the window receive bright light but not direct sun. A seemingly small detail, but if you reversed the location of the plants, they wouldn't be nearly as happy, particularly the creeping Charlies, which don't want too much sun. All of which underscores the importance of sizing up the environment you have to offer a plant before you decide on the plant you wish

From left to right: creeping Charlie, bead cactus, and string-of-hearts. A large-pattern wall covering makes these small quarters look bigger.

to put there.

Bathrooms are often higher in humidity than other rooms in the house. They are often low in natural light and are sometimes under-lighted, even with artificial light. Low-light, humidity-loving plants are obvious choices for these rooms.

In the small bathroom here, the plants were chosen carefully for their size and growth habit as well as for their environmental needs. The baby's tears and miniature peperomia are so small-leaved that they will not outgrow the limited space allotted to them, and boxwood is a very slow grower. The other plants—a minia-ture grape ivy and a medium-leaved Swedish ivy—are faster growers, but they thrive upon being pinched back and repay such cuts by be-coming full and robust-looking plants.

While all of these plants like the humidity of the bath and even welcome extra misting, they are not overly fond of water applied di-rectly to the pot. Refrain from watering them more frequently than necessary simply because the water is close by and convenient. Just re-member that more plant drownings take place in the bath than anywhere else in the house!

The baby's tears, peperomia, and box-wood fill three shelves which claim a mere 6 in-ches on the far wall of this small, narrow bath. Fluorescent striplights fastened to the underside of each shelf provide supplemental light for the plants. Each plant has a shelf of its own—the

Shelves of baby's tear, miniature peperomia, and box-wood.

boxwood on one shelf, the baby's tears on another. It's a neat, uncluttered way to stage lots of plants in a small space and to make sure each maintains a strong identity.

The miniature grape ivy, with its small, lacy, five-lobed leaves, occupies the lower, side-bracketed shelf; and the medium-leaved Swedish ivy, with its beautiful silver-gray foliage, fills the hanging basket. The owner's cat takes a few swats at this plant now and then, but like most cats, he finds that its leaves aren't nearly as appealing as ferns, palms, and other thin, straight-leaved plants. For a real feline treat, substitute catnip for the Swedish ivy. Hang the basket lower—make it a sturdy metal one—and mount it securely.

THREE HOUSE TREES THAT KEEP WITHIN THEIR BOUNDS

Just because your bathroom is small, there's no reason to rule out trees. There are many houseplants that are narrow and contained but still tall enough to qualify as house trees.

False aralia grows slim and tall and has interesting foliage. It's a plant you will like a lot or not at all. Its leaves are thin and spidery, either adding a lot of design interest for some plant lovers or making it seem nervous and a bit sinister to others. It can get along in low light or artificial light only, and since it also likes

FELINE TREAT

Catnip is an herb. The seed is widely available in garden stores, on seed racks in grocery and variety stores, and through seed catalogs. Plant the seeds according to the directions on the packet, and plan to protect the young plants from kitty for the first few weeks; otherwise the entire project may be eaten before it gets off the ground. After the plant has reached a good size, it can be hung in place. Some cats, once they discover they have a catnip plant all their own, go on a binge and eat the whole thing at one sitting. Most cats, however, are content to nibble in moderation, taking no more than what would amount to a natural pruning of the plant.

warmth and humidity, it's a good choice for the bath.

This plant tends to drop its lower leaves as it grows taller, so plan to add a younger plant, and yet another, to the pot as the original one stretches out. Three of these plants in one container will still not be too fat for a narrow space, and their different heights will look better than a single, older plant grown leggy. False aralia should be allowed to dry out between waterings. Give a once-a-month diluted feeding from March through October.

The cornstalk plant grows tall, and the leaves fan out at the top in an exotic date-palm effect. It takes up minimum floor space and makes a bold, luxuriant show. A yellow-green stripe shows up brightly down the center of its long, wide leaves when the plant receives good light (but not direct sun). It grows well in low light, too, but the coloring in the stripes will recede.

Fiddleleaf fig, despite its huge leaves, is actually rather slender. It takes up very little branching space and can make a wonderfully

Fiddleleaf fig.

Cornstalk plant.

dramatic plant for the bathroom—the large scale of the leaves is the secret. You can see the fiddle-leaf fig standing tall and slim on the floor tray on page 47. If you have space at all for a floor plant in the bath, be sure to consider this one.

NARROW VINES

A vine can double for a tree if you train it to climb instead of letting it spread out. Pothos, English ivy, and philodendron are good choices for trained vines. If you have strong light and will pay extra attention to humidity, consider stephanotis, jasmine, hoya, and passion flower. Train any of these vines to a moss stick, and you have a column of green that takes up a minimum of space while displaying plenty of foliage.

🌿 **Making a moss stick.** Buy hardware cloth; 10 inches of 3- or 4-foot width will do. Roll the hardware cloth into a cylinder, and fasten it securely by weaving a piece of supple wire through it. Stuff the column with dampened sphagnum moss. Poke cross sticks (short enough to fit inside the container close to the bottom) through one end of the cylinder to provide stability for the moss stick when it is stationed in the container. Place the moss stick in the container, and fill all around it with potting soil. Firm the soil around the stick. Space several plants around the moss stick to provide

Making a moss stick.

You can use hairpins to secure the vine.

Hardware cloth.

Cross sticks.

for a full, quick covering of green. If necessary, hairpins can be used to fasten the vines in place as they start up the stick. In addition to regular watering, occasionally water through the top of the column to dampen the sphagnum moss and provide moisture for the aerial roots the plants produce as they climb.

OTHER WAYS TO FIT PLANTS INTO SMALL PLACES

🌿 Ceiling-to-floor tension-rod pole planters come equipped with arms that adjust to any height and can swivel around to catch the light or fit a corner. They can be used at a windowsill, along a wall, or in a grouping as a room divider that can be easily dismantled when you or the plants move on.

🌿 Today's version of the classic French pot rack takes up a little more than 1 square foot of space with six to eight shelves stretching up in a tall tier. Though it was designed to hold large casseroles, soup pots, and such, it can double as a delightful plant caddy.

🌿 The three-tiered hanging vegetable baskets offer lots of vertical space. Use them in other places besides the kitchen. Display colorful face towels and scented soaps along with plants in the bath; scarves and bibelots and plants in the bedroom; hanks of yarn and needlework and plants in the living room.

🌿 Mounting one plant above another on a wall, door, or window frame is also a way of saving space. Here the simplest of arrangements makes a dramatic impact in the narrowest of quarters. Two vertical rows of browallia frame a window with blue flowers. Not enough light? Try pots of English ivy. Stick to one kind of plant in a small place. In summer, transplant the idea to the outside and surround a doorway to make an inviting entry.

Pots of browallia mounted on the window frame. False aralia.

Fantasies with foliage

At some point in life, you have the right to look at a particular room and decide to indulge in a bit of fantasy: a flight from caution; an escape from the rigid; a fearless approach; an I-like-it stance. For some of us this might mean merely gaining the courage to go beyond the ubiquitous avocado-and-gold color scheme that is the refuge of the timid or to trust our green thumbs with something more than a philodendron. A small step, perhaps, but each step builds toward a confident adventurer.

One place where flights of fancy in both plants and décor can be indulged with great success is the bath. And as most baths are small, a little flight goes a long way. Take those vintage peach-and-green tiled bathrooms that grew up in the thirties and forties. Frankly, there's not much you can do with those tiles. You can forget about painting over them, unless you plan to do it all over again when the paint begins to peel, which it will, despite claims to the contrary. If you can't fight the problem, work with it—with thirties' tiles, create a thirties' bathroom. Art Deco is what they called this style that spanned the period between the two world wars. Peach and green were its colors, and they're much in evidence in the pottery of that period—Roseville and McCoy are two popular names. Here these bowls make perfect cachepots for the most Art Deco plant of them all—sansevieria, both the tall type (snake plant) and the rosette kind.

Sansevieria—an Art Deco plant at home in an Art Deco bathroom.

TO MAKE AN ART DECO MIRROR

You will need a square piece of mirror large enough to do its job; a sheet of small mirrored tiles on a fabric backing (to be cut apart); a square frame made of flat molding wide enough to accommodate the mirrored tiles; a paint brush; some shellac, white glue, glass cleaner, and silver paint.

If you can't find a ready-made frame to fit the mirrored tiles, take the tiles to a frame shop and have a flat frame made to fit them and to accommodate the large center mirror.

Paint the outer and inner edges of the frame (wherever the mirror tiles won't cover) with a coat of clear shellac. Let dry, and then coat with silver paint. Do not get paint on areas where the mirror tiles are to be glued.

The next step is to go to a mirror and glass shop to have a center mirror cut and installed in the frame. Have screw eyes and wire attached for hanging.

Now for the Art Deco touch: Measure the sides, top, and bottom of the frame, and cut strips of mirror tiles to fit. (Cut through the fabric backing with a razor blade.) Apply an even coat of glue on the surface of the frame and to the back of each mirror strip. Set the strips in place, press them gently and firmly to align them evenly, and wipe off excess glue with a damp cloth. After the tiles have dried in place, touch up any wood that may show with shellac followed by silver paint.

OTHER FANTASY PLACES

The nature theme is obviously a favorite fantasy of plant lovers—a place that is green, serene, away from it all. One dreamer took a small bedroom with a double window in the middle of the wall and made her fantasy come true. Heavy planking (in a natural finish) was bolted to posts to form the bed (see the following page), and the ceiling was mirrored above it. Matchstick shades stapled to the walls match the blind at the window, and the shelf in front of the window provides lots of basking space for plants. The dreamer who lives here need only drop the blind, and the world goes away.

The fantasy plants growing on the next page were all chosen for an extravagance of one kind or another, whether in fragrance or foliage or form. For example, the false sea-onion, which is an old-fashioned windowsill plant, is merely spectacular. A large green bulb shows above the soil, and out of it grow long, graceful, arching leaves. Trim them back, and they curl into ringlets; let them be, and they will trail down 2 to 3 feet. The sea-onion's bloom forms on a long, curving stalk and is as dramatic as the foliage; and the bulb itself is something else. The plant multiplies by forming tiny bulblets attached to the mother bulb. The thin outer skin of the large bulb gradually peels away, and there, clinging to the side of the mother, may be as many as forty little baby bulbs. These can be potted up for new plants. Start them, several to a pot, covered over with soil. After they sprout, you can repot each one separately, placing the bulb up out of the ground now that it is on its own.

Keeping the sea-onion company is the gardenia, one of the most beautiful—and fickle—of plants. You can bring one home, love it, take care of it, house it well, feed it properly, and then for no apparent reason, leaves and buds suddenly begin to drop, despair sets in, and one day you are left alone writing an "Ode to a Dead Gardenia."

Enough people suffer through this experience to make the owning of a gardenia the source of some apprehension. But if you have never owned a gardenia, you should; when it flourishes, the beauty of the the fragrant, waxy flowers and the shine of the green leaves is pure joy.

Probably the first thing to remember about the gardenia is that leaf and bud drop is not inevitably fatal. If often happens in the first year you own a gardenia, while it goes through an adjustment from a greenhouse environment to your home environment. If you can put the plant outside in the summertime in a shady spot, do so; it loves the outdoors. Bring it in well before the heat goes on in the fall, and give it a sunny spot during the winter months. It likes humidity, so all the tricks to raise the moisture in the air apply: a pebble-filled tray for

A fantasy place to sleep.

Note: People who like heavy beds up against a wall must stay in shape, for a certain amount of agility is required at sheet-changing time. Helpful hint from the owner of the bed pictured opposite: Put on three bottom contour sheets, one over the other in one bed-making, and peel them off one by one at laundry time.

water to drain into; frequent misting; small, open jars of water tucked in under the plant's branches.

Gardenias also enjoy a weekly dunk in a pail of water or in the tub. A good tub soaking can carry them as long as a week in the winter, but never let the soil go completely dry. Yellowing leaves on gardenias are common; the treatment is a dose of chelated iron (available in garden stores; follow directions).

Gardenias like cool nights, which are also preferred by the lady-of-the-night orchid. The orchid takes its name from its sweet nighttime fragrance. Its flowers are fragile and white and bloom over a period of weeks during the winter. When not in bloom, as is now the case, the orchid is tucked back among the other plants, out of the limelight but not without care, which means filtered sunlight and frequent spraying.

The sensitive plant rounds out this bedroom fantasy display. Give the lightest touch to a pair of leaflets at the tip of a branch, and leaf-

lets along the line fold up in domino fashion, one after the other. Give the pot a rap with your knuckles, and the whole plant folds up in a total droop. Turn off the lights, and the leaves close up for the night, too.

This plant likes a sunny windowsill, lots of watering, and daily misting. It will flower in round puffs somewhat like a dandelion gone to seed. Unlike dandelions, these pink and lavender puffs are long lasting.

Many a family room could also do with a fantasy or two, particularly if the room is a small

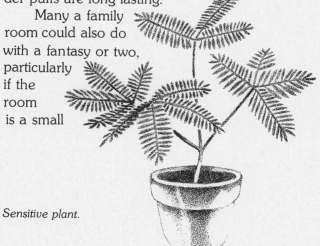

Sensitive plant.

one, and the family is just the two of you. The couple who turned the room on the next page into a fantasy getaway chose plants for a jungle effect.

The pencil cactus was an early choice. It makes a splendid house tree for a small room, since it creates the feeling of a lot of green without taking too much space. This strange, bare-limbed, succulent "tree" is made up of twiggy branches that look like glossy green pencils hooked together in a weird tinker-toy fashion. As the plant grows, tiny leaves appear on the tips of the new branches, but they remain only a short time and then dry and fall off.

The pencil cactus is easy to grow. It generously tolerates neglect, though it does like water now and then and a feather duster to whisk dust away. Rootings are especially easy with this plant, and you can make friends far and wide by sharing cuttings when your tree is large enough to spare them. Take a good hunk for a cutting, a piece about 8 inches long that has several twigs branching out. Dip the cutting in a growth hormone, place in a pot of perlite, and keep damp until the plant takes off.

It's hard to believe the ethereal calla lily can thrive here, in an ordinary window garden, but it does, and dramatically so. Although callas like a cool temperature, full sun is a must; and while they are in bud and in bloom, they need quantities of warm water.

Plan for blooming time. Plant each bulb 1½ inches deep in a 6-inch pot. Put pots in a cool, dim place for three or four weeks, and then they are ready for full sun. Give lots of water and plant food every few days. If you pot in August, you'll have blooms in October. When blooming stops, gradually stop watering. Leave the bulb in dry soil until the following August, and then start over again with potting

soil that is enriched with the addition of dry manure (available at garden shops; follow directions for mixing).

The third fantasy plant on display here is the lady slipper orchid. For your first try with this charmer, go with 'Maudiae,' with its strap-like leaves mottled green and white and its yellowish-green and white flowers. Many orchids are much easier to grow than is commonly thought, and this is one of the easiest. The foliage of this orchid is also better-looking than most, but unfortunately, this isn't saying a great deal because, on the whole, orchids are rather ratty-looking when they're not in bloom. But, oh those blooms! Not only are they beautiful, but they last and last—lady slippers for as long as three months.

OTHER SMALL FANTASIES

For touches of whimsy anywhere in the house, you can team up plants with accessories:

🌿 A ceramic duck or crystal swan, neck arched, reaching over to dine from a bed of baby's tears growing on the coffee table.

🌿 A Devonshire cow creamer in a meadow setting of ornamental grasses at the breakfast table.

🌿 A white porcelain rabbit hiding beneath a dwarf rabbit's foot fern in the bath.

The lower-level family room of a split-level home becomes a jungle abloom.

Letting in light: shutters, shades, skylights, and blinds

SHUTTERS

The young single who bought this older-apartment-converted-to-a-condominium took one look at the previous occupant's technique for coping with window and shelves and decided "there oughta be a law" against ready-made bathroom curtains that cover most of the window and spring-pole shelves that fit over toilet tanks.

Before.

The curtains and shelf were removed, and by the end of the day, light was pouring through the window and onto the wall-to-wall shelves that now provided the perfect perching place for plants. A simple louvered double shutter installed on one side of the window provides for complete privacy when needed, at a cost less than that of the curtains if you figure their life expectancy.

A floor-to-ceiling 1-by-12 was used for a divider and to produce a built-in, wall-to-wall look for the shelves. The shelves allow the plants to take advantage of all the light coming through the window. Their cost? Only a little more than the spring-pole shelves, with lots more space and a less cluttered look.

Window treatments that let in the light can help make bathrooms pleasant places where plants can thrive, adding softness and warmth to an otherwise cold, impersonal setting.

If the standard wooden louvered shutters are "too period" for you, there are other va-

A lost bathroom window is uncovered, and the whole bath greens up.

After.

rieties you could try. You can make shirred-curtain shutters by positioning tiny curtain rods inside a wood frame. If you have full sun at the window, a sheer fabric can help screen the plants from hot, damaging rays. To make the fabric panel, cut a piece of fabric twice the width of the frame opening, plus 1 extra inch for side hemming, and the length of the frame opening, plus 2 inches to allow for a casing at top and bottom wide enough for the rods to slip through. Hem all sides; slip rods in casings; put rods in frames; and your custom shutter is finished.

An old stained-glass window reborn as a shutter can be stunning. Should you happen upon a piece of stained glass, frame it in wood, and if necessary, add a fill-in frame at the window to receive it. Fasten one side of the stained-glass shutter to the window frame with hinges. Add a suitable knob, and you have a one-of-a-kind shutter that makes magical things happen to light.

SHADES

A tough window treatment that confronts many an apartment dweller is the wide window with heat and air conditioning vents stretched beneath. Countless apartments are built around problem windows such as these. And countless times Venetian blinds confront us as the uninspired answer.

True, you must do something to garner a bit of privacy and possibly to control the light, especially if your exposure is west and you have the strong afternoon sun. But before you settle for the usual draw draperies at either side of the Venetian blind (and remember the draperies will shut out some of your light per-

Shades can provide as much or as little light as you want and help create a greenhouse environment. Heat and airconditioning vents banished in one stroke.

DO-IT-YOURSELF SHADES

🌿 **For painted shades.** Painted window shades are not a new artsy pastime. Renoir was a practitioner of the art, and some of the shades painted in Europe in the eighteenth century are still on display in royal castles there. American craftsmen and itinerant artists of the late eighteenth century helped document the culture of our country at the time. Primitive scenes of American folk life as well as sophisticated landscapes found their way onto window shades, and toward the end of the nineteenth century, formal stenciled and bordered designs became the mode. The do-it-yourselfer should use vinyl-coated cloth shades—the room-darkening type. If you are painting a geometric or using a stencil, use masking tape to outline the design or to secure the stencil. Use acrylic, vinyl-base, or fabric paint; and make certain that tape, paint, and shade are compatible by running a test somewhere on the shade that won't be seen. After the paint is applied, allow it to dry thoroughly (twenty-four hours) before removing the tape. (If doing a freehand design, use a soft pencil or chalk for light sketching before painting.) To set the paint after it is dry, place a dry pressing cloth over it, and with a warm iron (set at low heat), go over the design, slowly moving the iron over the painted portion for a five-minute heat treatment.

🌿 **For appliquéd shades.** Use a vinyl-coated cloth shade, and choose designs from vinyl-coated wallpaper or a fabric such as chintz, polished cotton, or percale. If you use fabric, spray it with a clear acrylic spray to keep the raw edges from raveling. Use small, sharp scissors to cut out the designs you want. Arrange them on the shade, and lightly mark their positions with a soft pencil. Use a fabric cement and, following the directions for use, apply to the back of the fabric. Press each piece gently into position. When all are in place, press carefully but firmly to smooth out all air bubbles. Let dry, and then apply a protective coating of acrylic spray. For wallpaper appliqué, apply with wallpaper paste or white household glue. Let dry flat for twenty-four hours before rolling.

manently, no matter how tightly they are pulled open), consider the roller shade. Shades offer a lot of design interest while giving you the light and privacy control you need. Consider what happened to the window ledge on page 241 . . .

A wood shelf, 3 inches wider than the radiator, was stretched wall to wall a couple of inches above the radiator. (The overhang protects plants from direct blasts of hot or cold air.) Floor-to-ceiling 2-by-6s, nailed to a 2-by-4 at the ceiling, were placed at the sides and in the center of the window with the wide side placed flat against the shelf. Roller shades were then installed between the 2-by-6s, and the window took on an architectural interest of its own.

The roller shades, placed away from the window, introduced an unexpected opportunity to experiment with high-humidity plants. By simply lowering a shade or two, you create a small greenhouse space that stores the humidity produced by routine watering, misting, and filling pebble trays.

The shades can also be reversed with bottom-to-top pull if you have lots of high-hanging plants. The plants can get all the light they want at the top of the window while you have daytime privacy as well—a good bathroom window solution. Install the shade so that the roller faces to the outside for a smooth, finished look on the inside. For more finish and with only a bit more bother, you can add a thin strip of wood across the bottom of the window

to form a cradle for the roller.

So, all in all, there is a lot to be said for roller window shades. They can provide total privacy when you need it, and with a good spring that takes them clear to the bottom or top of the window, they admit maximum light for your plants. When fitted properly to the window, the shade can be more efficient than unlined draperies or Venetian blinds in keeping out cold, and they now come in enough colors and patterns to please all.

SKYLIGHTS

A skylight is the perfect therapy for a gloomy room. Flooding the room with natural light, it adds a whole new dimension to the indoor environment and indoor garden plans. Skylights are too often dismissed as being too complicated or expensive, but in fact they can be a bargain and are not difficult to install. They are far easier to handle than you might imagine, and for the enormous boost they give to the confines of a room and to the spirits of those who live there, they rank as a major improvement at minor expense. And while bathing a room in light and cheer and creating a super environment for plants, skylights can help save on energy bills.

When the thought of a skylight occurred to the owner of the small, old bath pictured on the following page, thoughts of plants in a sauna

Vanilla orchid, lipstick plant, fernleaf begonia, and Boston fem make their home in this skylit bath.

setting followed close behind. So along with the skylight came diagonally stripped wooden walls and rugged sisal matting. Among the plants that happily make their home here are the vanilla orchid, lipstick plant, fernleaf begonia, and Boston fern. They grow lush and luxuriant in the natural light, and the spotlights attached to the inside of the skylight walls illuminate them at night.

Skylights can actually help brighten whole layers of a house, as many town house and row house owners are discovering. They are the perfect antidote for a closed-in feeling. At the top of a stairwell, a skylight can flood a home with sunlight, creating lovely, light-filled shafts of space that brighten every room in the house and make every level an atrium to welcome plants.

Mirror the sides (the shaft) of your skylight, and remarkable things will happen in your home. The sky itself becomes reflected, and the sun bounces from side to side, throwing light all over the place. Suddenly the dark northern side of your house is as sunny as the south. And what's more—they're both sunny at the same time! The effect of a mirrored skylight is nothing short of pure wonder.

BLINDS

Most of us think that besides letting in the light and insuring privacy, window treatments

INSTALLING A SKYLIGHT

The idea of installing a skylight as a do-it-yourself project is more intimidating than the job itself.

Check with building supply firms for brochures from skylight manufacturers to help you decide the type and size of skylight you want. Choose one that is shatter- and weather-resistant and double-insulated for both winter and summer comfort. Use masking tape on the ceiling to mark the inside dimensions of the skylight opening and to give you a clear idea of the proportions of the skylight in relation to the rest of the room.

For a roof with no attic space between, you can get right to the installation. With attic space, you will need to build a light shaft first, remembering that the measurements are the most critical part of a skylight project. The size must be exact because the shaft must fit snugly at both the ceiling and the roof openings. After you have the shaft made (from ½-inch plywood or plasterboard), you can cut through the ceiling and tie off the joists with headers (crosspieces of lumber). Now slide the shaft up through the ceiling to the roof. Where the corners of the shaft meet the roof, drive long nails through the roof from the inside. Make sure the nails go through straight. On the outside, you use these points of the nails as they come through the roof from the inside as your guide for marking where to cut out the roof section from the outside for the skylight installation. Tie off the rafters with headers, and put the skylight in place.

Use metal flashing and asphalt roofing compound to make the joints around the skylight weather- and water-proof. Paint the inside of the shaft white for good light reflection or line with mirror tile.

Style 1. Straight shaft.

Style 2. Tilted shaft.

Style 3. Splayed shaft.

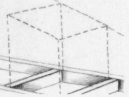
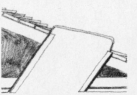
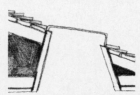

Tilted shafts are used where the ceiling opening cannot fit directly under the roof opening. With a splayed shaft, the ceiling opening is larger than the roof opening, to spread the light out over a wider area.

ought to look good, too. Included among today's best-looking window treatments on all these counts are roll-up blinds. The new versions, while a vast improvement over their country cousins—the old roll-up porch blinds—have lost none of their charm. Choices today range from wooden slats in tortoiseshell finish to natural matchstick to thin vinyl strips, all in a wide range of widths and lengths. With new cord-locking devices, the blinds are easy to roll way up to the top of the window and will stay put to let in all the light you want. They also unroll evenly and smoothly for total privacy. When in doubt as to how to screen your windows, you can't go wrong with a roll-up blind.

Faced with a tall, skinny corner window and no idea what in the world to do with it, this owner fell back on the garden theme and a solution that brought harmony to the whole room. The window was surrounded with a black and white wallpaper for a latticework effect, and the window itself was hung with a black matchstick blind. A row of young jade trees basks in the sun on the wide sill. The simplicity of the treatment as well as the plants themselves lends an Oriental serenity to the setting.

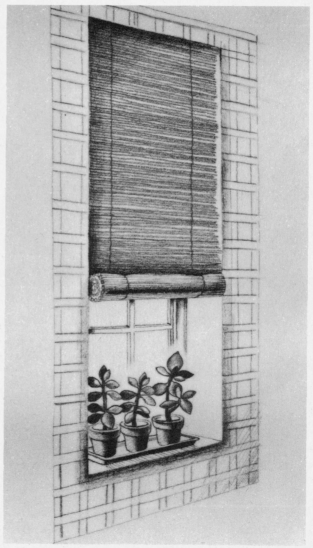

A latticework wallcovering frames a matchstick blind.

Bedrooms

Letting in light: cornices, curtains, lambrequins and swags

Dressing a window once required three sets of hangings. The first set of curtains hung against the glass and was covered with opaque draw draperies. Elaborate stationary side draperies were hung over these from behind either a cornice or valance or from a decorative pole. Hardly anybody does anything so involved with their windows these days except in restoration rooms, but we still take bits and pieces from the draped days and use them alone or in combinations that fit our lives today.

For example, the valance or cornice that was once the finishing touch can now be the total window treatment and could hardly be more compatible with a collection of plants at the windowsill. A valance is simply a "soft" cornice. It can be a simple gathered ruffle, a French-pleated heading to control the fullness, a short Austrian shade design, a swag, or a series of swags with a cascade at either end (see page 253).

A cornice is rigid and runs across the top of the window and returns to the wall at each side. It can be finished in any of a number of ways: painted or stained wood trimmed with molding; wallpapered with a border design; covered with leather, mirrored; or edged with an old gilt picture frame. Wooden cornices can also be padded and upholstered and trimmed with braid, fringe, or welting.

Valances and cornices can have a straight bottom edge or a shaped design, such as a Chippendale curve or a large scallop. They are usually 4 to 12 inches deep. If there is an upward curve, such as a deep scallop, that carries the eye up, then the valance or cornice can be a little deeper. Keep in mind, though, that if a valance or cornice is too deep, it can bring the ceiling, and the mood, down.

A sunny bay window makes an ideal spot for an indoor garden and a good place for a cornice window treatment. Here the scalloped, upholstered cornice offers all the luxury look any sybarite could want in the bedroom, and

A scalloped cornice frames a garden bay.

individual skinny white vinyl blinds control and filter the light for the benefit of the plants and people.

Cornices are especially useful in pulling windows and walls together without swathing the glass in layers of fabric and shutting out that all-important light that plants need. A cornice can be made to turn the corner right along with corner windows, which are often a problem area. If there is wall space between the windows, you can cover the wall with the same fabric that covers the cornice. Build shelves that also turn the corner beneath the windows, and you'll have a perfect garden corner.

Of all the various types of curtains, cafés offer the most flexibility in the control of light and privacy. They can be used alone or combined with shades or shutters. A sheer, filmy fabric softens the window glass and reduces glare while still letting sunlight filter through. Top tiers can be open; bottom tiers, closed. Cafés offer a pleasant kind of privacy. You can see out, but you are not on view.

The biggest part of the decision making involved in cafés has to do with placement. When hanging café curtains, look for an architectural feature as the place for installing the rod—for example, the sash bar in the middle of a double-hung window or the muntins, or strips, that separate the small panes of glass.

In this room, short little café curtains are

Café curtains topped with shades.

placed along the lowest muntin line with matching shades above. Even with the shades raised so that the hanging plants can bask in the light, the cafés still give those seated in the room a feeling of privacy. This charming effect is reminiscent of an old French restaurant. The cafés are low enough to allow the plants on the table to receive all the light they need.

If you don't have an architectural feature to dictate where your curtains go, think about proportion: one-third above, two-thirds below; or the other way around. As a matter of fact, the one-third—two-thirds proportion is a good guide for placement of other things besides café curtains. Chair rails, for example, are best placed one-third of the way off the floor. And if you do decide on tieback curtains or draperies, remember that tying back high—a third from the top—rather than tying back low—a third from the bottom—will let in much more light (and also suggest something that is French Empire in design, like the high-waisted dress that was Empress Josephine's preference in gowns).

As for lengths of curtains and draperies, there are three obvious architectural features that can help you decide, and then there is a fourth length that you can choose just for fun. First, there is the length to the sill. Second, to the bottom of the apron (the strip of horizontal woodwork under the sill). Third, to the floor (if you have baseboard heat, stop at the top of the heater). The fourth length is for stationary draperies or curtains—not the kind that draw. Let these be anywhere from 3 to 12 inches too long so they can rumple on the floor in a careless but elegant way.

Where you hang draperies, as well as where you tie them back, affects how much light you receive. To let in the optimum amount of light, the curtains should be outside the window, rather than inside, so that when they're pulled open they reveal the entire window and block none of the light. The inner edges of the draperies should just cover the woodwork at the sides.

French doors can often be curtained only partway up (in the manner of cafés) so that sky and treetops are always in view while privacy and light reign inside. If draperies are preferred, hang them in such a way that when pulled open, none of the panes is obscured.

A lambrequin is a sort of three-dimensional frame that runs along one side of the window, across the top, and down the other side, boxing it in. It is another window treatment that lets in the maximum amount of light for your plants. You can combine it with a roller shade for privacy; the shade can be kept rolled up under the lambrequin, out of sight except when needed. If privacy and glare are not problems, a lambrequin can be used all by itself as a handsome window treatment.

Lambrequins can be the answer to any number of problem windows: Mismatched windows can be outlined in frames so that they become look-alikes; small windows can be tied together in one treatment; windows can be given an architectural importance that will make them a focal point for the room.

As with cornices, all kinds of coverings can be used on a lambrequin. The inside edges of the lambrequin can be left straight for a contemporary look or shaped to fit whatever design period you want. Quarter-inch plywood can be used for the front of the lambrequin and 1-by-4s for the top and sides. Cut the side pieces the height of the finished lambrequin. Cut the top piece the width of the window. Glue and nail together.

For a shaped front, cut the design from brown paper, and trace it onto the plywood. Saw out the shape, and then glue and nail it to the side and top pieces. Use small wood blocks

Back view shows how angle irons secure lambrequin to wall.

The makings of a lambrequin (for the finished item, see page 216).

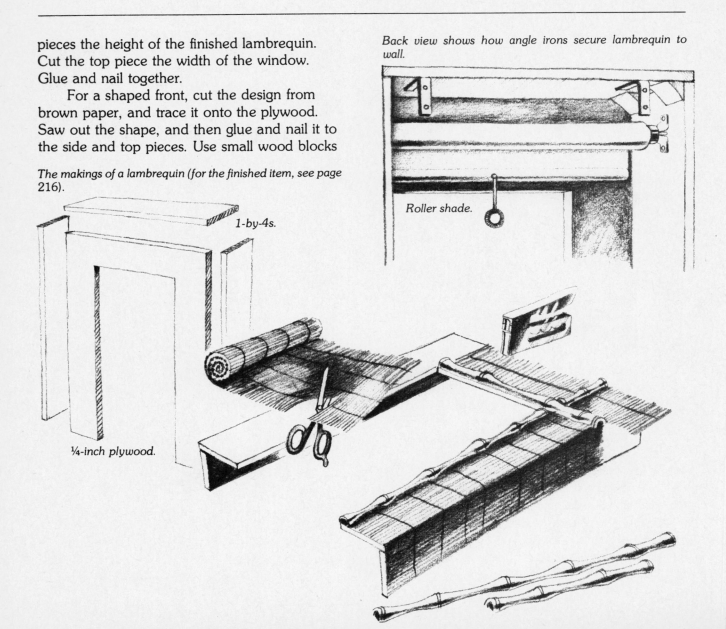

1-by-4s.

Roller shade.

¼-inch plywood.

or angle irons to reinforce the joints.

Attach brackets for roller shades to the inside of the lambrequin if desired. To hang the lambrequin, use two angle irons screwed to the top of the box and into the wall.

A swag and jabot—yet another window treatment—can produce a formal, elegant effect and still let in lots of light. You can also indulge in sumptuous fabrics without going bankrupt because this treatment calls for but a fraction of the yardage needed for full draperies. The swag is the part of the fabric that drapes across the window; the jabot is the cascading end piece that hangs on either side of the window opening.

Swags and jabots can be made of the simplest materials—muslin and sheeting—as well as of silks and velvets. A decorative edging on the jabots such as fringe or braid is traditional.

The simplest way to come up with a swag effect is by pulling a length of fabric through loops of cord that have been attached to the top of a window frame. You can use ready-made cord tiebacks, with or without tassels, at the top corners of the window. Pin or tack the fabric to the cord loops to hold it in place. Even simpler: Drape the fabric over a rod, ends going over the pole away from the room and toward the wall, so that the jabot drops along the side of the window from behind the pole.

Two windows looking like one. Note that the swag takes a double plunge.

Arrange the swag in folds by hand, and use thumbtacks to hold it in place where needed. You can tie two side-by-side windows together in an inexpensive yet classy way by draping one length of fabric across the two windows and holding it in place at the center and sides of the windows with ornamental tiebacks.

TO MAKE A SWAG AND JABOT

Decide how deep you want the swag to drape and how long you want the jabots to hang on either side. Jabots can hang anywhere from one-third the distance between the top of the window and the floor to all the way to the floor, in which case they double as draperies.

Use a 45-inch-wide fabric for the fullness you need, and cut a length that will reach from the end of one jabot to the other and that includes excess for the drape or plunge. Lay the fabric out, and mark off the center swag piece with tailor's chalk. Mark chalk lines from A to B, and cut the fabric here. Use the cut-away pieces to line the jabots, allowing ½-inch seams. Points B represent the places where the swag drapes over the pole. Gather the swag by hand at these points, and lay it over the pole; arrange folds, and tack in place.

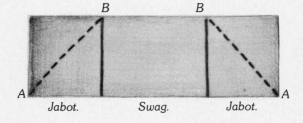

Jabot.   *Swag.*   *Jabot.*

Treillage

Treillage by any other name—lattice, trellis, arbor—translates on sight into garden and green world. What's more, treillage can perform all kinds of decorating magic. Tricks with treillage include the disguising of a wall in need of a repair job; the lowering of a too-high ceiling; the masking of a room's awkward architectural zigs and zags; and the dramatizing of windows large or small without eliminating a ray of light.

This bedroom bower for young romantics features a simple, inexpensive trellis stretched up the wall behind the bed and over the ceiling for a canopy. There's enough light coming through the large windows to keep a pair of velvet plants (also known as purple passion) healthy and thriving. The wall behind the trellis is painted a beautiful eggplant to echo the velvet plant's foliage, and because velvet plants are easy to root from cuttings, older plants can be replaced with new, vigorous ones at no added expense.

A bedroom bower.

HOW TO MAKE A LATTICE CANOPY

Install a frame for the lattice first. Use 1-by-3s on the wall at either side of the bed and across the top of the wall at the ceiling line. Position more 1-by-3s on the ceiling, lining them up with the sides, head, and foot of the bed. (You can create a small recess effect for the bed by using heavier posts at the head of the bed; 4-by-4s work nicely.)

Patch and paint the walls, ceiling, and framing before putting up the lattice. Buy lattice strips, and paint them before nailing in place. Pick a color that provides a good contrast with the wall. Crisp white lattice against shiny yellow or parrot green, chocolate brown or navy blue, or the deep blue purple of the eggplant. Trim off the sides of the 1-by-3s with molding.

The size and spacing of the lattice and the pattern you lay out is your own choice. The important thing about latticework is that once you begin, the spacing and pattern must be uniform. It is the repetition of treillage that makes it so appealing.

Cube rooms, zig and zag rooms, small rooms, difficult rooms—all can make good use of the see-through airiness that comes with treillage. Cane and windowpane patterns, Lucite and glass, wicker and wrought iron—these, too, will lend an open, garden spirit to any room.

This small dining room, with its standard sliding glass door leading onto the balcony, was reborn with a lattice treatment. It showcases a green view beyond, and a mirror and matching lattice wall doubles the indoor green and the feeling of space as well. Move in wrought-iron garden furniture, palms for floor plants and ferns for hanging, and you're dining *al fresco*.

A lattice treatment frames a glass door on the left and a mirrored wall on the right.

A private place for a kid

For a youngster who can't get enough of the green world, you can take the trellis right off the wall and turn it into a private place to study and think—a miniature arbor with room for all kinds of plants to climb, hang, and perch. When lattice is worked in squares instead of diamonds, as shown here, it produces a heavier, more solid-looking design. In this boy's room, it adds a sturdy, substantial feeling that nevertheless is still totally compatible with the openness and sense of freedom of treillage.

If you want the lattice look but not the hammering that accompanies getting the real stuff in place, then look into wall coverings. Though the fernery here was latticed inside and out with wall covering, covering only the inside or the outside would also produce an appealing garden air. Surround the outside of the fernery with lattice, and you create an arbor effect. Put the lattice inside, and you gain a bower look. Either way, or both, a little or a lot, lattice can help make any room bloom. This setting was designed like the one for the begonias on page

A fernery papered in a lattice motif.

314. It brings together one of the best plant-and-pattern combinations possible: ferns and treillage. And in one of the best indoor environments for both—the bath.

Most ferns like humidity, and the bath is a good place to house them. Not only is this room's humidity usually higher than the humidity in other parts of the house, but it is also a convenient spot for plants such as ferns that especially enjoy misting. Large ferns that are difficult to water from the top can be placed in the tub to soak up water from the bottom.

Ferns also do well under artificial light, which makes the bath another good choice for a fern's home because baths seldom, unhappily, have big, sunny windows.

Among the collection pictured on the preceding page:

Silver brake (*Pteris quadriaurita* 'Argyraea'). This is a silvery-green, two-toned plant that is exceptionally pretty as a houseplant. Its fronds are long, full, and graceful.

Button fern (*Pellaea rotundifolia*). The little round leaf parts of this fern grow low and spreading rather than upright, so you will want to place it where you can see the top of the plant and fully enjoy its lovely gray-green foliage. If you hang it, hang it low—the foliage is prettier when looked down upon.

Rabbit's foot (*Davallia canariensis*). You must have this fern, if only for its feet! As the fern grows, up over the rim of the pot will climb fat, fuzzy, brown runners. And then down the side of the pot. And then out along the shelf. It all may sound a bit creepy, but not so. The runners are lovely-looking and fascinating to watch grow, and once accustomed to the idea, you can break off a "foot" and pot it up for a new plant. The hare's foot (*Polypodium aureum* 'Mandaianum') is a good companion plant. The "feet" are bigger, and the foliage is more upright, with broad blue-green fronds (rabbit's foot is a lacy, floppy fern).

Birdsnest fern (*Asplenium nidus*). This plant is a nice one for any fern collection not only because it is a beautiful, easy-to-grow houseplant but also because it doesn't look at all like a fern. It has long, broad, shiny green foliage that spreads out from the crown to form the bird's nest. Look into the center of the plant before a new frond is ready to unfurl, and you will see it rolled up tight like a fat, green egg.

Boston fern (*Nephrolepis exaltata* 'Bostoniensis'). This was the most popular houseplant of grandmother's day. Everybody owned one or wanted to. The 'Boston Petite' is only one of many cultivars developed since then. These plants are satisfying to own because they fill their containers to the brim, looking rich and luxuriant. To help your plant grow full and fat more quickly, simply wind the runners (stolons) in around the base of the mother plant, and pin them to the soil with hairpins. New young plants will form from the runner buds. When the pot is full, extra runners can be cut and potted up in separate containers to increase your fern holdings or to give for any or all occasions.

THE AMERICAN FERN SOCIETY

If you have moved a bit beyond the admiration of ferns into the beginnings of a love affair with them, you will already know that they carry some of the most imposing, if not threatening, names in all of horticulture. (Orchids do outdo them.) Once past such simplicities as *Pellaea rotundifolia*, which is merely button fern, on to *Cyrtomium falcatum* (holly fern), and *Davallia canariensis* (rabbit's foot fern), the road is clear for becoming a pteridologist yourself.

One of the most rewarding facets of the study of ferns is that unlike most other houseplants, they are widely available for our enjoyment and observation in their native habitats, often not much farther away than a nature walk in the nearest patch of woods.

While the American Fern Society is basically a scholarly one (its *American Fern Journal* presents information on ferns that would leave a newcomer reeling), the lover of ferns will nonetheless find a warm welcome and much of interest by joining the Society. The *Fiddlehead Forum*, a quarterly newsletter, will be reassuring to the neophyte, offering how-to advice on indoor cultivation, easy-to-absorb articles on the nature of ferns, and fascinating tidbits on such things as how to prepare fiddleheads au gratin.

A Spore Exchange makes fern spores available at a nominal cost to those who wish to grow their own plants, and every so often a list of species in the collection is distributed to members. Fern Forays are also sponsored by the Society, and local chapters conduct all manner of activities, including projects on Phern Photography (the fern folks are not without their phun). Address: The American Fern Society, Inc., Dean P. Whittier, Department of Biology, Vanderbilt University, Nashville, Tennessee 37325.

Button fern.

Through a mirror brightly

Mirrors are good for plants and plants are good for mirrors. You can double the greenery while spreading the light around. Use mirrored shutters to show off a dwarf orange tree in full flower and fruit and you have the *Orangerie* of Versailles right in your bedroom!

Those of a practical turn of mind might like to know that mirrors on the inside of exterior walls reflect heat back into the room, so that the thermostat can be set lower than usual—a condition both plants and pocketbook will appreciate.

Mirrors can cover wide expanses—shutter, screen, or wall—or can be used on a smaller scale and just as effectively. In this formal pairing, two young neanthe bella palms sit on a low

A dwarf orange tree basks in the light bouncing off mirrored shutters.

Small 'Neanthe Bella' palms stand sentry in front of shell-framed mirror

two-door cupboard. Over it, reflecting the front door as you enter, is a large shell-frame mirror. Shells and mirrors go together, too. In the eighteenth century, decorating shell mirrors was a fashionable hobby in England, and the shell motif itself was especially popular in the Queen Anne and Louis XV periods.

In another solo performance a large, handsome floor plant gazes at itself in a mirror-topped table. (Almost any table can be inexpensively topped with sheet mirror cut to fit. Have the edges beveled a bit to remove the sharpness.) Plants can also sit on mirrors. A mirror makes a practical and dazzling tray for a collection of potted plants. Make one a centerpiece, combined with candlelight, for a most companionable accompaniment to good food and conversation.

Mirrors can make capital of architectural zigs and zags. A niche, for example, will enliven the décor when lined with mirror and plant shelves.

Mirrors also minimize the boxlike feeling that so many rooms in apartment buildings manage to produce. Start with that omnipresent "one big window," and position a mirror-paneled screen in one corner to bounce light into the room and reflect the greenery massed in front of it. Cover a 1-foot-wide panel (floor-to-ceiling height) with mirror tiles; frame with decorative molding; and mount it flat at the center of the window wall to divide the window in half. Attach either to floor and ceiling or to the window wall. Two simple additions, and the whole room takes on new interest.

Sometimes a wall, especially in a bedroom or foyer, consists mostly of doors. You can make the doors disappear by covering them, along with the rest of the wall, with mirror. (Remove the molding from around the doorways and use aluminum stripping for trim.)

A plant falls in love with its own reflection, and so will you.

SOME CITRUS TREES

A miniature or dwarf citrus tree makes a beautiful houseplant: glossy green leaves; fragrant, waxy blossoms; colorful, delicious fruit; and limited culture requirements.

It is easy enough to grow citrus trees from fruit seeds, and there is enormous satisfaction in bringing up a seed from a breakfast orange to a tree that is 6 feet or higher.

Unfortunately, trees grown from seed are not dependable performers: They do not always bloom; if blooming stage is reached, fruit does not always set; and finally, if fruit does grow, it is rarely "true" to the fruit which produced the seed. Better to go with a dwarf variety especially suited to pot culture. Three that are worth trying are:

Calamondin orange. This tree tends to grow tall and columnar; it produces an abundance of blossoms and fruit which are often in different stages of maturity at the same time—ripe fruit, green fruit, and blossoms—almost year round. The leaves are smaller than those of lemon or lime; the fruit is about 1½ inches in diameter.

Ponderosa lemon. This tree bears full-size fruit; a single lemon is often 3 to 4 inches in diameter and enough for a large pie. The flowers are waxen, trumpet-

Ponderosa lemon.

shaped, and beautifully scented.

Persian lime. This tree forms large thorns on some of the branches; it does not flower as heavily as the orange, but almost all of the flowers set fruit. The fruit can be spectacular—the size of regular limes or even larger and of the same beautiful bright green. Your lime tree can be in both flowering and full-fruiting stage at holiday time.

The two things citrus most demand are good bright light—preferably some sunlight—and lots of water, especially when they are blooming and fruiting. Although citrus trees can be grown successfully indoors throughout the year, their growth seems to spurt when put outside for the summer months. They can be moved outdoors once the weather is dependably warm. Watch out for insects and birds.

If kept inside year round, give the tree your sunniest window and rotate it about once a week to encourage the balanced development of the tree and the growth of blossoms and fruit. You may need to pollinate blossoms for setting of fruit. Use a soft watercolor brush and dab pollen from

Persian lime.

flower to flower.

Citrus plants prefer an acid soil. If leaves yellow, it may mean that the plant needs more acid. Dissolve ¼ teaspoon of aluminum sulfate in 1 quart of water, and wet the soil thoroughly. One application ought to carry through for a whole season. Fertilize once a month with an all-purpose fertilizer, and add a pinch of chelated iron.

One major pest you'll have to be on guard against is scale. Should you spot a sticky-looking substance on the leaves of the plant, scale is likely to be the culprit. Turn the leaf over, and if you look closely, you will see one or several small, round, light-brown spots. Look closely because when the scale is attached along the main vein of the leaf it is sometimes hard to see. In a bad case the scales will be attached not only to the veins along the undersides of the leaves but also along the branches and stems where they are especially easy to overlook.

To rid the plant of scale, use a warm, soapy cloth and clean each leaf and branch (if necessary), gently loosening each scale as you go. The job may take ten or fifteen minutes, but it's time well spent. One good, thorough going-over should rid you of the pest, but keep a sharp lookout so that any infestation won't get ahead of you again.

SHELL MIRROR FRAMES

If you can't collect beach shells yourself, you can buy them at a modest price. If you need a lot of shells for a large frame, find a restaurant in your area that serves steamed clams, and simply ask the management for the leftover shells. Use these for much of the base work, and buy a few bags of more fanciful shells to dress up the design.

To clean the shells, dunk them in a mild chlorine bleach solution (a tablespoon of bleach and a teaspoon of vinegar to a gallon of water) for ten or fifteen minutes, and then wash in hot, soapy water. Dry thoroughly. For a soft luster, polish the shells with a cloth barely moistened with mineral oil.

Choose a frame with a flat surface wide enough to accommodate a cluster of shells. Have the mirror installed. Arrange the shells on the frame before gluing to decide on the effect you want and to ascertain whether you have enough for the job. Spread white glue on the frame and the shell edges and put the shells in place. When gluing one shell on top of another, pull a little tuft from a cotton ball or swab and put it in between the shells to help form a strong bond. (Dab glue on the shell, put on a few thin-stretched fibers, and then dab glue on the second shell and press into place.) Use a cotton swab to remove excess glue. For an opulent effect, don't skimp on the shells; use lots of them. Make a base layer of large shells and fill in with smaller ones.

For shell-covered cachepots, use a clear, quick-drying waterproof glue—a type suitable for ceramic or glass.

OTHER MATERIALS FOR GLINT AND GLEAM

🌿 Silvery mirror-surfaced Mylar or a shimmery foil paper can bounce reflections back and forth to add depth and dimension. For beautiful reflections in a small foyer, cover all four walls and the ceiling, hang a mirror or two, add a crystal chandelier and a couple of palms.

Use the Mylar to cover the wall behind some white lacquered wood shelves, and you'll give your shelf plants lots more sparkle.

🌿 Stainless-steel tiles are another simple do-it-yourself project.

🌿 Inexpensive aluminum siding, plain or ribbed, comes in lengths as long as 16 feet.

This is an alternative for a quick cover-up of walls in bad shape in rooms with higher-than-average ceilings.

🌿 Corrugated galvanized steel comes in large sheets; available at sheet-metal supply houses or lumberyards.

🌿 Self-stick metallic tape in varying widths can be used to border any glint look.

MIRROR TILES

Mirror tiles are among the many good things that have come along in the last few years to cheer the heart of the do-it-yourselfer who loves plants. They are inexpensive and easy to work with. Just remember that the surface they're to go on must be clean, dry, and fairly smooth and that if you're doing a wall, a plumb line should be dropped every so often to make certain you line the tiles up straight.

The tense part of the job is cutting the tiles to fit, which won't be necessary for shutters and such if you make the base to fit the tiles. When it comes to covering walls, cutting will be necessary. Get a glass cutter, and practice on a spare tile. Score the glass (not the coated) side with the cutter, place the scored line on the edge of a sturdy flat surface, and press down firmly to break the glass along the cut mark. A couple of test runs, and you'll have it perfect.

For shutters. Use panels of ¾-inch plywood cut to the height and width desired. If you determine the height and width to fit the tiles, you can avoid any tile cutting. Finish off the edges of the panel with decorative wood molding or metal stripping before applying the mirror pieces. By doing as much as you can of the preparatory and finishing work on the project before putting the tiles in place, you cut down on the risk of breakage or damage.

To hang shutters, screw wooden strips to the inside of the window frame, abutting the edge of the frame at the front. Leave a ⅛-inch space at top and bottom to allow the shutter to open and close freely. Put half-hinges in place on both shutter and window strip. Match the half-hinges together and drop the hinge pin in place.

How to hang shutters.

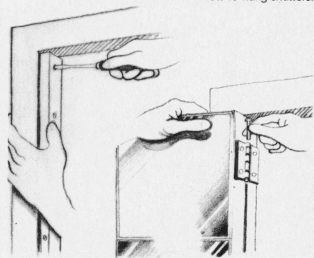

For screens. Two or more panels will make a free-standing mirrored screen. Use double-action hinges and fasten together before mirroring the panels. Place one hinge in the middle and place the top and bottom hinges equidistant from the center. On a 7-foot panel, put the hinges about a foot from the top and a foot from the bottom.

If you don't have a window suitable for the mirrored shutters—orange tree treatment, then try a corner with a mirrored screen. If you don't have enough direct sunlight for the orange tree, then try a luxuriant angelwing begonia or a beautifully trained topiary of English ivy.

Mirrored ceilings. If you're thinking about mirroring above, take a look at the new type of acoustical ceiling panel with an aluminized surface. The panels come in sizes 2 feet by 2 feet and 2 feet by 4 feet and are installed the same way that other lay-in ceiling panels are. They are shatterproof, easy to keep clean, and well worth considering as a substitute for mirror. They can be used on walls, too.

For more on mirrors, with good ideas on how to use and care for them, write to the National Association of Mirror Manufacturers, 807 Jefferson Building, 1225 19th Street N.W., Washington, D.C. 20036.

Kids' Rooms

Hanging plants

Hanging plants add grace to any room, but there is something especially nice about having them in the bedroom. You can stretch out to rest, to think, to brood, with soft, gentle, greenery in view. There is something therapeutic about hanging plants. They do nice things for your psyche while doing nice things for your décor.

Almost anything can be hung from almost anywhere. Though it may be the conventional chic in the plant world to espouse the sphagnum-moss hanging basket for its *au naturel* look and to eschew the white plastic pot as a jolt to esthetics, the picture is much bigger than either. The country seems full of clever people turning out clever ideas for pots; or making do with recycled bleach bottles and margarine tubs; or seeing a new use for familiar objects from colanders to fish baskets to wire salad baskets, from old mixing bowls and upside-down china lampshades to odd pieces of pottery and glassware and brand-new, sleek-looking Plexiglas cubes. Nor is the lack of handles on any of these containers an obstacle to hanging. The marketplace runneth over with all sorts of yarn, twine, leather, string, wire, chain, rope, and other hangers and harnesses into which all manner of containers will fit. (You can also make your own, see page 274.) There are wood and wrought-iron brackets available, as well as the new Lucite suspenders that hang from clear nylon line.

The young occupant of this room was no slouch when it came to displaying plants. All of

A ceiling-suspended pot rack with lots of hooks for plants.

her hanging plants have been corralled and suspended from one large ceiling pot rack. Up there along with her plants are her baseball mitt, butterfly net, and a low-flying goldfish bowl. Other plant favorites in this eclectic collection are a Patio tomato in a cast-iron kettle and a Norfolk Island pine the same age as the owner.

Kitchen utensil racks are available in a wide range of shapes, sizes, and prices: some with large 6-foot, two-tier sliding tracks so that hanging items can be shifted about; some as small as a 20-inch-diameter circle for under $20. If you, the room, and the plants need a large rack, choose one made of aluminum to reduce the weight hanging from the ceiling.

Another teen took a look at an old bicycle wheel, removed the rubber tire, spray-painted the metal rim and spokes, and hung it, flying-saucer fashion, from the ceiling of his room, providing lots more places for plants to swing from.

In the closet, in the kitchen, among the sporting goods, all kinds of potential hangers wait to be discovered. Drapery poles and expandable clothes-closet poles can provide maximum hanging space with a minimum amount of effort. Coat hangers with curled ends can dangle pretty plants. There are free-standing hatracks and reproductions of the lavish Victorian wall-hung coat hangers that plants can share with towels in the bath. Outings to junk and garage sales could net a coatrack salvaged from an old bus, a basketball hoop without a net—or items yet unthought of.

Plants can dangle from almost anything.

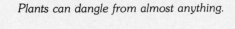
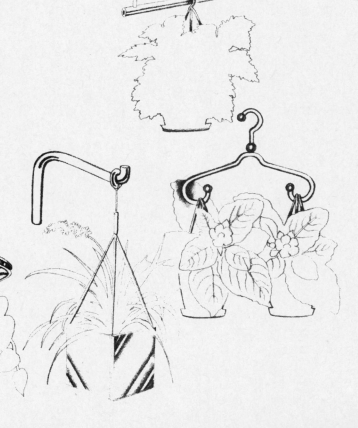

WHEN PLANTING A HANGING BASKET

Use potting mix rather than ordinary soil; the mix is much lighter in weight. Fill only to within an inch of the top so that water will not run over the sides each time you give the plants a drink. Stay away from the wire sphagnum-moss-filled hanging baskets unless you're willing to take them down for each watering and give them the dunk-and-drain routine. Watering them from above produces a major drip problem which invariably results in less frequent watering of unhappy, parched plants.

Before you hang your plants way up high, decide how you will water them. Many a hanging plant has died of thirst for want of easy access to it. If it involves taking up an uncertain and rickety stance midway between windowsill and whatever else your other foot can reach, then you might as well kiss your plants goodbye.

A pulley installation is an excellent solution for getting high hanging plants down within reach. Small pulleys with lockable cords are available at shade and awning shops. When you wish to inspect or water your plant, you simply lower it by means of the pulley cord.

Scale becomes especially important when your plants are hanging and highly visible. You should choose a container that is right for the size of the plant and vice versa, and also right in relation to the size and nature of the window or wall or wherever the container will hang. If the background is brick or wood, for example, and the texture is rough and coarse, you wouldn't want a dainty little plant or pot.

If the ceiling is higher than usual, choose large-scale containers and plants. If the ceiling is low, often the case in basement rooms, maybe you should decide against hanging plants; they'd only accentuate the low ceiling. Focus on floor plants instead, and prop those you'd ordinarily hang on low stools and stands to show them off.

Be extravagant when planting a hanging basket; use several plants of the same kind to produce a full, robust look.

Plants can be positioned for different effects. Here they form a rich green drapery pulled to one side of the window.

TWENTY-EIGHT EASY SWINGERS

Grape ivy
Cissus rhombifolia

Kangaroo vine
Cissus antarctica

Creeping Charlie
Pilea nummulariifolia

Bead cactus or green marble vine
Senecio herreianus

Wax begonia
Begonia semperflorens

German or parlor ivy
Senecio mikanioides

Burro's tail
Sedum morganianum

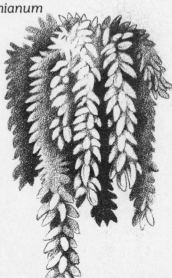

Burro's tail.

Puerto Rican or miniature peperomia
Pilea depressa

Swedish ivies
Plectranthus australis
P. purparatus

Wandering Jew and inch plant
Zebrina pendula discolor
Tradescantia fluminensis variegata
T. albiflora 'Albo-vittata'

Wandering Jew.

Rosary vine or string of hearts
Ceropegia woodii

Peperomias
Peperomia fosteriana
P. obtusifolia
P. prostrata
P. rotundifolia

Goldfish plant
Columnea microphylla

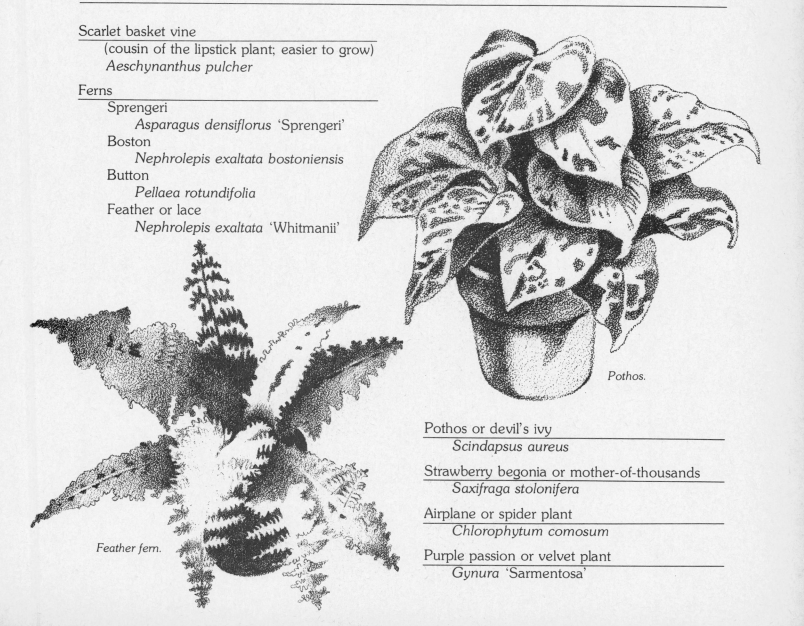

Scarlet basket vine
(cousin of the lipstick plant; easier to grow)
Aeschynanthus pulcher

Ferns
Sprengeri
Asparagus densiflorus 'Sprengeri'
Boston
Nephrolepis exaltata bostoniensis
Button
Pellaea rotundifolia
Feather or lace
Nephrolepis exaltata 'Whitmanii'

Pothos.

Feather fern.

Pothos or devil's ivy
Scindapsus aureus

Strawberry begonia or mother-of-thousands
Saxifraga stolonifera

Airplane or spider plant
Chlorophytum comosum

Purple passion or velvet plant
Gynura 'Sarmentosa'

MAKING A MACRAME HANGER

If you can tie a knot, you can do macramé, which, simply stated, is the art of tying knots. The following directions will produce a hanger that costs next to nothing and the know-how to make as many more as you need. One of the most obliging things about macramé hangers of this type is that they adjust to the size and shape of almost any kind of container, from a fat, squat mixing bowl to a tall, slim glass bottle.

You start with four long strands. The length of your completed hanger will be about one-quarter the length of the strands. For example, if you start with 8-foot lengths, your hanger will be about 2 feet long. You can use twine, macramé braid, clothesline, or leather thong—whatever you like. You can use decorative beads along with the knots. You can tie several knots in a row and use no bead; or you can tie several knots and use several beads.

Fold the four cords in half. Separate and straighten the strands while holding the loop ends together in one hand. Now tie an

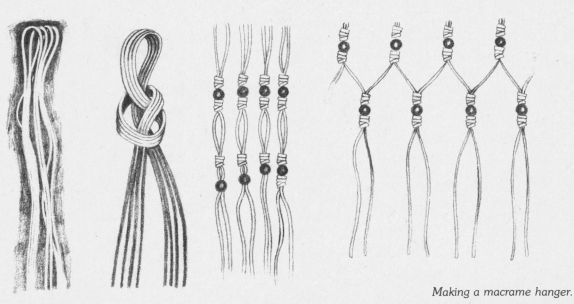

Making a macrame hanger.

overhand knot, with all of the cords together, about 2 or 3 inches below the folded
end of the loop. This is the top of the
hanger.

Slip this end loop over a chair back
spindle or a door or drawer knob or some
such while you work with the end strands.
Work the strands in pairs for the suspension part of the hanger. Measure down as
much as you like below the end loop, and
tie each pair of strands together in an
overhand knot. If you are using beads, slip
one over each pair of strands, and then tie
another knot below it to hold it in place.
Repeat in this fashion every few inches or
as you choose, depending upon how long
the hanger is to be and how plain or
elaborate you wish it to be.

To make the webbing or cradle that
will hold the plant container, stretch out
the pairs of cord side by side. Now take
one strand each from adjacent pairs and
tie them together in an overhand knot;
add bead and bottom knot if you like. Repeat for each adjacent pair of strands.

Next, measure down 3 to 5 inches,
depending upon whether the container is on
the small or large side, and repeat, knotting
together one strand from each adjacent
pair to form a pattern of alternate knots.

To complete the bottom of the container cradle, gather all the strands together
2 or 3 inches below the last round of knots,
and tie in a single
overhand knot. Let the
ends of the strands hang
loose for a tassel at
the bottom. Trim ends
to uniform length if
necessary, and fray for
a fringe effect.

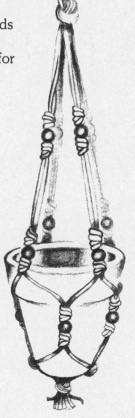

Flower on flower

Gloxinias in bloom.

One of the most rewarding ways to have beautiful flowers indoors all year around is to choose plants that grow from bulbs and tubers and rhizomes. These are the plants that die back and rest for a time after blooming. By choosing carefully from a rather large assortment of these obliging bloomers, you can schedule flower performances throughout the year. The scheduling and care may be a bit too much of a hassle for the more harried gardener, but it presents a fresh challenge and lots of action for the young teen-ager who belongs to this room. At the moment, gloxinias are creating a spectacular scene on the Formica-topped counter under the window. (She made the counter herself, too, using an old iron sewing machine base for support at each end.) The gloxinias, her favorite bloomer, are cousins of the African violet, producing huge, velvety, bell-shaped flowers, sometimes dozens of them on one plant. The gloxinias will be followed in the fall by temple bells, another member of the gesneriad family, which includes the African violet and gloxinia. Kafir lilies and amaryllis will take over through the holidays. In January she'll have bowls of paperwhite narcissus ready to enjoy, followed by an all-through-the-spring display of crocus, hyacinth, daffodils, and tulips.

The cornice in this room, by the way, was covered in quilted chintz and appliquéd to match the coverlet by the fourteen-year-old who lives here. The needlepoint flower pillows are also her work; a favorite flower print was used as a guide.

BULBS, TUBERS, AND RHIZOMES

🌿 True bulbs are modified fleshy leaves that contain within them the buds of next season's plants in miniature form. The roots form at the flatter end of the bulb, with new growth coming from the pointy end. An onion is a bulb.

🌿 A tuber is a fat, somewhat knobby underground stem that has a number of buds (eyes) from which new growth develops. An Irish potato is a tuber.

🌿 A rhizome is an underground rootlike stem that usually grows horizontally, stretched out close under the surface of the soil. From its joints (nodes), the roots and stems of new plants grow. Ginger root is a rhizome.

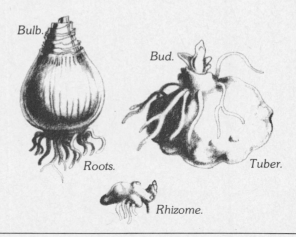

Bulb.

Bud.

Roots.

Tuber.

Rhizome.

TRANSFERRING A DESIGN TO NEEDLEPOINT CANVAS

Designs for needlepoint can be found anywhere—in magazines, artwork, books, or wallpaper. Most often, the design will need to be enlarged. The easiest way to do this is by having it blown up by photostat.

If you don't have photostat services in your community, or if you want to save yourself the cost, you can enlarge or reduce your design freehand with the help of a grid. With a sharp pencil and a ruler, divide the design you want to enlarge (or reduce) into equal squares. On another sheet of paper, mark off the same number of squares, proportionately larger or smaller, as desired.

Number and letter the squares in map fashion to help you keep track of where you are as you copy the design. This you do freehand, matching square for square. When you have finished the drawing, go back over it again with dark, thin lines. You are now ready to transfer this design to your needlework canvas. (If you are using a photostat, follow the directions from here on.)

Buy a piece of canvas at least 2 inches wider on all sides than your project will be. Tape the raw edges with masking tape so that they don't ravel. Place your drawing under the canvas. Line up the design in the position you want, then tape the canvas to the paper.

Trace the design onto the canvas with an indelible marking pen. Use a pen the color of the background you plan or a lighter shade than the yarn or thread to be used. After the design is on canvas, you can use waterproof acrylic paint to brush in the approximate colors you will be stitching for the final design. This makes an easy color guide to follow.

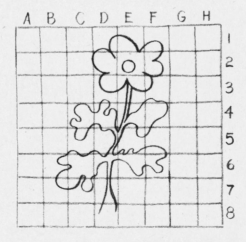

AMARYLLIS

Among the members of the flower world, the amaryllis is one of the most dramatic in performance and appearance. Its growth is so rapid it can be measured almost daily, and its huge, lilylike blooms provide enough impact to impress even the most blasé among us.

In our young friend's room, two scarlet amaryllis are programmed to bloom for the Christmas holidays, and a beautiful soft-pink variety with white-tipped petals blooms at Easter.

Amaryllis bulbs are on the expensive side. They are rarely found for under $5 a bulb and range upward in price. But if you are going for the spectacular, you might as well have the most spectacular, and amaryllis certainly qualifies. Besides, if you take care of the bulb, you can have repeat performances from it year after year. Amaryllis bulbs appear on the market in the fall.

The amaryllis bulb is large but it does not require a pot with more than 1 inch to spare all round. You can use ordinary garden dirt mixed with one part sand to three parts dirt and add a tablespoon of bone meal, which is good food for all bulbs. A regular potting mix will also be satisfactory; add a weak fertilizer solution each time you water. Plant the bulb so that the top third of it is above ground.

Put the bulb in a warm place (the top of the refrigerator is a good spot) until the new growth appears. Now move it into the light in front of a window; keep the soil moist but never soggy, and watch the plant grow. It will reach a height of 2 feet and be blooming magnificently, with flowers 5 to 8 inches across, within a matter of three to five weeks. That is quite a performance, and kids, especially, are crazy about this plant.

After the blooms fade, cut them off—stalk and all. The leaves will continue to grow, and you should continue to feed and water the plant regularly up through mid-May, when the pot can be put outdoors, either in or above the ground. The leaves will stay green all summer.

In the fall, when you bring the plant back in, start easing off on water, and eliminate feeding. When the leaves begin to yellow, stop watering altogether, cut off all but 1 inch or so of the leaves, and let the plant go bone-dry to rest for ten to twelve weeks—no water, no food. If you live in an apartment and have no outdoors for the pot, you can still carry the amaryllis through to the next year by following the same procedures. Being outdoors just gives the plant more light, and it is likely to have stronger roots and a stronger bulb for the following season. After its rest period, add water to begin the growth process all over again.

GLOXINIAS

Gloxinias grow from tubers. They do best when started in spring so that they will have long daylight hours for growing and so will not become too tall and leggy. (Gloxinias also do beautifully under fluorescent lights, on a sixteen-hour day.)

Start with a good-quality tuber, which cannot be judged by size because that will vary with the variety. Buy from a reputable grower, and pay the going price. A good gloxinia tuber is a good investment. With care, you can keep it growing and blooming for many years.

You can use a regular potting mix or a special African violet mix. Fill a 5- or 6-inch pot two-thirds full. Place the tuber so that the convex side is up; that's where the sprout will come from. Fill in with more soil, and cover the tuber with about ½ inch soil.

You can expect a full-grown gloxinia in four to six months. It will bloom continuously anywhere from three to ten weeks. Gloxinias are relatively heavy feeders and thrive on regular dilute-feeding at every watering. When the plant is through blooming, with no more buds developing, gradually reduce watering. The leaves will begin to yellow and die. Remove them as they dry out. You can then store the pots away in a cool, dry place and water only sparingly, just enough to keep the tuber from shriveling. Gloxinias do not remain dormant on schedule; anytime within a few weeks or a few months the small mouse ears of a new plant may appear. Bring the pot back out into the light; water and feed; and your gloxinia will be off and blooming again.

Temple bells, another member of the African violet clan, blooms in late summer or early fall and on into winter. They like the same bright indirect or filtered sunlight that the Kafir lily and gloxinia do. These plants are grown from a rhizome. After they flower, don't let the soil go bone-dry as you do with the amaryllis bulb, but water sparingly, keeping the soil just moist enough so that the rhizomes won't dehydrate.

KAFIR LILY

The Kafir lily is not nearly so well known or generally grown as it should be. It is easy to grow, has large, long-lasting, brilliant orange-and-yellow flowers, is evergreen and attractive year round. It actually prefers not being disturbed, so it can go without repotting for three or four years. You can simply let it increase in clusters until it fills the pot to overflowing. The care of the Kafir lily is compatible with that of the other plants here. Give it strong light but not direct sun; water it well during spring and summer but only sparingly during the winter.

PAPER WHITE NARCISSUS

Paper white narcissus are among the easiest bulbs for bringing to bloom indoors. Buy good-quality bulbs when they first come on the market in the fall, choosing the biggest ones you can find. Use a large container to accommodate a maximum number of bulbs for a truly beautiful effect. Try for at least a dozen. Paper whites can be planted in soil in a shallow container or grown in a water bed of pebbles or marble chips. Place the bulbs close together but not touching one another. If planting in soil, firm gently around each bulb, leaving just the tips of the bulbs showing. Dampen the soil thoroughly, and put the container out of the way in a reasonably cool place.

Many people feel that paper whites do best if stored in a dark place until they have sprouted, but others find that the foliage is more compact and attractive if the bulbs are left in a bright, cool place. One lesson in gardening is that there is really no single *right* way of dealing with any living thing. You may garden for years and years, following great gardening truths, only to be astonished each time that you, either by chance or design, take a different route and pull off a triumph in your own plant world.

Whether light or dark, paper whites do, however, like cool rooms. A temperature as cool as 60 degrees F. would suit them fine, though it would be hardly comfortable for people. Set the thermostat as low as you can take it, put on a sweater, save some fuel money, and enjoy the spring narcissus. If you plant the bulbs by mid-November, they can make the first part of your January sit up and sing with their sweet fragrance and beautiful blooms.

Paper whites are not cold-hardy and will be a one-time flower fling for you unless you live in the warm climes and can plant them outdoors. They cannot be carried over indoors for next year's bloom as can the amaryllis.

FORCING BULBS: HYACINTH, CROCUS, DAFFODIL, AND TULIP

Anyone having even a nodding acquaintance with houseplants knows that hardy outdoor spring bulbs can be forced (or brought into bloom ahead of schedule) indoors. Most of us don't do anything about it, though. We don't think about it until sometime in late winter, when we begin to see potfuls of blooming tulips and hyacinths and crocus begging to be bought, and then it's too late to grow our own. Or we may think about it in plenty of time, but we remember something to do with burying the pot in the ground for a couple of months. Well, if you are an apartment dweller with no ground, or if you have the ground but no ambition, then the whole thing is not going to come off.

There is an easy way to see to it that your bulbs get the cold period they need, and that is to use the refrigerator instead of the ground. You can tuck away more bulbs than you might imagine without giving up a great deal of space. The trick is not to plant the bulbs in the pot first— it is the pot that takes up most of the room. Keep the bulbs in a double brown paper bag, rolled up and tucked in the corner farthest from the ice-making part of the refrigerator. If you are among the fortunate ones with a second refrigerator, down in the basement, in the bar, or in a weekend or vacation home, be sure to make full use of any spare refrigerator space. If the refrigerator is going to be running anyway, with space to spare, then stuff in as many bulbs as you can, and boost the return on the investment of energy with an enormous boost to the spirits when you bring spring out of your refrigerator and spread it around your house some dull, gray day in February.

In the fall, buy the biggest, firmest bulbs you can find as they come on the market. Mail-order houses will ship at the proper time. The words often used to describe the size of bulbs, such as *jumbo, mammoth, gigantic,* are generally of no more help in determining size than they are when used to describe canned olives. Don't rely on such descriptions. In catalogs, look for a listing of bulb dimensions—1 inch, 2 inch, and so on—and choose the largest for forcing. The reason is simple. The flower-to-be is already tucked away inside the bulb. It was formed in the previous growing season, so the bigger the bulb, the bigger the flower-to-be.

When choosing bulbs in a store, select from

Three spring bulbs: daffodil, hyacinth, tulip.

among the biggest, those that are plump for their size. Look them over in much the same fashion as you might onions from the grocery store. You want no soft spots, no scabs, but bulbs that are round and firm and fully packed.

Put one heavy brown grocery bag inside another; add enough moistened potting soil to make 2 inches; set the bulbs in the soil, close together but not touching; barely cover with soil; pull the sides of the bag together; fold over to make a flat, compact package. Keep the bag right side up, and store in the refrigerator away from the ice or freezer section. Turn your refrigerator temperature back a notch or two from the coldest temperature for three or four weeks; then set it at the coldest setting for the remaining seven or eight weeks. By keeping the bags flat and compact, you will have room for two or possibly three bags in one stack on the shelf.

An alternate cold treatment for the bulbs, of course, is the aforementioned sinking of pots into the ground. You can also store them above ground, well wrapped to protect from freezing, on patio or porch. Just remember, they must have a cold treatment—below 50 degrees but not below freezing. The refrigerator is obviously the only way to go if you live in warm climes that provide no cold season for the bulbs.

Hyacinths, crocuses, and daffodils will require about three months in the refrigerator; tulips, closer to four months. If your bulbs went into the refrigerator about the middle of October,

then about the middle of January you can begin to bring them out—a nice, bracing activity to counter the blahs that often follow the holiday season.

Settle the bag in a wide, shallow bowl, carefully rounding it to fit the contours of the bowl. Unfold the top, and tear the bag off at the rim of the bowl. Tuck any ragged edges into the soil, or trim off with scissors; press any misarranged bulbs back into position. Water the bulbs.

A good thick root system should have formed while the bulbs were doing cold time, and warmer room temperatures will bring the shoots popping out (sometimes the bulbs will already be sprouting when you take them from the refrigerator). Put them in a bright place (a sunny windowsill is fine in northern climes where the winter sun is not too hot to damage tender sprouts). Growth will be rapid. When blooms appear, move the plants back away from the sun so that the flowers will last longer.

After the blooms have faded (you'll have as long as a week of pure beauty), cut off the stems. Let the foliage be. Put back in a sunny spot, and when the weather is warm enough, if you can do so, plant the bulbs outdoors where you can enjoy their blooms again in future years—if not the following spring, the ones after that. You will not be able to coax blooms out of them again indoors, however; so plan to start at least a few new bulbs each fall for an early spring in every room.

Greening the underground

Basement rooms are the last outposts—the rooms that get finished off only when family growing pains demand more space. In this family's case, a young botanist bid on the downstairs space for a room of his own. To make the place bright for his plants, he painted it white—block and brick, paneling and shutters—and with the help of strategically placed track lights created a solarium out of the shadows.

Along with plants, microscope, test tubes, terrariums, books, and botanical prints, this young man brought to his new underground room an adventurous eye that spotted design ideas in the design problems the room presented.

Problem number one was a structural support pole in the middle of what was to be his room. His idea: If one pole is a problem, two might be the answer. He boxed in the first pole to make a column, then added a second column so that glass shelves could be installed between them. The inside of each column (the sides facing each other) was mirrored, and fluorescent lights were installed inside a deep cornice. He wound up with plenty of space for the green things as well as a divider that softly defines sleeping and hobby areas. (A neighbor took one look and went straight home to execute another approach. Instead of boxing in the first pole, he left it bare and merely added a second pole. He covered the ceiling in a green-and-white fern print wallpaper, stationed green plants by the poles, and strung up a hammock between them.)

Problem number two was a small, unattractive below-ground-level window. His idea: an eye-level conservatory. The metal outdoor window well was lined with adhesive-backed brick veneer, and a protective roof was made from a hard plastic covering, carefully caulked to protect

A miniature greenhouse made from a window well.

against rain and drafts. The end result is a miniature greenhouse where seedlings are started in early spring and where cool-loving plants such as cyclamen, azaleas, and English ivy thrive during the winter.

Problem number three was the low ceiling. His idea: Place a center of interest close to the floor. Unaware that he was actually following the Oriental custom of placing art where the floor-sitter can see it, this young decorator hung his botanical prints low on the wall (as shown on the next page), following his own logic that he and his friends usually sit on the floor anyway.

The prints themselves are particular treasures, due largely to his exposure at a young age to the life and work of the great eighteenth-century Swedish botanist Carolus Linnaeus. In remarkable detail Linnaeus described, classified, and illustrated thousands of plants. In one book alone, *Species Plantarum,* Linnaeus described more than 7,300 plants.

For the plant lover, botanical prints say it all; they represent a most felicitous marriage of science and art. Their history really began with the great herbals published in the late fifteenth century and on through the Renaissance. With the seventeenth century came the great flower books known as the florilegiums. Pierre Vallet's florilegium was dedicated to the Queen Marie de' Medici, and later florilegiums were used by designers and craftsmen as inspiration for embroidery, textiles, and wall coverings.

The contributions of Linnaeus in the eighteenth century gave another enormous boost to interest in matters botanical, and then came the superb flower prints of Pierre-Joseph Redouté, who somehow managed to survive the Revolution, going from honorary painter of flowers to Marie Antoinette, on through the reign of the Empress Josephine, to serve as teacher to the Empress Marie Louise.

With the invention of lithography at the end of the eighteenth century, more and more flower books and botanical drawings came from the presses, particularly during the first half of the nineteenth century. Today, reproductions are widely available, and fine old prints can still be found. Best place to browse: bookshops that specialize in old prints.

Botanical prints are any gardener's favorite.

Also helping to create a floor-level composition along with the botanical prints in the basement room is a grouping of plants and cuttings (shown at left), basking in light from wall-mounted, cool-beam floods.

Nothing green escapes this botanist's eye for increase. Even some cut carnations that arrived as a gift for a family dinner party were intercepted as they were ready to be discarded. Small sprouts showing between leaf and stem were snipped off carefully and planted. Some of the stems were also cut into pieces and planted, with at least one node (joint) covered with moist potting mix. Cuttings rooted in February were ready for transplanting to an outdoor garden in June, then were put back into pots in September for placement in a sunny window, with blooms coming along in December. Sprouts from these new plants were duly collected for rooting, and apparently a years-to-come carnation cycle is under way.

This budding botanist's interest—career goal, actually—began as a preschooler when he learned that lots of plants could be made from one.

CUTTINGS

Cuttings, both leaf and stem, are one of the easiest ways to propagate plants (make more from one). The cuttings can be rooted either in a light, porous soil mix or in water. The water route is the more interesting, allowing you to see the progress of the roots as they form. You will also find the roots of many plants quite beautiful as they emerge and develop. In the botanist's room, racks of test tubes hold stem cuttings, one to a tube.

There are two things you can do to maximize the decorative assets of cuttings. You can choose something for the cuttings to live in that is suited to their size. This means that an empty cheese or jam jar for a leaf from an African violet will not do; the size of the jar is just too big for the size of the leaf. You can group bottles of cuttings for impact, much the way you would other accessories.

For the small child whose room will house a cutting collection, the acquisition of bottles for the cuttings can be a pursuit of some interest. The collecting instinct runs strong in all of us, but never stronger than in childhood. Remember how it was when you kept a sharp eye out for matchbook covers, cigar bands, strange insects, stickers, postcards, marbles? All that is needed, then, is the suggestion to watch out for small bottles that will hold a single leaf or a sprig of a plant—from tiny perfume bottles, to bottles in import stores, to those in souvenir shops and other places where you might be on the prowl for something for yourself. (Note: Since medicines of various sorts come packaged in small bottles, it's a good idea to go around again on the safety lesson with small children: The acquisition of bottles is to be cleared with you, and the contents of same are not to be touched in any way.)

You can stage collections of small bottles in other parts of the house. For example, small cobalt-blue bottles can be grouped together on a blue glass plate, or in a white porcelain quiche dish, or in or on whatever else you may recognize as just right for this use. If you want small bottles on hand right now without the wait involved in collecting, visit the pharmacist at the drugstore, tell him or her your purpose, and ask to buy a few of the small containers that prescription medicine is packaged in.

Equip a small child with an eyedropper so that he can keep up the water level in the bottles. He will enjoy administering the water in this fashion. You'll enjoy it, too, because it will eliminate a good deal of spilled water.

When the cuttings have at least five or six roots on them (½ to 1 inch long), they are ready to pot up. Many types of cuttings will put out long roots rather rapidly; others do not. African violets, for example, are slow in forming their roots, and they will take a good while to reach a length of 1 inch. On the other hand, Swedish ivy will have formed its roots by the time you have checked on it two or three times.

Have on hand a couple of muffin tins (small size) and a package of peat disks. The latter are easy to work with and especially appealing to children. They are made of compressed soil nutrients and peat and are about 2 inches in diameter and ¼ inch thick. When put in water, they expand. In a few minutes you have miniature flowerpots about 2 inches in height encased in a thin netting that holds the soil and nutrients firmly together. You can use a pencil to poke a hole in the center of each peat pot and then tuck in a rooted cutting. The peat pots can then take their place in the muffin tin, where they will be easy for the youngster to care for. These peat pots dry out rather quickly when exposed to air in this way, so they will need to be checked often to see that they do not get too dry and that the new cuttings do not go too long without water.

After the cuttings have become established in their peat pots—when they have put out new growth and are strong and vigorous—they can be potted up into larger containers, peat pot and all. You can try your hand at creating a generation-after-generation family of plants, beginning with the original cutting. Children especially will take to the suggestion when it's pointed out to them that a cutting from each successive plant labeled and dated can be another collecting adventure, to see how many generations from one plant they can acquire.

Begonias (angelwing and wax—not rex), Swedish ivy, patience plant, coleus, African violet, wandering Jew, and inch plants are all good plants to water-root from cuttings.

MORE FROM ONE BY LAYERING

Plants with rambling stems, such as creeping Charlie or miniature peperomia, and those that

TO MAKE CUTTINGS INTO ROOTINGS

🌿 Choose a stem neither too young (light green and soft) nor too old (brown and tough).

🌿 Use a sharp knife, not scissors. Cut a 4- to 6-inch piece just below a node (leaf joint).

🌿 Remove leaves that will be below the waterline.

🌿 Dip the cutting in hormone powder (available at garden shops) to stimulate root growth.

🌿 Let the cutting rest an hour or so to allow the cut end to absorb some of the powder and seal over a bit; then put into water.

put out plantlets, such as the spider plant and strawberry begonia, can be propagated simply by pinning down the stem at a joint or setting the plantlet joined to the parent into moist soil mix. After roots form from the node, the new plant can be separated from the mother plant and potted up separately. This method is called layering in soil.

Some houseplants can also be propagated by air layering, and this can be the answer to salvaging one of your taller plants that may have shed some of its lower leaves and is beginning to look a bit scraggly.

In air layering, the root forming is done above ground. You will need some milled sphagnum moss and some hormone rooting powder, also a 6-inch square of plastic wrap, electricians' plastic tape, and a sharp knife.

Soak the sphagnum moss in hot water, getting it thoroughly wet, and then drain off the ex-cess water. Select the place where you want new roots to form—several inches below the leaves of a leggy plant, for example. Make a sharp cut into the stem 1 or 2 inches long and about a third of the way into the stem. Dust the open cut with the hormone powder to help guard against infection and also encourage root growth.

Now bunch the wet sphagnum moss around the entire stem. Form a ball out of it, and squeeze out excess water. Cover the damp moss with the square of plastic wrap, and seal the edges with the electricians' tape where the wrap comes into contact with the stem, making a waterproof seal. The little plastic-wrap pouch will allow you to watch the developing roots as they form. When there appears to be a good amount of roots, cut the plant off just below the new root package. Remove the plastic wrap, and pot up the new plant. If you continue to water the remaining stem sparingly, it will eventually put out new growth, too.

For the Collector

Bromeliads

Bromeliads grow out of the hollows and crevices of a tree stump.

Bromeliads are the bold and beautiful ones, the plants that lend themselves more than any other to one-of-a-kind collecting. The different types have such strong identities that one of each is quite enough to own, and at that, you still have literally hundreds from which to choose. Each family member is singular, and yet they all blend beautifully with one another for quite a show.

Many of the bromeliads are epiphytes (air plants that have only minor root systems). In nature, they cling to other plants, usually trees, for support and gain their nourishment from rain and air-borne organic matter. Because they are not earthbound and need not be confined to pots of soil, they offer all kinds of interesting design possibilities when brought indoors. They can be fastened to almost anything, placed high or low. They offer a nearly unsurpassed range of spectacular foliage and long-lasting, flamboyantly colored flowers and bracts and berries. (A bract is a form of leaf that is often mistaken for the flower petal; the bract of the poinsettia is probably the best-known example.)

The collection here began with the tree, which is actually part of a huge stump the owners found in the wake of a highway clearing project. It

TEN BROMELIADS FOR THE NEW COLLECTOR

Aechmea chantinii A handsome plant: dark olive-green foliage with silvery-white bandings across the leaves; spectacular when in bloom. Likes both warmth and humidity, so keep away from cold, drafty windows, and have a mister close by to use often.

A. fasciata Silver-banded leaves, soft blue flowers on a pale pink flower head; probably the most widely grown of all the bromeliads, which is no reason not to own one yourself.

Ananas comosus (sativus) Your fruity friend, the pineapple. It's grown as easily as the avocado from what's left behind in the kitchen sink.

Cryptanthus bivittatus minor This is one of the earth stars, a beauty to look down upon. Low, arching leaves forming a small rosette of pink and green in bright light, or soft yellow and green in lower light. As with most earth stars, offshoots develop in between the leaves. These can be pulled off and rooted in dampened potting mix to make new plants. Remove these offshoots from the parent plant before they grow too big if you want to maintain the symmetry of the original plant.

Guzmania lingulata Produces a cluster of white flowers surrounded by brilliant orange-red bracts.

Neoregelia carolinae Lavender-petaled flowers and red bracts with leaves that turn a brilliant shade of vermillion just before flowering begins. One of the easiest bromeliads—turns in a spectacular performance.

Tillandsia aeranthos Small, gray-green leaves about 3 inches long. A strong grower, good bloomer, producing numbers of pups (what bromeliad growers call baby plants) in a short time.

T. ionantha Small, curled gray-green rosettes growing in clusters. Grow and display on a small piece of bark as part of a mobile or in bonsai.

Vriesia carinata A small, dainty, colorful plant with light-green leaves, crimson bracts, and bright-yellow flowers.

V. psittacina Good for indoors as a small-to-medium-sized plant. It likes it warm and on the shady side. A good choice to tuck to the back of a tree display. Light-green leaves and a showy feather flowering that lasts for several months.

was turned upside down on the hearth so that what were once the roots of the tree are now branches where bromeliads nestle.

More than a dozen plants of different sizes and species have been arranged in the hollows and crotches, fastened in beds of sphagnum moss and secured with thin strips of nylon stocking.

Another bromeliad—a guzmania—floats low in the air over a side table. It was mounted on a piece of fern bark and suspended from the ceiling by clear nylon fishline. Only a little below it, on the table, are two small tillandsias, also mounted on small pieces of bark. They rest against miniature tabletop picture easels. And finally, sharing the table space, is one large earth star, spreading out in perfect symmetry and completely covering the small clay pot that holds it.

OTHER WAYS TO SHOW OFF BROMELIADS

🌿 Spotlight a cryptanthus collection by planting it in pockets of lava or feather rock and displaying on a low bench in the foyer or on a large cocktail table. These lovely earth stars need more soil than most of the other bromeliads and do well when potted. The wavy symmetry of their leaves is beautiful to look down on.

🌿 Tillandsias are good candidates for bogus bonsai. Plant them on small pieces of driftwood, on a gnarled branch, or even in pine cones, laid flat in slabs of wood or "planted" in a

Bonsai made with tillandsia.

bonsai tray.

🌿 Make a mobile out of a collection of tillandsias to hang in the kitchen window or in a child's room. Mount on small pieces of fern bark, and hang from small branches by nylon line. Or use spray-painted wooden dowels and small pieces of wood in clear sherbet colors. While these plants are beautiful on the plain bark, don't let the "natural is best" trend dissuade you from adding some zip with a raspberry, lemon, or lime touch if your room and your spirit say yes.

TO MAKE A TREE

Find a piece of driftwood, an inverted stump, or a large branch with limbs. Put it in place, and arrange until satisfied as far as branches, position, stability, and ease of care are concerned. If the tree is too big or wobbly to stand alone, one answer is to place the base in a container and secure it with some plaster of paris, which you can then cover with river stones or pine-bark mulch. A large and slanting tree may also require some support from the wall; a leather thong wrapped around a branch and attached to a large screw eye in the wall will do the trick neatly.

A bromeliad tree can usually be watered and misted with a minimum of drip, but it has to be done carefully. If you are worried about wood or carpeted surfaces, put the whole tree and its pot in a floor tray. These can often become decorative masterpieces themselves, filled with river stones, smaller pieces of driftwood, large seedpods, or other oddments.

When choosing the plants for your tree, take your time. Look in plant shops and through reference books and catalogs. An incredible variety is available by mail order, and most bromeliads travel well, so you

Wrap roots with dampened sphagnum moss.

needn't confine your selection to what is available locally.

Think about composition: a large aechmea at the base, for example, some of the smaller tillandsias for the top branches, and in between some choices from among the vriesias, guzmanias, billbergias, and nidulariums.

Choose places for the plants in the natural niches and crotches of the tree; you can also drill or bore out small holes (1 inch or so) in places where no natural hollows exist and where a plant would look fine.

Wrap the roots completely in sphagnum moss (soaked first in warm water). Fasten the roots to the tree with strips of nylon stocking. These are strong but soft and won't injure the plants.

N.B. If you haul home a log or part of a fallen tree from the woods, make certain that you are not trucking termites and/or other undesirables into the house. If the piece of wood seems much too lightweight for its size, forget it. If it has small, round, needlelike holes in it, forget it. Once you get your choice home, leave it outside, and treat it with an insecticide recommended for termite control. Follow label directions carefully.

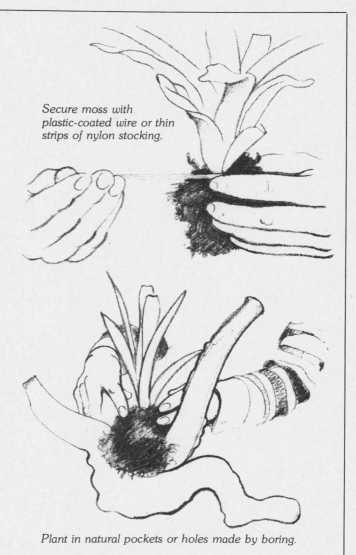

Secure moss with plastic-coated wire or thin strips of nylon stocking.

Plant in natural pockets or holes made by boring.

Make a wall planting for a den or library. Back a piece of quality cork wall paneling with Masonite to keep the cork stiff and protect the wall. Fasten a wall hanger to the back of the Masonite.

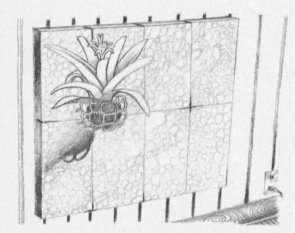

Shape small pockets out of pieces of chicken wire, and staple the two sides and bottom of each pocket firmly to the cork. Line the pockets with dampened sphagnum moss, fill with a small amount of potting mix, and then add the plants. Tuck them in firmly, and if necessary, secure them to the pockets with plastic-coated wire or thin strips of nylon stocking.

Hang the panel low on the wall. Keep a mister handy, and use every day. Use a nondrip, long-spouted watering can to fill the plant cups. Occasionally take the board off the wall and to the kitchen sink or bathroom for a general sprucing up. Moisten the sphagnum moss, dust, and clean.

BROMELIAD CARE

Most bromeliads like strong light but not direct sunlight. They also do fine under artificial light. Many of them can make it in a relatively low-light situation, but their coloring brightens and the plants thrive in stronger light. They also love humidity and enjoy daily misting.

Though many bromeliads grow as epiphytes, they can also be grown as potted plants. In fact, some of them will grow much larger in soil than they will on bark. Their insignificant root systems develop after planting, and then their growth takes off. (Some bromeliads, notably the earth stars and the pineapple, are by nature terrestrials—plants that grow in the soil.)

To pot bromeliads, use a prepared orchid mix or a mix made of equal parts of sphagnum peat moss, fir bark, and perlite. As many bromeliads have practically no root system, the first potting is mostly for anchorage. Once secure, roots do begin to form.

Use only a small amount of fertilizer, and be stingy about how often you use it. If you have a collection of bromeliads, it would be worth buying a soluble orchid fertilizer for them. Apply at half strength and only once a month. Use a spray bottle of the window-cleaner type. If your plants are of good size and in good condition, infrequent feeding will adequately maintain them. Any more feeding, and the growth can actually become a problem; some bromeliads can double what you might think is their adult size when they are put on a heavier feeding schedule.

For bromeliads with a vase or urnlike shape, keep the center cups filled with water, and occasionally water the soil in the pot, too. For plants that are grown as epiphytes, dampen the moss in which the plant is wrapped at least every two weeks, and mist daily.

PLANTING A PINEAPPLE TOP

Here is the simplest possible way to root a pineapple top. Twist the top off the fruit. Pull off the bottom leaves to expose 1½ to 2 inches of the stalk (this is where the roots will develop). Place the stalk in a small glass of water. Within a few weeks, sturdy roots will have formed around the sides of the bare stalk. When the roots are a couple of inches in length, pot the stalk in a porous soil mix. Feed, water, and provide light according to the directions in "Bromeliad Care."

The next growing season after rooting, you can induce flowering and fruiting by putting a ripe apple in the center of the plant and enclosing the whole in a plastic bag for five days. The apple releases ethylene gas as it ferments, and that's the signal that turns the pineapple plant on. Now you can remove the plant from the bag and resume normal care.

A month or so later, the inner leaves of the pineapple will begin to show a blush of red. Then a flower spike will grow straight up and out. Finally, fruit will form at the top. In four or five months, all told, you will have a small but tasty pineapple (with another stalk atop it!), ripe enough to eat.

Pineapple.

THE BROMELIAD SOCIETY

Varying classes of membership are available, beginning at a mere $7. This sum includes a subscription to the *Journal of the Bromeliad Society* (six issues a year and one of the world's best print bargains). The *Journal* is a sort of do-it-yourself, miniature version of the *National Geographic*. Members contribute stories and pictures of encounters with the exotic bromeliad in far-away places—from the mountains of Ecuador, Colombia, and Peru, the Amazon jungles, the rain forests of Central and South America. Other members from Belgium to Australia to South Africa share with American enthusiasts their experiences with these exotic plants. Color photographs of beautiful foliage and flowers mingle with snapshots of the plant explorers.

Editor Victoria Padilla is also the author of *The Bromeliads,* a classic on the subject, with over five hundred species described in simple, nontechnical language. Editor Padilla has collected bromeliads for some thirty years. Her book, she says, "is the type of reference work that I wanted when I started my collection. It is primarily a book to help the beginner in his selection of plants."

In addition to the *Journal,* a Bromeliad "Round Robin" provides an informal exchange of information, primarily for bromeliad fans not close enough to others to join in shows and other plant meetings. A Seed Bank service is also available for the sale, exchange, or purchase of seeds, with a list of available species from which to choose. Address: The Bromeliad Society, Inc., P.O. Box 3279, Santa Monica, California 90403.

African violets

African violets—deep-purple, double-bloom variety.

Love affairs with African violets often begin as chance encounters: a gift plant from a friend, an impulse purchase at a dime store, the successful rooting of a violet leaf, and the subsequent delight that comes when a tiny new plant pops into being.

What happens after that? The owner discovers that African violets bloom almost constantly, take up little room, are easy to care for, survive home atmospheres; that they are, in short, close to being the perfect houseplant.

What's more, it's easy to make lots of new plants from the first one; there are literally thousands of other varieties, each more tempting than the one before, and suddenly the casual African violet owner has become a full-fledged violeteer.

The plant that not too long ago was

stereotyped in the province of little old ladies shod in tennis shoes shows up as a sophisticated collection of jewellike flowers ensconced in plain white earthenware pots. No shrinking violets these—nothing shy about them or the room either. The all-too-familiar unfinished split-level family room shown on the preceding page has turned all violet, vim, and verve. Three successive coats of whitewash for the cinder-block walls, loveseats covered in a sturdy soil-repellent fabric piped in purple, and bare flooring all provide a clean, clear background for a year-round bloom of violets. At the window, a 1-by-8-inch board was placed atop the sill, nailed securely in place along the back edge, and painted white to match the walls and window trim.

The violets chosen for the window are all large show plants, all deep-purple, double-bloom varieties.

This is an east window, and during hot summer days the sheer white curtains are drawn to protect the violets from too much sun. (This same window arrangement with violets, sill, and curtain was created for another violet lover whose window faced north and did not admit quite enough light to coax year-round bloom from the violets. Track lights were installed on the ceiling, 1 foot out from the window, to provide supplemental light for the plants. Come night, they splash the wall with light. Specimens of polished rock and semiprecious stones share the windowsill space, and their colors vibrate, too, against the white pots and plain background.)

Several varieties of trailing violets stand on marble chips and glass beads on a white china platter on the coffee table. (The marble chips are sold by the bag in dime and hardware stores, and the glass beads are a bargain buy from a junk jewelry shop.) Each pedestal highlights a superb specimen plant, the flowers ranging in color from pink to purple to magenta. The pedestals themselves can be made according to the directions on pages 80—81. Each one is a different height and has a hole cut in the top to catch the rim of the pot and support it. The pedestals can be constructed without backs for easy access to the pots. (Use pots that come with attachable saucers. A glass pie plate on the floor inside each pedestal provides extra insurance against an occasional overflow of water.)

Pots of African violets sunk into pedestals.

VIOLETS AND OTHER ROOMS

Use your violets everywhere in your home, but don't downgrade their beauty by crowding all available surfaces with a hodgepodge of pots and rootings afloat in cheese jars and cake tins. Take the time to think about how to do justice to them. For example, where you might have a large display in one room, in another room you might limit your show to a single plant.

Think of unexpected places for your collection. A large bloomer in the bath, for example; or two or three violets nestled among the herbs in the kitchen; or several miniatures serving as shrubs for your child's dollhouse or train station.

A tea cart makes a splendid mobile home for a violet collection. Or perhaps the perfect plant for the living room would be a miniature, displayed under a glass dome (a cheese dome does fine; so does an upturned glass salad bowl).

From the kitchen, a still life can be put together featuring your violets and a mélange of violet-hued fruits and vegetables: eggplants, turnips, red cabbage, or plums.

In a bedroom where mostly naturals and neutrals have been combined for a peaceful, uncluttered look, try a clay strawberry planter full of trailing violets for a study in pinks or blues.

For a small, out-of-the-way place, a tiny powder room for example, hang one or more of the new mini-trailer types for small, compact clusters of green covered in bloom.

SOME VIOLET ADVICE

Gardeners who have known the addictive experience of harboring African violets offer the following among their top pieces of advice:

🌿 Always buy named varieties. First of all, it is more fun to know what you have; but, in addition, if you move into hybridizing (cross-pollinating plants to get a new variety—a painstaking but not difficult pursuit to which many violeteers succumb), you will want to know your offspring's true parentage.

🌿 Don't take up precious growing space with inferior plants or poor performers. With only a little effort you can choose really superior plants. For example, every March, the African Violet Society's magazine carries a list of registered varieties. These are plants that have been grown at least three generations and thus can be depended upon to be true to variety (i.e., the offspring will not differ from the parent plant). In November, the magazine features a list of "Best Varieties." Each variety on the list has received votes of at least fifty members of the Violet Society, so you can be certain that these varieties are good choices.

🌿 Start acquiring violets slowly, to give you an idea of which types do well for you, as well as which types you prefer. You will find that not only do the flowers come in different colors, sizes, and forms but that the leaves can be as varied and beautiful as the blooms. Some are bright apple green and fan out from the center of the plant in a flat, beautiful cartwheel. Others may be a darker gray green, with leaves forming more of a rosette. Still others have variegated leaves, ruffle-edged leaves, smooth-edged leaves, and infinite variations in between.

🌿 When mail ordering, check through the ads in the African Violet Society's magazine. Often violet *leaves* are offered for sale—an inexpensive way to introduce yourself personally to a number of varieties. Keep the ones that develop to your taste; gift away the others.

🌿 Discipline is essential in both the acquisition of new plants and the multiplying of old ones, or else you will have more than you can handle. "Fewer but better" is a good motto when your holdings threaten to outgrow your space. True collectors cannot overemphasize self-restraint because violets are so easy to grow and so tempting to propagate (see pages 287–288). The very names of the varieties make them difficult to resist: 'Garnet Elf,' 'Giant Butterfly,' 'Coral Cascade,' 'Jersey Devil.'

🌿 Set aside an out-of-the-way place where esthetics don't count so that you can indulge your hobby en masse: down in the basement, out in the garage, in a spare bedroom. Here you can have tiers of plant shelves and fluorescent lights (African violets actually do better most of the time under fluorescent light than in natural light) and keep dozens of violets happy in one spot. From here can come the selections that can make every room in your house a violet room.

🌿 Collect a reference library so that your knowledge grows along with your plants. A good first book to own is *the African Violet Book* by Helen Van Pelt Wilson (New York: Hawthorne Books, Inc., 1970).

CARE OF AFRICAN VIOLETS

🌿 Use potting soil that drains fast. Special potting mixes for African violets are widely available. If mixing your own, here is a good, simple recipe: two parts milled sphagnum peat moss, one part perlite, one part vermiculite. Rub the dry peat moss together between your hands to remove any lumps, then mix thoroughly with other ingredients. Moisten thoroughly with warm water when ready to use.

🌿 Clay pots were once considered de rigueur for African violets, but if you have a lot of violets to care for, you will prefer plastic pots because the plants won't dry out so fast and you won't have to water as often.

🌿 African violets need to be kept more on the moist side than dry—meaning, don't let them go all the way to dry before watering, but also *never* have them soggy and *never* let them stand in water. For violets gathered in one spot, consider wicking (see pages 33–34). Violets seem to love this type of watering and feeding; they grow and bloom like crazy.

🌿 Fertilize all year round for year-round bloom. Use a water-soluble fertilizer in a weak solution (as weak as one-twelfth strength when watering twice a week) as a regular watering routine. The solution is not stong enough nor the soil dry enough for the roots to burn.

🌿 Provide good bright light, but protect from hot sun. When growing in natural light, give each pot a quarter turn to the light source each time you water so that the plant will develop symmetrically. African violets will tell you very quickly and emphatically whether they are content with the light they have. If they are, they will bloom profusely. If they aren't, they won't. If they are getting too much light, the leaves will have a pale, bleached look. If not enough light, plants fail to bloom, or bloom sparsely, and the stems of the leaves grow long and lanky. A well-lighted, well-developed plant will have leaves that overlap so that no soil shows between the stems.

🌿 Violets are shallow-growing and finely rooted. They like to be potbound (their roots crowded in the pot) and seldom require a pot larger than 4 inches in size. Plantlets should start out in the 1-inch size. Repot only as roots appear in drainage holes or the crown of the plant crowds the rim too tightly. Use only the next largest pot.

🌿 Remember that you can continually renew your collection by rooting single leaves, so plan to have offspring of your favorite violets coming along to replace any of the old-timers that may begin to fail with age.

THE AFRICAN VIOLET SOCIETY OF AMERICA

Join this society and you become a member of one of the friendliest, down-home, plant-loving groups imaginable. The *African Violet Magazine,* a lovely, fat journal with beautiful color photographs, is packed with article after article on plant culture, dealing not only with African violets but also with other members of their family, the Gesneriaceae, including columnea, sinningia, and episcia.

All kinds of pots and other plant paraphernalia are advertised in the society's magazine, much of it worth knowing about and not always easy to find in the usual plant shop. Also advertised are dozens of varieties of violets available from commercial growers all around the country.

A single evening spent with the *African Violet Magazine* will make you feel that you belong, along with more than fifteen thousand other members. Members write in to share their successes with you, to describe a new idea for easier care or better growth, and to tell about a special plant they are grooming to enter in a show. Address: African Violet Society of America, Inc., P. O. Box 1326, Knoxville, Tennessee 37901.

Cacti and other succulents

The world of cacti and other succulents offers an invitation to unlimited beauty in exotic plant forms, although in the case of cacti, plant lovers are seldom aware of it when they first take up with this plant family. Often their first experience with a cactus involves a spiny-looking, round, gray-green lump that's part of a dish-garden planting. Awesome it's not. Nonetheless, if you take care of that cactus and bring it through its budding and flowering stage, your perception of its appeal will undergo a good bit of change.

Not all cacti are slow-growing, dry, and unresponsive, as many people think—if they think of them at all. Cacti and other succulents number among their members some startlingly beautiful plants. Many of them produce large, showy blooms; they can be dramatic, exotic, bizarre, amusing, and most of all, they're easy to grow.

The indoor gardener here, equipped with some inexpensive and widely available plants, executed a *tour de force* in a kitchen window. The *pièce de résistance* is the living totem pole of echeverias, sempervivums, and sedums. Balancing it in the opposite corner is a large jade plant which is due to be ousted from its place shortly, since the owner has just discovered the lemon vine cactus and has fallen in love with it. The jade tree, which can make it with less light, will be moved to a bedroom window and the lemon vine installed in its place. (The lemon vine can be pruned to keep it in shrub form rather than let it go to vine.)

A living totem pole.

This seemingly innocent addition sets a risky precedent. The owner is not yet aware that in the succulent world, once you move beyond the hens and chicks, crown-of-thorns, and jade tree, there is no way to stop. In no time at all she'll be searching for room for the panda plant, burro's tail, and bunny ears. And what about the pencil cactus and golden stars? Dozens and dozens more not-so-hard-to-find species await her. There is no end to the enjoyment to be found in the beautiful and bizarre world of the succulents.

TO MAKE A TOTEM POLE

Buy a piece of fine-mesh chicken netting a couple of inches longer and 8 inches or so wider than the piece of lumber you will use for the base. Staple the netting to the back of one side of the plank; stretch it out flat alongside the plank.

Mix milled peat moss and perlite, half and half—enough to make a thick, rounded layer (a couple of inches thick at the center). Moisten the mixture thoroughly, and pat by handfuls onto the board. Shape into a mound so that the finished pole will have a rounded effect.

Soak unmilled sphagnum moss in hot water until it becomes flexible, and then top the peat-perlite mixture with a layer of the sphagnum moss.

Now carefully pull the netting over the moss, and staple it to the back of the other side of the plank. Staple the ends in place. Attach a heavy-duty screw eye in one end of the plank for a hanger.

Use a sturdy tool—a screwdriver or the handle part of a wooden spoon—to make the hollows you will need for planting. Snip a wire where necessary to make planting room for larger plants.

Choose plants of the rosette and trailing types for planting: green jade from the echeverias; hens and chicks from the sempervivums; small burro's tails from the sedums. Some of the small, round mammillarias will work, too. Heavier, upright growers won't be suitable; their own weight and center of gravity will pull them loose.

Choose the side of the window that gets the most sun, and hang the totem on the reveal (inside wall of the window). Attach so that it can be taken down easily for watering. With cacti and other succulents this will not be a too-demanding job. Lay the slab flat on the kitchen drainboard (or in the bathtub) to water; let drain thoroughly before rehanging.

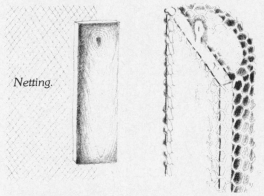

Netting.

First layer: peat moss and perlite, half and half. Second layer: unmilled sphagnum moss, soaked in hot water

Most households have only just so much sunny space, the space most succulents favor. The problem in letting your enthusiasm outgrow your capabilities for care is that you may be tempted to thrust some plants back into dimmer light than they'd like. Although they may survive for some time, inevitably they will give out. So cactus lovers must keep a firm grip on what they can handle.

One collector, for example, collects only Mexican snowballs—all from multiples of the original plant. As time went by, she wound up with a stunning, no-cost floor display that would be hard to match at any price.

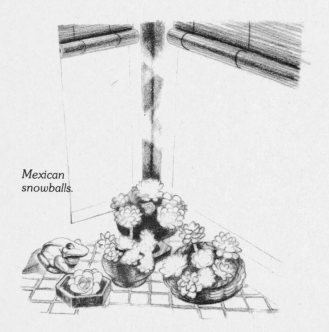

Mexican snowballs.

Another collector with minimal space samples various types of cacti and other succulents by planting them in the pockets of a large strawberry jar. The strawberry jar sits atop a sturdy lazy susan so that it can be rotated easily each day to let all the plants have a regular dose of sunshine.

CARE OF CACTI AND OTHER SUCCULENTS

Most cacti and other succulents like it bright, and they like it dry. So you can generally choose the brightest spot in the house and water only when the soil is thoroughly dry. However, don't overdo the simplification. Succulents thrive on restraint, not neglect.

They can go without water longer and better than most other plants simply because they are able to store moisture and can draw on this supply to take them over the dry times. If you care for your plants, however, try not to put them through this trauma.

Take the trouble to pot your succulents in a soil mix that will provide perfect drainage for them. As for feeding, do so, but sparingly, and with a specially formulated fertilizer—one with a low nitrogen content in relation to the other two major ingredients, phosphorus and potassium. Most fertilizers designed for houseplants contain too much nitrogen for succulents; it forces green growth and can cause the plants eventually to go soft from overdevelopment. Even tomato plant food is better for succulents than the usual indoor foliage houseplant food because its nitrogen content is relatively low.

Most succulents travel well, so that they are generally easy to acquire by mail order. When they arrive, trim back any roots that may have dried out before you pot the plants.

There's one downbeat note to add about cacti, which grow in the wild in nearly every state in the Union. While many people are concerned about the plight of various animals and birds that may be facing extinction in their native habitats, few are even aware that many plants are also threatened. Of all endangered plants in the United States, none are so actively threatened with extinction in their native habitats as members of the cactus family.

The sheer force of population spread and the attendant developments of housing, highways, and shopping centers are responsible for much plant destruction, but cactus collectors in the field—commercial as well as private—are also

TO INCREASE YOUR COLLECTION

If the plant has branches or plantlets or pads, take a whole segment for a rooting.

If the plant's stems are jointed, take enough of the stem to include at least one joint.

If the plant is a columnar type, cut a piece off the top.

If the plant has a long, unjointed stem, the stem can be cut into several pieces for rooting.

After you have cut off from the plant the piece to be rooted, put it aside for a few days in a shady place to let the cut edges dry out. (If you have cut several pieces from one stem, mark the edge of the bottom side of each with a piece of tape or with a felt marker to indicate which end goes into the soil to root.)

Let the cut edges dry completely before putting the piece in a pot to root.

Fill the pot with cactus soil mix, except for the top 1½ inches. Here, put in a 1-inch layer of sand or vermiculite for the cutting to root in. Don't use too big or too deep a pot.

Push the cutting into the sand or vermiculite only about a ½-inch deep. Moisten, but don't overwater. As the roots form on the cutting, they will reach down into the potting mixture and a new plant will be off and growing on its own.

lending a hand in this depredation. Cacti by the thousands are dug up from the wilds, potted, and sold locally or in faraway cities at enormous mark-ups. Depending upon state laws, this is being done legally (e.g., Texas) or illegally (e.g., Arizona).

So how can you acquire members of the beautiful, exotic cactus family without doing violence to your own conscience? How can you escape feeling that you may be purchasing the equivalent of a leopard coat for your living room by buying an unusual specimen? One way is to acquire cacti that have been propagated from seed. They are generally small-sized and of uniform appearance. Another is to patronize only reputable dealers who do not traffic in large specimens collected in nature, such as the sought-after and expensive barrel cacti. Another is to become acquainted with those species that are endangered and neither buy nor recommend them to other collectors. (Obtain a copy of the *Report on Endangered and Threatened Plant Species of the United States,* issued by the Endangered Flora Project, Department of Botany, Smithsonian Institution, Washington, D.C. 20560.) And, certainly, don't dig and cart off plants from the wild yourself; such actions seldom can be rationalized as conservation because many varieties are so specifically adapted to their environment that few survive the attempt to transplant them.

SOME CACTI AND OTHER SUCCULENTS TO KNOW AND GROW

Cacti

Epiphyllum
Orchid cactus, *E. hybridus*

Mammillaria
Golden stars, *M. elongata*
Powder puff, *M. bocasana*
Old lady, *M. hahniana*

Opuntia
Bunny ears, *O. microdasys*
Teddy bear, *O. bigelovii*

Pereskia
Lemon vine cactus, *P. aculeata godseffiana*

Schlumbergera
Christmas cactus, *S. bridgesii*

Christmas cactus.

Succulents

Ceropegia
Rosary vine or string of hearts, *C. woodii*

Crassula
Jade tree, *C. argentea*
String of buttons, *C. perfossa*

Echeveria
Green jade or molded wax, *E. agavoides*
Mexican snowball, *E. elegans*
Plush plant, *E. pulvinata*

Euphorbia
Crown-of-thorns, *E. millii splendens*
Pencil cactus or milk bush, *E. tirucalli*

Kalanchoe
Panda plant, *K. tomentosa*
Christmas kalanchoe, *K. blossfeldiana*

Sedum
Burro's tail, *S. morganianum*

Sempervivum
Hens and chicks, *S. tectorum*

Senecio
Bead cactus or green marble vine,
S. herreianus

*Christmas
kalanchoe.*

Begonias

Begonias are for the romantics among us. There is an enormous variety from which you can choose—all beautiful in foliage and flower, all romantic.

There are trailing begonias to hang from baskets to brighten the upper reaches of a room on even the darkest winter day. There are compact, nonstop bloomers that are heartbreakingly beautiful lined up in a row. There are begonias with foliage so dramatic it creates its own focal point, with color and texture rich enough to build a room around. There are begonias big enough to use as floor plants, with branches arching out and blooms to coax romantic thoughts.

Happy is the collector who chooses begonias to fill a bedroom, for there is nothing like a glimpse of their vibrant color and lush foliage to get your day going. Such an awakening can be almost assured with the semperflorens begonias, which are, as the name indicates, always in flower. They're also known as wax begonias, and they do nicely in almost any exposure, growing and blooming well with only a little sun or even bright light and without constant surveillance. They are probably the most underrated of all houseplants—a case of simply being taken for granted. While they have been grown as house-plants for generations, in recent years new and more exotic varieties have been claiming most of the attention. However, if you feel you have no luck with plants, if your house is on the warm, dry side and hostile to temperamental plants, if you are an apartment dweller with not much control over your temperature and humidity environment, if you want to grow the plant your great grandma no doubt grew, then do not be without everblooming begonias.

The semperflorens varieties are widely available in garden shops or can be ordered from garden catalogs. There are single or double blooms, in white and colors ranging from pale pink to deep rose red. The foliage also varies in size, texture, and color, ranging from delicate green to dark bronze and two-toned combinations in between. All are downright indomitable, astonishing in their determination to bloom. When cut back, they grow and bloom even more vigorously. It is no accident that they were saved for the last rooms in this book because no matter how many rave notices (all heartfelt), appear in the preceding pages about other plants, everblooming begonias are still the best. They never let you down; they are cheerful, ebullient, and beautiful. For them, destiny is blooming.

In the bedroom pictured opposite, baskets of the everbloomers are joined with a tall, beautiful angelwing. As the name implies, the leaves have wing-shaped lobes. Some resemble fat, lopsided hearts; others have slim, more arrow-shaped leaves; some are silver-splattered. The variety of leaf form, texture, color, and bloom make it possible for the collector to specialize in angelwings only.

Angelwings are also called cane-like be-

Wax, or everblooming, begonias grace the bedroom scene along with an angelwing.

gonias. Their thick, jointed green stems are something like bamboo. They can be coaxed into a luxuriant, full effect by pruning them in the fall to encourage more shoots to come up. You will have blooms on them from spring to fall, and the plants themselves grow anywhere from 2 feet to over 4 feet high.

Next to consider in the begonia world are the Riegers, which are relative newcomers, gaudy and gorgeous. These are named after Otto Rieger of Nurtingen, Germany, who developed the plants; they are patented and can be reproduced for sale only by licensed growers. They are definitely not the begonias grown by grandma, but she certainly would have loved them.

Riegers were the inspiration for this begonia bower in a bath, which was created out of a linen closet and clothes hamper. This homeowner decided there was really no need to keep all those towels and sheets in there, and why waste the rest of the good space on dirty clothes?

The doors came off, the shelves came out, and a simple frame to conceal vertical fluorescent lights was put up around the opening. Spackling compound and plasterboard tape smoothed out cracks and holes, and a shiny vinyl wall covering transformed the underutilized closet space into a glass-shelved, flower-filled alcove that brought beauty to the bath, joy to the person who thought up the idea, only a few beginning grumbles from those who were now keeping their own laundry.

Rieger begonias claim a linen closet.

Now, what about these Rieger begonias? These nonstop bloomers? The two types you are most likely to hear about and see are the Aphrodite and the Schwabenland. Schwabenland red was the choice for this bath. It's a beauty, a low-growing plant with rich green foliage and brilliant blooms. Their compact growth and symmetry make these begonias ideal for display in rows. They do well under lights, and you can experiment with the time needed to produce the most blooms. A minimum of ten hours is required for bloom, and if you give them much over fourteen or sixteen hours of light, you will likely get more foliage growth than flower. Riegers need to be watered well; then they need to dry out *thoroughly* before they are watered again.

The rex begonia was the choice for a third begonia hobbyist—a challenging one, since rexes are not the easiest plants to grow. What enticed this young enthusiast's interest was the unusual method of rooting them. She started with a single leaf from one of the best known of the rexes—Merry Christmas—and from that leaf, on her first try, she produced six plantlets, three of which she brought through to adulthood.

The next rex she acquired was the Iron Cross, another widely grown favorite, famous for its quilted foliage and the striking two-toned design in the leaf. From then on, it was all adventure, largely through membership in the American Begonia Society and the acquaintance of other rex fanciers who generously provided choice specimens to challenge her. She has had a number of failures, due largely, she thinks, to low humidity. A humidifier for her room, which is heated by forced hot air, has helped her plants. (Her mother thinks it has also helped cut down on winter colds.)

Rex begonias don't like direct sun, but the rich color variations in the leaves do not show up brilliantly unless they have enough light. They are excellent candidates for the artificial light garden, and that is where this begonia fan grows hers—under a long, low shelf that has two 8-foot fluorescent tubes mounted behind the apron.

Making lots of rexes from one leaf: Choose a well-formed leaf from the plant, not an old one that is on its way out and not a new one. What

Propagation of rex begonia leaf.

THE AMERICAN BEGONIA SOCIETY

For the beginning begonia fancier, *The Begonian,* published by the American Begonia Society, may be a somewhat baffling mixture of information. It's a little like sitting down for a companionable cup of coffee with a friend, chatting over everyday matters of mutual interest, and then suddenly, to your bewilderment, your friend switches to a foreign language.

Thus it is with *The Begonian.* Mixed in with helpful hints from delightful people who share all sorts of practical advice about soil mixes, containers, and begonia culture in general, you will also find detailed accounts of specific varieties of begonias that you may feel you will never have the time, or even inclination, to become acquainted with. Then there are the somewhat scholarly articles on taxonomy and horticultural classifications. The genus *Begonia* includes an enormous number of plants, and there is, to put it bluntly, chaos and controversy in attempts to standardize the nomenclature within it.

All of this information, however, comes packaged in a small, friendly monthly journal, put together in a loving, disjointed, and very personal fashion. After reading a few copies, you will begin to recognize the names of some of the top specialists in the field and marvel at their generosity in taking time to discuss their successes and failures and to provide hints to help the rankest beginner. You will also begin to recognize different species and varieties; and you will love the "Round Robin," a sort of "Hints from Heloise" for the begonia fan.

No time spent reading here will be wasted time, and one of the most important things you will discover is that there is no one way to handle any plant. *The Begonian* is not pretentious. Contributors put on no airs; they claim no mystique; they share experiences that have been successful for them; and they always make you feel that while what they are suggesting in plant culture has worked for them, you should strive for confidence in trying your own way of making your own plants happy. Address: American Begonia Society, 11506 McDonald, Culver City, California 92030.

you want is a good healthy-looking, middle-aged leaf. Put the leaf stem in a glass of water for a few hours so that the leaf will take up as much moisture as it can hold.

Prepare a small, shallow pan of moist vermiculite or sand. With a sharp knife, make two or three cuts through the large vein that runs down the center of the leaf and a cut or two through several of the larger branching veins. Each cut is the site of a potential new plant.

Dust the leaf cuts lightly with a hormone rooting powder. Lay the leaf with the underside flat against the moist vermiculite or sand. Push the stem down in the pan so that it will help the leaf retain moisture. Pin down the leaf, too, using small hairpins, so that the cut edges will stay in contact with the vermiculite or sand.

Slip the pan into a plastic bag, and wrap loosely. Place out of direct sun. If the leaf shows signs of drying out, remove the pan from the bag, mist lightly, and return to the bag. New plantlets should begin to show within three or four weeks. When a pair of leaves have formed, you can open the bag and gradually adjust the new plantlets to room environment. When they each have a couple of sets of leaves, you can transplant the plants to separate pots.

Mail-order sources for houseplants

Listing mail-order catalogs is an uncertain venture at best, given the vagaries of prices and postal services, and the passage of time. The following sources, however, have proved successful for the authors, with addresses and prices current as of spring, 1976.

John Brudy's Rare Plant House specializes in unusual plants that can be grown from seed (Kafir plum and gungurru gum, for example). The catalog costs $1 which is refundable with an order. Packets of seeds are generally priced at $ .75. Address: P.O. Box 1348, Cocoa Beach, Florida 32931.

Fischer Greenhouses specializes in African violets, and their catalog (price: $ .15) presents new varieties and old favorites in dazzling color closeups. Their "Gardening Aids Catalog" has extensive listings and is available for $ .25. Address: Linwood, New Jersey 08221.

Gurney's catalog is old-fashioned and folksy with a bit of everything, from trees, shrubs vegetables, and berries to cherry pitters, bean stringers, bird houses, and houseplants. The catalog is for free. Address: Gurney Seed and Nursery Co., Yankton, South Dakota 57078.

Hemlock Hill Herb Farm will send you, for $ .50, an illustrated booklet that features a fine listing of both aromatic and culinary herbs. Plants only; no seeds. Address: Hemlock Hill Road, Litchfield, Connecticut 06759.

The Houseplant Corner's catalog has lots of plant pots, hangers and other accessories mixed in with a nice listing of plants, potting mixes, and plant food. Price: $ .25. Address: Box 5000, Cambridge, Maryland 21613.

Jones and Scully, Inc., has the catalog you want if orchids are your thing. The catalog is a great buy at $3, with hundreds of orchids illustrated in full color. A full range of prices, too, from $3 seedlings to specimens costing several hundred dollars. Address: 2200 Northwest 33rd Avenue, Miami, Florida 33142.

K &L Cactus Nursery, run by Keith and Lorraine, is a family venture, and the catalog reflects it with pictures of the kids as well as the cacti. Seeds are sold as well as plants. Good, clear, close-up pictures with names and descriptions right alongside make the catalog especially useful. Price: $ .50. Address: 12712 Stockton Boulevard, Galt, California 95632.

Kartuz Greenhouses lists a wide variety of plants, including begonia, African violet, lipstick, columnea, and gloxinia. Price: $1. Address: 92 Chestnut Street, Wilmington, Massachusetts 01887.

Logee's Greenhouse publishes a handsome catalog of houseplants, including many unusual ones. The Logee family has been in business since before the turn of the century and is one of the few concerns that actually grows what it sells. Price $1.50. Address: 55 North Street, Danielson, Connecticut 06239.

Loyce's Flowers is a person-to-person operation. Miss Loyce Andrews carefully packs each plant for shipment. Her unpretentious catalog is sprinkled with personal observations of how individual plants have performed for her. The hoya collection is unbeatable and there are lots of other treats, too. Price $ .50. Address: Route 2, Box 11, Granbury, Texas 76048.

Merry Gardens will send you for $1 their "Pictorial Handbook of Rare Indoor Plants," featuring begonias, geraniums, ivies, ferns, cacti, and succulents. A rare foliage, flower, and vines price list: $ .50. Address: Camden, Maine 04843.

Walter F. Nickes' catalog carries all the accoutrements of gardening; the handtools, hose fittings, pruners, misters, and other items worth owning and nice to give. Price: $ .25. Address: Box 667SK, Hudson, New York 12534.

George W. Park Seed Co., Inc. publishes just about the best all-round gardener's catalog, with lots of showing and telling of vegetables and flowers, herbs and houseplants, grow lights and whatever else a gardener could want. The catalog is for free.

Address: Greenwood, South Carolina 29647.

The Tool Shed Herb Farm, run by Helen Whitman and Charlotte Lee, lists at least one or two species, sometimes more, of almost all of the most widely used epicurean herbs. Tossed in for good measure are simple rules for making herb vinegar, jellies and butters as well as for drying and freezing herbs. Price: $ .25. Address: Salem Center, Purdys Station, New York 10578.

Wayside Gardens, formerly of Mentor, Ohio, has a beautiful catalog featuring shrubs and bulbs and is a real bargain for $1. Address: Hodges, South Carolina 29695.

White Flower Farm's catalog offering actually amounts to a subscription to two "Catalogues" and three issues of "Notes." They make delightful reading, and though more outdoor plants are listed than indoor, the offerings are as choice as the advice. A good buy at $4 annually (deductible with the first $15 order). Address: Litchfield, Connecticut 06759.

Index